Devil's Snare

*Best New England
Crime Stories*

Edited by

Susan Oleksiw
Ang Pompano
Leslie Wheeler

Crime Spell Books
Cambridge, MA 02138

Crime Spell Books
Cambridge, MA 02138
www.crimespellbooks.com

Printed in the USA.   First Edition

ISBN 979-8-9881991-0-6

Devil's Snare

Contents

Introduction

We often think of crime fiction in terms of the nefarious doings of the villain, a man or woman with a capacity for conduct that chills us, or perhaps intrigues or entertains us. In this collection of twenty-four stories, we focus on men and women most of whom are living ordinary lives until something extraordinary flips the narrative.

The supposedly good guys aren't very good, but their struggle is relatable, and to our surprise we may want them to succeed. The traditional tale of a sleuth, amateur or professional, uncovering a crime and the guilty party, however serious that is, is still satisfying. Clea Simon's cub reporter follows advice and breaks open a case in "The Shorty Beat." Ang Pompano's policewoman in "By the Light of the Silvery Moon" needs to be observant and quick, and she is. Nikki Knight's radio anchor in "Public Affairs Homicide" reinterprets an earlier experience to confront a murderer and her own past.

It helps to understand the culture when a young student friend tries to help a fishmonger find out who's trying to destroy his business in Paula Messina's "Fish Eyes." Another student observing a crime offers an entirely different perspective in Stephen D. Rogers's "The Princes and the Corpse." Quieter in her role is the church lady in Mo Walsh's "Lessons from Nature."

For some, life is safer on the periphery, though these individuals are never far from danger. An ex-con manages to stay out of trouble, barely, in Sean Harding's "The Ave," as he tries to help a friend from prison. A man searching for a friend's brother to tell him about an inheritance in Chris Knopf's "What Made Sammy Run" avoids the pitfalls of a failing neighborhood and still manages to set a few things right. The sole employee in a laundromat in Nancy Brewka-Clark's "One Shy of a Load" thinks it's his lucky day when he encounters a certain family of crazies.

Not everyone wants to know the truth, especially after they uncover it. The daughter in Shelagh Smith's "Snapshot" could not have prepared herself for what she discovers when she takes on the task of clearing out her late father's home. The college student in Emily Ross's "Let the Chips Fall" struggles with a brain injury that folds around the truth and its pain. The truth is searing for the wife in Kate Flora's "Widow's Walk" and for the PI in Michael Ditchfield's "Chinese Exclusion." Some find it easier to leave the truth for others to cope with, as in Gabriela Stiteler's "The Business of Others." A family chooses action, discreetly, in Susan Oleksiw's "Coda for a Love Affair." The ending in Hans Copek's "A Capital Offense" is haunting, an injustice that is ironical and needless.

The reader wonders at the kind of future that will exist for the owner in Christine Bagley's "The Cottage," and the wife in Connie Johnson Hambley's "Obscura Eclipse." Bruce Robert Coffin's ending is inevitable in "Novem Vitae," and the reader can only speculate on the protagonist's future in Christine Eskilson's "Peregrine Point." But the young woman in Alison McMahan's "Hellfire & Holywater" finds her way home in every sense.

Three stories take the reader into another realm: "A Christmas Cat in the Woods" by Eugenia Parrish, "Gonna be a Heck of a Band" by Sarah Smith, and "The Book Club" by Leslie Wheeler.

These stories challenge our sense of reality, justice, fairness, and fair play. The characters we love don't always get what we want them to have, and others seem to get away with their deeds—for a while, at least.

As editors we enjoy the variety of stories, the different perspectives on behavior that may or may not be criminal, and the outcomes that arise, which are not necessarily legal consequences but point to the intricacies of modern life. Writers explore different problems and varied solutions, and from these we gain a deeper understanding of a world growing increasingly complex and oftentimes downright confusing.

Susan Oleksiw
Ang Pompano
Leslie Wheeler

Let the Chips Fall

Emily Ross

I pick up a green poker chip from my desk. It's the good clay kind, not one of the cheap plastic ones. It feels like a polished stone on my palm. Pete says the clay chips have grace. Only Pete could find grace in poker.

I've been studying so hard for the SAT my head is swimming with words, but I can't resist the urge to look up *chip*—a small, usually thin and flat piece, a token, a flaw left after something has broken off. Flaw, I never would have thought of that.

Since I got hurt, Pete's gone radio silent on me. My friends say he won big and went to Vegas to live with his dad, but I bet he can't face seeing me this way.

I squeeze the chip between my thumb and forefinger to stop my hand from shaking. In the hospital they told me this could happen, but it still unnerves me that a blow to my head can send tremors all the way down to my finger tips.

My phone buzzes and the chip slides from my hand. It's Shady, commanding me to come out.

"Can't, studying."

"There's going to be a fight down by Wolly Beach," he says.

1

Shady's been calling every day since I got out of the hospital, asking if I'm better yet, if I remember anything. If I figure out who beat me up, Shady says he'll teach him a lesson. I touch the shaved spot on my head. Fine stubble is already growing back. The doctor told me the memory of what happened could come back anytime or never. All I know now is what my mom told me. The police found me unconscious in the parking lot behind the Emerald Shamrock.

"Liam, you there?" Shady says.

I go over to the window in my room. Rooftops cascade down the hill to the flatlands below. Beyond them is a fuzzy strip of light blue. The ocean. Shady and the rest of them are down there somewhere, no bigger than grains of sand.

I press my hand on the glass. It's warm for October. My room is unbearably stuffy, but since I got back from the hospital I have an irrational fear that if I open the window, I will lose control and jump. I don't want to. I'm just afraid I will.

"I'm coming," I say too loud. The test is tomorrow, but I convince myself I'll meet up with Shady, chug down a few brews, watch the fight (not get in it), and study using the app on my phone. I've always been a sucker for my own bullshit.

I stand in front of the sliding glass door. It rained and the grass is a rich drenched green. I compulsively search my phone for the right word: *verdigris, emerald, viridian*. None of the above. The answer is *baize*, the color of billiard and card tables. I feel the soft green felt beneath my palm, see the cards fanned out on it. Playing poker with Pete and Shady in the back room of the Emerald Shamrock that night is one of the last things I remember.

As usual, Pete was taking everyone's money including mine. When he got up to leave, he gave me a nod that meant I should leave too. But I have trouble stepping away from the table when I'm losing. Just one more hand, I told myself that night as Shady and his friend Mike followed Pete out. If only I'd left with them, I'd be fine now, but I was stupid. I want to pound the door in frustration. Instead I slide it open.

Wet grass brushes my ankles as I walk over to the old playhouse at the back of the yard. I take a deep breath, push aside the broken rope ladder, hoist myself onto the platform, and pull the *Curiously Strong Altoid Mints* case out from under a pile of leaves. I've kept my stash in here ever since Mom found my weed in my bureau drawer and flushed it.

Smoke from my joint drifts through the holes in the tattered canvas roof of the playhouse. The world is backing off the way I want it to, when I see Pete standing in the middle of the yard, his hands buried in his pockets. I can't believe my eyes.

I jump down. "You're back."

"You might say that." His face looks greenish, more mint than baize, and his clothes are wet. He must have gotten caught in the rain.

"You look noxious, man," I say. He raises an eyebrow. "Harmful, poisonous, lethal." I don't even have to look it up. I know this shit.

"Aren't you the smart one."

"Been studying for the SAT tomorrow." I hold out the joint, but he shakes his head no. "So, where you been?"

"Around."

"Can you be more specific?"

He runs his hand through his slicked back blond hair. "Maybe later."

I tell him I just got out of the hospital and he says he's sorry, he had no idea. How could he not know?

He sighs. "Remember in middle school when we used to come here to go through your dad's *Maxim Magazines*, smoke, and talk about the models we'd bang, the Cristal we'd drink, the Lamborghinis we'd drive."

"Two twelve-year-olds dreaming of being players in an abandoned playhouse. How ironic." I eye him. His yellow and blue striped Rugby shirt with a white collar actually looks like something he would have worn when he was twelve. Pete and I used to talk about how poker would be his ticket out of Quincy and words would be mine. But he doesn't look like someone who got out. He looks like he's been sleeping in a dumpster.

I tell him I'm meeting Shady and he says, "Cool. Let's roll."

Devil's Snare

His wet sneakers make squishing sounds as we walk past the pathetic takeout Chinese restaurants, bars, and smoke shops that pass for the center of town.

When we get to the beach Pete says, "Man, I missed this place."

A beach where tampons and used needles are as apt to wash up as seashells isn't exactly something you miss. But as Pete goes down to the water's edge to eye the splendor of it all, I miss it a little too. He turns and I notice something on his cheek.

He plucks it off. "Mermaid's hair." There are green seaweed threads on his palm.

"You been getting it on with a mermaid?" I say.

"That might be difficult," he replies. It would be funny if he didn't look so miserable.

Shady is waiting for us in front of the Clam Shack, eating French fries from a striped box. The hood of his black sweatshirt is pulled down low over his face.

"You look like the grim reaper," I say.

He grins. "Thanks for the compliment."

"Who you fighting?"

"Jack Provo."

"You can take Jack, no problem." I can't believe Shady is even bothering to fight someone like him.

"No duh." Shady raises his fists. "You want to fight me instead?"

He's not serious. Everyone knows I can't fight since I hit my head, or play soccer, or do anything worth doing unless I want to die. He must feel bad because he offers me some of his fries. I jam a bunch in my mouth and get ketchup all over me. I look down at my sticky hands, and smell something metallic. The hamburger I wolfed down for dinner comes up the back of my throat and I rush into the Clam Shack's stinky restroom, and barf into the rust-stained toilet bowl. I rinse my hands under cold water until I can breathe again. Since the accident I have a problem with anything red, *carmine, scarlet, vermillion, ruby, incarnadine*—so many words for the color of blood.

4

We follow Shady down a street that leads past a marsh to our old elementary school. Kids stand under the hoop beneath floodlights, smacking balls against the cracked asphalt. It's not much of a basketball court.

"I don't get why we keep coming back here," Pete says.

Usually I wouldn't have an answer, but tonight I do. I show him the word on my phone, *nostalgia*, "a wistful affection for the past." It's a soft word, like wind through leaves.

"It's funny how something can really suck and then you end up looking back thinking those were the days," he says and I nod.

Everyone steps aside as Shady elbows his way through the crowd. He's Jason Shade, the guy who can level anyone with a single blow, a good friend to have, a bad enemy. I'm glad he's on my side. I've known him almost as long as I've known Pete. We've played on soccer teams together since preschool. I'm good but Shady was way better until he quit the varsity team. Now he gets high from the small pharmacy he keeps in his room.

When I see Jack I call out, "*Comment allez-vous?*" and he waves ridiculously. Jack was in my honors French class last year. His nose is too big and his baggy b-ball shorts practically come down to his ankles. He's the sad sort of geek who recognizes his geek-hood and wants to rise above. He thinks fighting Shady will make him one of us.

We form a circle around Jack and Shady as they square off. Shady flings back his hood. Sweat glistens on his shaved head. Jack takes a swing and misses. Shady ducks, then rams his fist into Jack's face. Blood sprays out of his nose. Jack doubles over, but Shady doesn't let up. He pins Jack on the ground and keeps wailing away at him like he's punching the whole damn world into submission.

Pete lays a hand on my shoulder and it's so cold a chill goes through me. His skin is white, pellucid to be exact. I can see his veins. My friends cheer, but as Shady beats Jack bloody I can't stop shaking. Air won't go down my throat. My ears are blocked. What is happening to me? Pete is saying something but his words scramble. I can't hold myself back.

"You're going to kill him!" I scream as I hurl myself into the fight and pull Shady off Jack.

5

Jack drags himself up as if mortally wounded and thrilled at the same time and yells at me for ruining everything.

Shady grabs me by the shirt. "What'd you do that for, Liam?"

I'm breathing so hard I can barely think. "I don't know."

Shady shakes his head. "I'll let it go this time but don't do it again."

I should be grateful the almighty Shady isn't going to beat the crap out of me for disrespect or whatever. Sometimes I get so sick of everyone I know. I look for Pete. He's the only one of my friends who's at all like me, but he's disappeared. Figures.

Blood is gushing from Jack's nose so I give him my shirt. It turns red as he balls it against his face.

"You look like a plucked chicken." Shady points at my bare chest.

Shady's sidekick, Mike, the only guy tougher than Shady, and dumber, says, "You need to work out."

"Hard to work out when you're in the hospital," I say.

"Sucks for you, Liam." Mike turns the corners of his mouth down. I've reached a new low. Mike who is dumber than a trilobite feels sorry for *me*.

Jack hands me back my bloody shirt and says, "Here you go, chickenshit."

"Thanks, Ichabod," I say. The blood smell from my shirt goes up my nose. My hands shake so hard I drop it on the ground. Mike snatches it up and throws it onto the telephone wires next to some old sneakers that have been there forever. My hands feel like my phone on vibrate, only worse. I shove them in my pocket before anyone sees, but it's too late.

"Hey Frank-Einstein, how does it feel to come back from the dead?" Shady lurches forward, flapping his hands. Mike flaps his hands, too. Soon they are all flapping their hands.

"You're a moron," I say to Shady. My role is to play along as he tears me to pieces, but I can't do it tonight.

"What'd you call me?" he says.

"I called you an imbecile, an ignoramus, a cretin, a simpleton, a drug-addled waste of a human being." Shady raises his fist. "Go on, put me out of my misery," I say. He gives me a baffled look. I prepare myself for death.

"Stop being a dickwad, Liam." Shady shakes his head as he stares at me. "I get it. I should have had your back that night. I'll make it up to you. I'm asking around. But so far no one knows who did it or they're not saying." I nod. People here don't rat each other out but if anyone can get to the bottom of this Shady can. "Come on boys. Let's get out of here," he says.

As we head out I say, "Hey, wait for Pete." I scan the crowd for him but can't see him anywhere.

Shady whips around. "Pete?"

"He was right here," I say. "Give me a sec. I'll go find him."

Shady strokes the dark stubble on his chin. "Liam, Pete wasn't here tonight." My heart beats so hard it feels like it might catapult out of my chest. Shady goes on. "He won big the night you got beat up, took off for Vegas with his money, and we haven't seen him since."

"He's back now. He was with me."

Shady lets out a small sigh like I'm such a loser. "No, he wasn't."

Mike and Shady exchange a look, and Mike says, "First you're forgetting things. Now you're seeing things."

I feel clammy all over. I turn to Jack. "You saw him. Tell them."

"I didn't." He won't meet my gaze.

"Must be your broken head, bro." Shady pats my shoulder. His fake sympathy makes me feel like crap.

"I'm not broken," I say. Every muscle stiffens. They're messing with me the way they always do, but I refuse to be the stupid, laughable, defective, flawed person they think I am anymore. I really wish Pete would show up now when I need him, but that dude is gone. "He was right here and you were too stupid to notice."

Shady glares at me. "Say one more word and I'll break that stupid head of yours again."

"Pete was here, dumbass," I say.

Shady goes to punch me but stops. "I told you to keep your mouth shut," he says. "And I'm telling you again. Now listen."

As I walk away he yells, "What's wrong with you Frank-Einstein?"

When I get home, I take off my sneakers, pull on a clean T-shirt, and climb into bed. I'm drifting off when I hear a clicking sound. I shove the sheets off and sit up. The room is freezing cold. The blue curtains billow out as if in a breeze but the window is closed. My hand shakes as I flick on the light by my bed. Pete is stacking poker chips on my desk.

"You came back," I say.

"You might say that." He pats the chips into a neat pile and says, "Best to stack them by value." He pulls a strand of seaweed from his hair.

I frown. "Thanks for ditching me. Now those guys think I'm crazy."

"Sorry." He keeps stacking the chips, click, click, click. "I wasn't going to come back at all but I wanted to thank you for trying to save me."

"Trying to save you?" I stammer. "You won big that night. If anyone needed saving it was me."

"You need to learn when to walk away." He turns a green chip round in his hand, and it shimmers.

My voice shakes as I say, "I shouldn't have stayed for one last hand. I should have left with you." The green chip shines so bright it hurts my eyes. "But I went all in, because that's what I do, and I lost, because that's what I do, too." I pause. "It was only fifty bucks but it felt like everything."

Pete sighs. "I'm the one who lost everything that night."

The floor is icy beneath my bare feet. I'm shivering uncontrollably. Drops of water shine on the polished wood. "I thought you won big."

"I did but they took it all."

"They?"

"You know," he says with a rueful smile and the strange thing is I do.

Shady's words come back. "I'll break that stupid head of yours, again." *Again.* A simple word with a simple meaning: another time. Shady's the stupid one. As I cup my hands over my mouth and breathe into them, I remember Mike and Shady following Pete out and see myself stepping into the nearly empty parking lot later, hoping they haven't left yet.

Bottles are breaking. Someone shouts, "cheater." Shady and Mike stand at the far end of the lot by Mike's car. There's a dark shape that looks like a jacket on the ground in front of them. But when I get closer it's not a jacket. My chest feels so tight I can't breathe. A dark pool spreads beneath Pete's head. Shady stuffs a wad of bills in his pocket. Mike leans against the hood of his car, smoking.

Blood keeps bubbling up no matter how hard I press my hand on the artery in Pete's neck. As gray clouds sail across the sky, it's like I'm being pulled up with them, like I'm floating away.

"He fell on the broken glass." Shady wipes his palms on his jeans. "It was an accident."

Still pressing on Pete's neck, I say, "No it wasn't."

He yanks me off Pete and throws me down so hard my head bangs into the asphalt. He bangs it down again. "You keep your mouth shut."

Pete stands by my bedroom window now. His skin is milk pale with a wet sheen. A dark stain spreads on his shirt. "I would have given Shady the money if he'd asked. Winning is what I care about. The rest is . . ."

"Inconsequential?" I say.

"Yeah, something like that." He eyes the sparkling green chip. "They threw me in the ocean. The water was mad cold." He pulls aside the blue curtain and looks out.

Everything in the room feels wet as if a mist rolled in. Waves of panic crash inside me. "Now what do I do?" I ask.

He looks at me sadly. "You open the window."

As I walk toward him, words swim through my mind. *Shine, shine, lachrymose, shine.* I don't even know what *lachrymose* means. More words appear and split apart. They're not even words. They're silver boats sailing out to sea, glass shards from smashed stars, flowers

9

for the forgotten—more than answers to a test. For the first time since this happened I cry. Pete my best friend from forever is dead.

"Open the window," he says again.

The frame sticks but shoots up when I shove it hard. As Pete swings his legs over the sill, he gives me a backward glance. "You stay there," he says. "I need you to tell the police everything."

He tosses the chip out the window and jumps into the green shimmers as they vanish in the air.

I rush out into the yard and push aside the baize blades of grass looking for the chip. It has to be here because one of the chips on my desk is missing, but I can't find it. I never do.

The next morning someone walking their dog discovers Pete's body washed up in the marsh. I tell the police what I remember, and they find blood in the trunk of Mike's car. Shady and Mike are arrested. My friends are no longer my friends. But I don't care. It's time to walk away. ❖

Snapshot

Shelagh Smith

Burying my dad wasn't the hardest part; it was cleaning out his cottage.

The place was a wreck, not in a filthy hoarder kind of way, but in an old man who's lived by himself too long kind of way.

I sat amid a pile of old magazines—*National Geographic*, *Smithsonian*, *Guns & Ammo*—and paused for breath. Salty, my blissfully dimwitted mutt, lifted his head, and let out a soft whine. "I know," I told him, and then to my best friend Carla, "Would someone want these?"

She looked up from going through his old roll-top desk, dust motes swirling around her face, and wiped her brow with the back of her hand. The air was thick with the humidity of the late June day creeping in around us, and Salty's moist doggy breath didn't help.

"Maybe the library?" she suggested, and then held up a box of paper clips. She set it atop the other twelve boxes. "Did your dad steal these or what?"

"No idea."

"I'm done here," said Carla, standing and stretching. "I'm going to the bedroom, but before I do, let me ask. If I find something that's a little . . . um, sensitive? Would you want to know? Or just toss it?"

"What do you mean?"

Carla arched an eyebrow. "He was a guy."

"You mean like porn or something?"

"Or something."

I considered it and finally said, "Use your best judgment."

Carla disappeared upstairs. I heard the floor creak overhead as she moved about the bedroom where he'd passed. A sudden swell of emotion rose in me, so I hauled myself to my feet, called Salty, and together we went outside. I leaned on the deck railing as Salty leapt down to survey the yard. I watched him crisscross the lawn until he found something interesting and started to dig.

"Hey!" I yelled. "You're trashing the property value!"

Unimpressed, he continued to dig, then lost interest, and began another circuit. There wasn't much space for him to roam, but childhood memories painted the space much more grandly.

The yard had seemed immense then, when it was just me, my older sister, and a rusty swing set that had eaten up hours of my childhood. I swore I could still hear the creaking swings echo against the woods around us. The memories, so sweet at first, began to sting as I realized our lives—all I knew and loved—were ebbing away. First Mom, then Dad, and now it was just me and Colleen, but even she had been drifting in and out of my life since we were young.

Gone nearly five months now, Dad had died alone here, going to sleep one night at eighty-three and simply never waking. There were a lot worse ways to go, I supposed, and he'd died the way he'd spent most of his life: alone.

He'd divorced Mom when I was eighteen, had had a series of relationships that never lasted, and ultimately married his job. Being a beat cop in a small town wasn't particularly challenging, but he had loved it, and I'd always loved him for it. He'd been there to break up fights, pull over drunk drivers, bring lost dogs home. He'd been the model of a good small-town cop, something many people nowadays forgot ever existed, and I treasured our times together, here in this very cottage, after my sister departed on bad terms for the West Coast and the life she wanted.

"Hey, Moll?"

The unsettled note in Carla's voice twisted my guts. Oh god, I thought, please don't let it be . . . Well, I didn't know what it *could* be, but whatever it was sounded upsetting. "Well, shit," I muttered, and then called Salty.

Salty gave up the spot he'd been digging in a flower bed and ran to me.

I found Carla in my dad's room, perched on the bed, a pile of scrapbooks splayed open around her. She held a photo—an old-fashioned snapshot where you drove to a tiny parking lot kiosk, handed over a roll of film, and prayed for seven to ten days that the pictures had actually come out. This time it had. The white border around the photo and date on the back placed it almost exactly fifty years ago.

It was a young blonde woman, hair ringed by daisies woven into a chain. She smiled at the camera, blue eyes alight. It was impossible to miss that she'd been in love when this was taken, and it made my heart hurt. I had never felt that, not even once, but here she was, eyes shining as though she'd finally figured it all out. It took a few seconds for me to realize who she was, and when I did, my stomach clenched.

"Oh my god," I whispered.

"Who is that?" asked Carla.

"Delilah Festis," I said softly, recalling the case that had rocked our small town and ended my carefree childhood days playing alone outside, even in our own backyard. "A missing girl from a long time ago. They never found her."

Carla gestured to the scrapbooks and photo albums. "Looks like your dad had a thing for her."

For some reason, her words sent a chill down my spine. I shook it off as I looked at page after page about the case, about Delilah.

"This was so long ago." I breathed, pausing to examine a black and white school photo from the newspaper, staged, formal, and worlds apart from the one in my hand.

"He was obsessed," she said.

"It was a pretty big case," I said. I flipped through clippings and newspaper photos of Delilah, forever eighteen. The editors seemed to like the black and white graduation photo, which to me seemed

13

unfair. The photo I held showed her alive and in love. Why not use the one that told more of her story?

In the snapshot, she stood against a woodsy backdrop, hair teased by an unseen wind. Sun dappled the leaves, throwing shadows against her cheeks, and shrouding eyes that seemed lit from within. Flowers bloomed at her feet, buttercups, and just out of frame, the hint of a strangely angled pole, white and red like a candy cane, nearly matching the woven red band and dangling half charm around her wrist. That band, more than anything else, made me sad. Who held the other half of that friendship bracelet? Were they missing her still today?

"Oh my god," said Carla in a suddenly hushed whisper. "Moll, do you think he killed her?"

I stared at my best friend. "Are you insane? Have you actually gone insane?" I asked in something close to amazement. "You're talking about my *father*."

Carla looked chagrined, but only for an instant. "No, I'm just saying, it happens. Didn't you see that documentary where the woman found her serial killer dad's souvenirs from—"

I cut her off. "You watch too much murder TV. It's rotting your brain."

"I'm sorry, I just . . ." Her voice trailed off, and I found a smile for her. I supposed if my very best friend couldn't bring up such outlandish ideas, who could?

"It's fine." I continued to turn pages.

"Do you think the town PD would want this?"

I considered the new detectives—an entirely new evolution from the cop my dad had been, in the same way wolves had evolved into domesticated dogs—poring through his collection. No, I thought. They wouldn't appreciate an old man's obsession.

Plus, the killer was undoubtedly dead.

I made a show of looking at my watch. "You've got to pick up your kids."

"Don't remind me," she said, but she stood and brushed dust from her shorts. "Pick it up again Saturday?"

"You bet."

We shared a brief hug, she gave Salty a scratch, and we watched together as she backed down the narrow drive.

Across the way, afternoon light shimmered on the pond where I'd learned to swim. How many times had I woven my way through thick brush to the water, causing my mom to yell after me, "Dear God, Molly Gallagher! You better not drown!"

Parents back then were a different breed too.

"C'mon, dog," I said, heading inside to stare at the photo albums.

But still Carla's words rang in my ears. *Moll, do you think. . .*

I resisted the urge to light up a smoke. I'd quit when Mom passed of lung cancer, not from smoking, but some genetic fuckery that left her in misery for the last year of her life, not long before Dad's passing. I wondered if her dying had hastened his. Even though they'd stopped being married they'd always remained close, despite the unique challenges of managing a fractured family.

There had never been any noticeable acrimony between them during or after the split; all that venom had been spilled when my sister, older by twelve years, left home for her new life. Perhaps that ugliness was enough for one lifetime.

Occasionally, though, a word or two would bubble up about each other. "So he's seeing *her,*" Mom would say with a sniff. Or my dad might say, "Well, she got what she wanted" whenever Mom married the new man in her life.

I wondered idly if Mom had blamed Dad for my sister, Colleen's, leaving, but she had never mentioned it to me. Who can say what might have passed between Colleen and Mom when the prodigal daughter returned with wife in tow to nurse Mom through cancer treatments?

I pushed the thought aside, turned to the albums, flipping to a newspaper article dated nearly a quarter century ago.

Missing Girl Case Enters 25th Year—Waiting for Answers

Delilah Festis—"Daisy" to friends and family—was only 18 years old

15

when she vanished from Rocky
Point on a scorching July day in
1974. Today, she would be 43.

And today, there are still no
answers. With no new clues, it's up
to Daisy's family to keep her
memory alive.

"Everyone loved her. She
marched to her own drum, you
know?" said her sister Patty. "She
was a free spirit. She trusted
everyone. I guess she trusted the
wrong person."

I studied the accompanying photo of Patty and my cigarette
fingers itched again. She looked sad, old, worn. A cigarette burned in
the ashtray beside her, and I wondered how that had slipped by the
editors, even back then. Smoking was verboten now, the same way
hitchhiking became forbidden in the late seventies and eighties when
horror stories of missing girls started to come out. Was Delilah—Daisy
—one of those girls?

I turned the page to avoid the pull of nicotine and stumbled
into a series of Dad's handwritten notes, all dated the same July day in
consecutive years, like some grim anniversary.

July 12, 1975—spoke to Det. Carver—no leads.
July 12, 1976—called Det. Carver—no leads. Still working.
July 12, 1977—called Det. Mercantonio— no call back.

They went on for years—decades—until eventually the notes
stopped because the detectives stopped returning calls. I felt a pang of
regret for Dad that he was ignored when he so clearly cared about the
case that happened on his watch, in his town. They ended with one last
note, just three years ago.

July 12, 2021—Done.

I turned next to printouts from online missing persons' forums where the bored and lonely lived—and died—vicariously through others' misery. Most posts were links to anniversary articles. Some offered suggestions. One writer, SleuthSlayer, had an abundance of theories, all printed and annotated with Dad's increasingly wobbly hand.

> Did anyone check her sister? Younger than her but kids do crazy things. Look at the Kennedy family murdering that Moxley girl.

And my dad's note: *Crackpot.*
And later:

> What are cops not telling? Small town cops must have known this girl. Looking like that, she probably had a lot of male attention.

And the response:

> We're assuming male attention.

Dad's note in the margins: *Revisit.*

I leaned back in my chair, idly stroking Salty's head in my lap. I wondered if Dad had softened enough in his later years to consider that very idea, that it might not have been a man who took her. It seemed his acceptance of other people's lives had grown as he aged, although as far as I knew, he'd never reached out to Colleen to make amends.

Revisit.

Did he mean the case? Or did he mean his broken relationship with my sister? I supposed either could have been true.

17

I didn't sleep well that night, a victim of my often unchecked anxiety, thinking over all the things I had to do. The thoughts came relentlessly, clawing at my peace, and the one that cut deepest: *Moll, do you think . . . ?*

I finally dozed off in the last hour before my alarm chirped, and that pissed me off. I fed Salty, drank a rank cup of coffee that had been in the pot since yesterday, and planted myself in front of the computer to tackle the detritus of living. Paying bills. Checking emails. Reading social media. When I'd exhausted those distractions, I dived into the thing that had kept me spinning in my sheets overnight.

Why Delilah? Why *that* case? And Carla's words: *Moll, do you think . . . ?*

I researched the sleuth forums. As I skimmed, I dug into foggy memories from that time in my life. I wondered how many people actually remembered with any clarity what they did in the summer of their eighth year.

I recalled vague conversations among grownups, back when things like missing and murdered women weren't celebrated with such macabre glee. Aside from a cursory "Don't hitchhike," there were no stranger-danger talks. I used to think I was lucky to have grown up during a time when the only instructions were to get home before the street lights came on. Parents didn't care where you were; they were just happy you came home at all.

Well, most parents anyway.

I thought of Delilah's parents. They'd gone to their reward without ever knowing what happened to her, and soon, no one would remember her at all. After fifty years, how many follow-up stories could a newspaper print?

With nothing new online, and my own memories sketchy at best, I did the only other thing I could think of. I drove to my sister's house.

Her wife answered the door. I hadn't seen her since the funeral.

"Hey, Laura," I offered. "Colleen here?"

She ushered me in and summoned my sister. She came out of her office wearing a tight smile and I knew she wasn't entirely happy to see me. That was okay. The last time I'd been here had been to tell her I'd found Dad dead in his bed. Her reaction then had been reserved, but at his memorial service, she'd wept openly and spoke about the loss of the father she'd loved, then hated, then . . . what? What had evolved between them in his later years I would probably never know.

"What?" she demanded.

"I wanted to check in about the house," I said. It was a weak excuse. She hadn't cared about the house before and she didn't care now. But it would get the conversation rolling.

"Do what you want."

Laura threw her hands up and said, "You two. I'm going to put on some coffee. You want?"

"Sure," I said. To Colleen, I added, "It's going on the market next week. I'm cleaning it out."

"I don't want anything."

"Okay."

Silence hung between us until she let out an exasperated sigh and said, "Stop worrying I'm going to hate you for something later. Do what you want. Keep it if you like."

"I don't want it," I said, and the vehemence in my own voice surprised me. Where had that come from?

"Then sell it."

"Yeah, but—"

"But nothing." And then, raising her brows over the frames of her glasses, said, "What's *really* on your mind?"

There it was. She'd always been able to see through me, but maybe that was part of being so much older. She'd left home shortly after I'd started eighth grade—she needed to be free, Mom said. Dad had said much worse.

"I found some stuff."

"Porn?" she said with a sly grin.

"Oh, my god."

"Please tell me it was gay porn." A genuine smile lit her face, her eyes gleaming. I couldn't help but smile too.

"I'm sure you'd like that."

19

She cackled wickedly, and suddenly the ice was broken between us. She gestured to the living room as Laura brought our coffee. She backed out, saying "Family business," even though we encouraged her to stay.

Colleen sipped and grimaced. "How does she fuck up a perfectly good cup of coffee?" she whispered conspiratorially, and I had to agree. The coffee was shit. "It's a Keurig for fuck's sake."

"Do you remember the Delilah Festis case?"

Colleen blinked slowly, and I thought she might be trying to place the name, but the way she set her cup down made the hair on my arms stand up. "Daisy?" she asked. "Why do you ask?"

"He had a ton of stuff about her."

Colleen hesitated again and said, "Not surprised. He was a cop."

"Yeah, but I mean *a lot* of stuff."

He was obsessed. Moll, do you think . . . ?

"Like what?"

"Newspaper articles, internet posts, photos."

She pressed her lips tight together and said with a hint of bitterness in her voice, "He always wanted to be a detective, just couldn't pass the tests. He wanted to be something he wasn't—wanted *us* to be the family we weren't, right?"

Suddenly, I regretted excavating bad memories. "I didn't mean to upset you."

She forced a smile and said, "It was a long time ago."

I struggled for something to say, then returned to the reason I came. "What was Delilah like?"

Colleen shifted in her seat, crossed and uncrossed her legs. I could sense her unease from across the room. "She was nice. Pretty. She was . . . missed." Colleen stopped talking suddenly, and I wondered if she was struggling with her emotions. Spots of color rose in her cheeks. "Her absence was felt by the whole town."

"Was she a good friend of yours?"

"We knew each other," she said, blowing out a sigh and slapping her hands on her thighs. "Long time ago. I barely remember 1974. Too many drugs," she joked.

"One thing I didn't find," I said, "were any photos of us. Isn't that strange? Dad didn't have a single photo of *us.* Just *her.*"

"Mom had those. Wait here."

She hurried to another room and emerged with a photo album, not unlike my dad's. In fact, they were identical. Synthetic fabric backing gone dingy with age. She plopped down beside me, leaning into me, and it brought a tear to my eye. How long had it been since we'd sat like this? I wiped it away before she could notice.

She opened the book, and under see-through pages lay the story of her—of *our*—youth.

"Oh my god, is that Patches?" I asked, studying a picture of our old dog in the back yard of the cottage. "And this was Mom?"

The photo was my mom in an evening gown, a metallic pink party hat atop her head. The banner in the background read Happy New Year! I couldn't remember her ever looking so young.

"And Dad," said Colleen, pointing to my father, tuxedoed, arm around another woman. "That's Mrs. Sullivan. She lived next door."

"Oh, wow," I said, and heard my sister mutter under her breath, "Swingers no doubt."

"Oh!" I cried, and nearly slammed the book shut. "That's disgusting."

"That was the seventies. Free love, baby."

"I don't believe you."

"You don't have to, but I was there," she said, and together we turned pages until she found a picture of us together.

We were in the back yard, my feet climbing the sky as she stood behind me, pushing me on the swing set. I could almost hear the creaking metal as the set tried to break free of its mooring, feel the burning chains in my hands, and whooshing of air as I leapt off, midswing, landing amid a field of sunny yellow blooms.

"Do you remember this?" I asked.

"How could I forget? You loved that stupid swing set. You thought you were a bird. I thought it looked like demented candy cane."

I stifled a grin. Colleen was right. It did look like a demented candy cane, its red stripes over rusting white metal. It was an eyesore, but it had been my eyesore, until suddenly it vanished one day, another victim of the hysteria that followed Delilah's disappearance.

Carla's words came to me again, causing my stomach to drop to my feet. I knew if I didn't ask it now, I never would, and I'd regret it forever.

"Colleen, do you think Dad had anything to do with her disappearance?"

She stared at me, her face a blank slate, and not for the first time I wished I could read her the way she could read me. "Why would you ask that?"

"You know why."

"Because he was obsessed?"

I nodded, unable to speak.

"No," she said with certainty. "He was a lot of things, but he'd never hurt a woman."

With that, she slapped the book shut, handed it over with a tight smile, and said, "I've got to get back to work. Do what you need to do. I'll be happy when it's gone, and I think you will too."

I wanted to be hurt by what she said, but she was right. The cottage had been important to me then. Now it seemed like something else, something I didn't want to consider too deeply. "Thanks, Sis," I said, and she hugged me tight before I left.

I couldn't sleep again that night. I lay awake in the dark, listening to Salty's snoring. It was strangely comforting, and I wondered if everyone felt this way about their dog. They *had* to. There were few things in life better than the unconditional love of a pup. I thought back to Patches, back to the album that sat untouched on the coffee table. I couldn't bring myself to look at it, to revisit old memories—the good, the bad, and the ugly—of our childhood.

I knew that raising teenagers was hell, and it couldn't have been easy raising me, but raising my sister must have been much more challenging, especially back then. Colleen was different, a lot like Delilah, I thought. She, too, walked to the beat of her own drum. Sometimes I admired her eagerness to go out on her own and find herself, her life, and her truth. Honestly, I was still a little jealous.

It was sometime before dawn when I nudged Salty out of my way, crawled out of bed, and slipped into the past.

The photos were dated, of course, documenting a time when things were easier or, maybe not *easier*, but hidden. I studied pictures of my sister, a freckled Irish girl like me, with dark hair, splotchy skin, and stance that said she was uncomfortable in her skin. Her shag 'do fell over her eyes as she slouched in jeans and T-shirts in the back yard. If teen resentment was a person, it was Colleen. Some photos were of us together, Colleen the tomboy, me in frills and lace that did little to hide my plump figure and unfortunate hair. We Gallagher girls would never be Delilah.

I turned pages, fingers fondly stroking Patches, then Thumbs, an old cat who long ago crossed the Rainbow Bridge, and then I settled on the photo of me and Colleen, at the swing set I loved and she hated. This one I would frame for a gift, I thought.

I laughed out loud at how miserable she looked, not at me, but past the lens to the photographer. I imagined if it were a selfie today, she'd throw up a middle finger, but certainly not back then, and certainly not if Dad was taking the picture. I looked with some chagrin at my own goofy smile, just happy to be around my older sister, and then to her hands, one resting on my shoulder, the other on the candy-striped swing set pole.

Then I saw it.

Around her wrist was a flash of red, a woven band, and hanging from it, the other half of a silver charm.

I stood on the back deck of the cottage watching Salty make his circuit. I didn't hear the car door shut, but Salty did. He ran to greet Colleen.

"Where's Laura?" I asked but words were hard to get out. It felt like I had gravel in my throat.

Colleen shrugged off the question, took a bracing breath, and leaned back against the railing, staring at her reflection in the sliding glass door. "Why am I here?" she asked.

I took the photo of us on the swing set from my pocket, handing it to her. She looked at it once, then handed it back. "What about it?"

"I was going to have it blown up for a gift, but thought better of it." My words caught, but then I managed. "I thought we shouldn't memorialize evidence that Dad killed Delilah."

A soft gasp, not quite a laugh of disbelief, escaped Colleen. "What are you talking about?"

"Look at it." I shoved it at her. Color rose in her face, redder than I'd ever seen, and maybe, for the first time ever, I *could* read my sister. "You know it too, don't you? That's why he was obsessed."

"Moll," she said slowly. "You need to let this go."

"Oh, come on, Colleen," I said, and felt tears start to build. "She was *here*. She was in this yard. With us. With *you*. Look!" I pulled out the photo of Delilah, held it beside the one of us, and pointed out the swing set's matching legs. I pointed to the friendship bracelet, a forever-promise, on both their wrists. "She was here, Colleen. He killed her. Why else would he track the case so carefully? Why?"

Colleen shook her head. I could see her swallowing hard again and again, and was afraid she'd be sick.

"Tell me I'm wrong," I said, clutching her arm.

Then, with a dead certainty in her voice that stopped me cold, she said, "You're wrong." She wiped angrily at her eyes, so full of sudden tears that they spilled down her cheeks, and when she met my gaze, I felt my knees go weak.

"I'm not wrong," I said, but deep inside, I knew I was. I knew what she would say next, and I wanted to scream no, no, no to drown out the words that would come. I clamped my mouth shut, bracing myself for it, for the truth.

"It was me."

I felt the world spin. I steadied myself on the railing. I wanted to scream that she was lying, just fucking around, but the desolate expression in her eyes told me otherwise.

"What are you saying?" I whispered.

"Daisy and I weren't just friends. We were . . . seeing each other," she said, her voice barely audible. "We were over there." She gestured feebly to the spot where the swing set once stood. "We were messing around, you know, and Dad saw us. He flipped out."

I took a breath, imagining the scene, imagining his rage when he came upon them. He had mellowed in later years, but still I recalled the ugly words he'd spoken to my sister when she told him her truth. I could see it. I could hear it.

"He grabbed her. I tried to stop him. There was a struggle." Colleen fought for the words. "I tried to push her out of the way and she fell. She . . . fell." Colleen covered her mouth with her hands, and I watched as the horror of what had happened came alive in her mind. "She hit her head on the swing set. She started shaking. Convulsing."

"No," I said, but I *could* see it in my mind, like a movie playing endlessly before me.

"She died so quickly. I still can't believe it," she said, and short, ragged sobs tore out of her.

"Why didn't you call the cops?" I demanded, suddenly angry.

"Because Dad *was* a cop," she said as though I was an idiot. "Do you know what that would have been like? He was a town cop, Moll. His lesbian daughter gets caught with the homecoming queen and she dies *here,* in our yard. What do you think would have happened to him? To us?" She fought back more tears, and said brokenly, "You once asked if I knew Dad loved me. Moll, I know he did. He covered it up for us. For *me.*"

The next question was obvious, but still it stuck in my throat. I couldn't ask it because I already knew the answer in my heart and soul. My hands shook as I gazed at the photo of Delilah here in our yard, beside the swing set, among the field of buttercups at her feet.

I looked at the yard today, at the spot where the set had once stood, and saw Salty digging, digging, digging in a patch of flowers that bloomed in the shape of a young woman's body. ❖

What Made Sammy Run

Chris Knopf

When an old friend who's done you a million favors calls you from San Francisco asking for one in return, you just do it. I was living in New Haven, and he wanted me to find his brother, last known location somewhere in Middletown, Connecticut, about a half hour away.

"Our mother died," he said. "The Alzheimer's finally got her."

"Sorry, man. I liked your mom."

"Me, too. As you recall, we were both adopted, but she raised us like we were blood. As good a mother as you'd want."

"That's true. Was always good to me."

"I haven't talked to Sammy in a few years. Lost track of him. He needs to know."

"And you think Middletown?"

"That's what somebody told me. Supposedly has a gig cooking for a restaurant on Main Street. That is the beginning and end of my information."

I'd worked in kitchens and behind bars in New Haven and parts north to pay tuition and keep myself from starving before landing a teaching job at the college. I'd never worked in Middletown, but I knew how to get there. I was loafing through spring break, so the timing was perfect. I told him that.

"Excellent," he said. "I really appreciate it. By the way, Mom actually left us some money. Not enough for a private jet, but not nothing."

"I know Sammy loved your mother, but that part would be of particular interest."

"If I were a dollar," he said, "I wouldn't get too comfortable in Sammy's wallet."

"I'll do my best."

Leveraging my experience in the hospitality trade, and remembering Sammy's regular routines, I headed straight for a bar on Main Street, Middletown. After breaking the ice with some shoptalk, I asked the bartender if he knew Sammy Anderson, explaining his general appearance.

"Maybe. Could describe a lot of guys around here."

Despite the burden of sampling beers in every bar in every restaurant up and down the street, this was the response I usually got. But I was just getting started, so I didn't get discouraged and came back the next evening. Though it was the same deal. Nobody seemed to know Sammy Anderson.

Crossing a side street before making one more loop, I looked to the left and saw a neon sign sticking out that should have announced Cathy's Bar & Grill but with all the missing lights it read, Cat y's B r G il . I realized then my mistake. My earlier attempts were too upscale. Sammy's cooking had yet to attract the attention of the *Bocuse D'or*, and his standards for ambience never rose above key rings, Metallica T-shirts, Bud on tap, Slim Jims, and the aroma of barely swabbed beer and tobacco breath.

Cathy's was just such a place. In fact, Cathy herself was on duty behind the bar. Now confident, I got right to the point when she set down my beer.

"You know a guy named Sammy Anderson?"

She leaned toward me with hands flat on the bar, one holding a soggy dish towel. She was not a svelte person, and though the graces of youth hadn't entirely fled her face, it recorded a long, hard drive.

"I might, depending on why you're asking," she said.

"His brother Bill's looking for him. He's out in California and sent me to hunt around."

"I didn't know he had a brother," she said, proving she did know Sammy.

"We all grew up together in New Haven. The three of us."

"Didn't know he came from New Haven."

"I have a message for him."

I could have told her about the mom's passing, but thought it better to deliver that myself, if possible.

"You could write him a letter," she said.

"We would if we knew the address."

She tapped on the bar.

"You're sittin' in it."

I looked around as if expecting to see Sammy's bed and a chest of drawers.

"He gets his mail here," she said, amused by my confusion. "Where he sleeps, I couldn't tell you."

"He doesn't work for you?"

She stood up straighter and flung the towel over her shoulder.

"He used to cook on the day shift, work your side of the bar at night."

"So he'd have a W2?"

She smirked.

"We try to avoid those bureaucratic complications. Sammy got paid in cash and most of it ended up back in the till."

"You said he used to cook here."

"Disappeared about three weeks ago. Maybe more. Hasn't shown up since."

"And you don't know where he lives."

"His friends might. Stick around and some of them might be coming by. I'll send them over."

"That's good of you. Thank you."

She should have left to attend to the other customers, but paused, looking me over.

"He doesn't owe somebody money or any of that? You're not a leg breaker?"

I stopped myself from saying "exactly the opposite"; instead I made a little laugh and said, "He probably owes both of us some money, but with Sammy it's the cost of doing business."

She nodded as if we'd just shared confidences.

"Everybody loves Sammy," she said, and wandered down the bar.

The place did fill up after that, and true to her word, Cathy brought over a young couple and made the two people next to me give up their seats. I don't remember their names, but I imagine him to be a Todd, and his girlfriend likely a Jennifer.

"Dude," Todd said, "you know Sammy?"

"I do. I'm looking for him."

"He's a riot," said Jennifer.

"Do you know where he lives?" I asked them.

They conferred with their eyes, then looked at me with regret.

"Not really," Jennifer said, "though I think I know which street."

"That'd be great," I said. "Can I buy you two a drink?"

"Is the Pope a twenty-first century Argentinian ecumentalist in counterreformational clothing?" Todd said, obviously not for the first time.

"He's always spouting theological subversions." Jennifer sighed. "I think it was his upbringing. Though it gets tautological."

"You guys go to Wesleyan?" I asked, taking a flier.

Todd looked down at his working man's outfit, as if it was an effective disguise. I wrote down the street Jennifer referred to, and saw on my phone that it was toward the north end of town. I bought them matching Heinekens, the closest they could come to craft beers at Cathy's. I asked them how they thought Sammy was doing. They were noncommittal.

"Don't know, really. He's just a guy we see around here. Likes to tell stories and joke around."

"So you don't know why he's been gone for a few weeks?"

"He's been gone?"

I spent the next day walking up and down the street suggested by the young theologians. It was a tired place, barely holding things together. The residents were a mix of Black people who looked well established, and a scattering of white people, seeming more desperate and transitory.

I didn't ring any doorbells, though I stopped people on the street asking about Sammy Anderson. Everyone was friendly and tried to help, but as in every American neighborhood, they only knew a few of their neighbors.

"You best check with the community health up on Main Street," said one helpful woman pushing a baby carriage with a bright-faced little girl on board. "They know where everybody's at."

I thanked her and moved on down the street. I paused at one of the more dilapidated buildings and went up on the porch. There on the bank of buzzers was the name, right out there in the open. Samuel Anderson. I rang it with no result. So I pushed the buzzer immediately below, the last one in the stack.

When a young woman said hello, I asked if she knew Sammy, who surely lived in close proximity.

"Who wants to know?" she replied, though with no hostility.

"I'm looking for him. Sent by his brother."

"I didn't know he had a brother."

"I need to talk to him. I just want to pass along a message."

It took a while for her to come back on, but she eventually said, "I'll be out."

I don't know what I expected, but I was surprised by her appearance, which was both tattered and comely. Her face had the type of bone structure favored by fashion photographers, lots of angles and definition, though she badly needed a hairdresser, and her eyes, a vivid eggshell blue, needed Visine.

She opened the door the whole way and stepped out onto the porch, forcing me to shift back in order to preserve personal space. She clenched herself around the middle and looked ready to abandon the conversation at any moment, though she never did.

"He's not here," she said, without preamble.

I heard an accent, something Eastern European, which matched her face. As I took her in, I noticed that her skin was a light shade of olive, and clear as Sophia Loren's in her first feature film.

"I'm sorry to bother you," I said, launching what I'd prepared, despite the way she'd started the conversation. "I only have a message from his brother, which I need to tell to his face. Do you know where he went?"

"He didn't say. He just left. Rent is all paid till the end of the month, so we don't care."

"Is this your house?" I asked.

"My husband's. He looks after everything. What does this brother want?"

"Just to talk to him."

"Does Sammy owe him money?"

I wondered how many people in Middletown would raise the same question.

Having known Sammy my whole life, I wasn't surprised. There wasn't a rose he didn't stop to smell, and if the situation warranted, buy the flower a drink. Though the time spent was worth the price. Sammy always left you feeling as if your spirit had been given an intravenous torrent of *joie de vivre*. The penalty was you paid all the tabs, advanced a fifty here and a fifty there, and frequently fell for grand investment schemes, until you realized you had to stop doing that.

"No," I said, and this time gave in to the impulse. "There's money in it for Sammy. That's one reason I need to track him down."

"Money. Really?"

She moved a little closer, as if the promise of Sammy's potential good fortune conveyed to me, and that I might be a person she should get to know better. She fussed with her hair, ineffectively, reinforcing the impression. I instantly regretted what I'd said.

"Not a lot of money," I said. "But he should know."

She was undeterred.

"My husband might know where he is," she said. "He doesn't share these things with me, though, why should he? I just clean the apartments before the next tenants move in and plunge the toilets."

"Can I talk to your husband?" I asked, not wanting to pressure her, but having little choice.

She shrugged an extravagant shrug.

31

"I'm going with him to Cathy's bar like we do every night. You can ask him yourself," she said, starting to give me directions to the joint, which I cut off midsentence.

"I know the place."

She liked that.

"Of course. Around eight tonight. You know me. He's the fat guy who doesn't know how to dress."

Then she turned and disappeared in a graceful swivel into the building.

I had time to kill, so for the hell of it, I went into the community health center and asked if they had a Samuel Anderson on record. The woman at the counter said that was confidential information. I played the whole tape about being sent by his brother to tell him their mother had died. It fell on deaf ears. I said I just wanted to pass along a message, which moved her not an inch.

She did smile when asking me if I was Samuel's spiritual adviser.

I realized anything out of my mouth would be wasted breath, so I just said, "His bookie," and left.

I got to Cathy's well ahead of the Eastern European woman and set myself up in the same spot at the bar. Cathy came over with my prior order and I didn't have the heart to tell her a scotch on the rocks would have been preferable. Though when I stared blankly at the beer she got the message, and said, "Something stronger?"

The preternatural powers of the common bartender are highly unappreciated.

I only had a chance to drink half the tall scotch when the Eastern Europeans came bustling into the bar. She was nearly radiant in an untucked blouse that was almost like a little skirt, cheap makeup, and tight jeans. The husband was what I expected, with a pockmarked complexion and lumpy features. He wore a gym outfit with a Denver Nuggets logo you could see from space. I waved them over to the bar. Cathy slid on up and said, "Hello, darlings. The usual?"

They nodded and a cosmopolitan and draft beer followed. We all clinked glasses, the woman with exceptional poise, given the overfilled martini glass.

"You lookin' for Sammy the welch?" the husband asked.

His wife pushed into him with her shoulder.

"You already talking business?" she said. "We just sat down here."

"What, you don't like money?"

"I like money," she admitted. "But talk about something else first."

The husband didn't seem to notice her criticism, though he looked around the bar, maybe hoping a better prospect would materialize.

I smiled through their back and forth, then said to the husband, "Your wife thought you might know where he went."

"As far away as Kansas, if he knows what's good for him," he said, like he meant it, completing the thought with a heroic downing of his beer. "No, I don't know where he is. But if he comes back and pays me, I won't put him in the river."

"I said his rent was paid," the woman said to me, in a half whisper, "but not so much the utilities. And maybe a little loan."

"No such thing as a little loan," he said.

The husband had very large hands, with noticeable scar tissue on the knuckles. The last time I'd seen eyes like his were on a deer I'd hit on the highway. Brown and dead. That Cathy called him "darling" proved her indiscriminate affections, and their long tenure at the bar.

"I'm taking a piss," he said, sliding off the bar stool. "You two talk, but don't get too friendly," he added, looking at me.

When he was gone, the woman slid her cosmo over to me and said, "Here, drink this. He always orders them, but they make my head go funny."

I did as she asked, immediately feeling my head go funny.

"So you really don't know where Sammy went," I said.

She looked at me as if trying to read a note in fine print on my nose. Then abruptly turned her head away.

"I can't talk about it."

"Your husband seems like a pretty serious guy."

She whipped her head back at me.

"He wasn't kidding about the river," she whispered. "He did such things in Ukraine."

Before the husband came back, I made sure I'd scooted my bar stool a few more inches away from his wife. He twirled his hand at Cathy and another beer soon followed.

I don't remember what else we talked about, but eventually I needed to visit the john myself. I was about to open the door when the woman was suddenly there beside me, crammed into the passageway outside the restrooms. She gripped my shirt at the shoulder.

"I know something about Sammy that nobody else does," she said, in the raspy sotto voce she'd used at the bar. "It's why he's gone. And we'll never see him again, I'm sure."

Then she did something that explained the whole thing. She pulled up her shirt and the bulge was obvious, even to my inexperienced eye. I looked at her and she nodded.

"The fat man hasn't touched me in years. You figure it out."

My surprise was proportionate to my horror that her burly and murderous husband might suddenly appear in the narrow hallway, mindful of the two-block proximity to the Connecticut River. I told her in an urgent hiss that there was a possible remedy, but it would mean an instant and resolute decision on her part. Not waiting to see her response to this, I scribbled a note on the back of a receipt crumpled in my back pocket, and pressed it into her hand before escaping into the men's room.

I was glad to see she wasn't standing there when I came out. I didn't want the two of us returning to the bar together. She was back at the bar with another cosmopolitan, which I wondered how she'd dispose of this time around.

Cathy brought us the cheeseburgers we'd ordered, so eating substituted for conversation. The husband managed to squeeze in two more beers to accompany the meal, his version a towering thing that likely taxed the establishment's condiment supply. His wife barely picked away at her dish, though she asked for an extra pickle.

Happy to politely slip away, I left them there, along with an abundant tip, and made my way back to New Haven.

The next day I called Bill Anderson.

"You find him?" he asked.

"Not exactly, but I know what to do. How much cash is available?"

"A bit north of fifty thousand," he said. "The rest will come when we sell the house."

"Can you send me a bank check? It'll be good for Sammy."

"Sure. It's his money. How did he take it?"

"You know Sammy," I said.

"Yeah, I guess I do. Tell him to call me."

"As soon as I can."

I met her at the train station in New Haven. She'd already bought her off-peak ticket into Grand Central. I handed her a fat envelope which she stuck in her rolling suitcase.

She wasn't nervous, though a spark of excitement had brightened her eyes. We didn't have much to say to each other, but I stayed with her and pulled the suitcase out to the platform when they announced the train's imminent departure. Before she boarded, I asked her, "Do you know if it's a boy or a girl?"

She put her hand on her belly.

"Who cares? Either way, the name will be Sammy."❖

Hellfire & Holywater

Alison McMahan

It felt good to scream.

The game on the local TV was Analy Tigers versus the Cardinal Newman Cardinals. A high school game, but it didn't stop the guys watching it from screaming every time there might be a touchdown.

I slid onto a stool at the end of the bar. I glanced back at Dad, sitting in a dark booth at the back. Maybe if I sat there long enough he'd drink until he passed out. Then I could get us both home. I screamed at the game because I was making fun of those screaming guys, but gradually I got into it and started cheering for real.

"Blow on it for me."

This hot guy plopped onto the stool next to mine. Really hot: strong jaw, a shock of reddish-blond hair, gray eyes that always seemed to be looking into the distance, which just made me want to make him look at me.

"Excuse me?"

He waved some bills under my nose. "Blow on it for me. For luck."

He wasn't much of a smiler, but I was used to that.

They were all waving money around. Making bets.

I blew on it, hard, like I was blowing out birthday candles.

"That's what I'm talkin' about!" The guy slapped the money on the bar and placed his bet.

We watched the game and screamed together some more.

The bartender slid a drink in front of me.

"What is it?"

"Holy water."

I was about to tell him I was underage, but the bartender winked and tilted his head toward Betting Guy.

"Least I could do," said Betting Guy. "You brought me luck." He waved his wad of bills, thicker than ever.

The sight of all that money made me dizzy.

Betting Guy stuck out his hand. "I'm Grayson."

I shook it. "Zoey." I picked up my drink and took a long slug, trying to look like I knew what I was doing. Grayson watched my performance with interest.

"Hey, do you need a ride someplace? I should get out of here while I'm ahead."

I didn't even look back at Dad. If he could blow off all his responsibilities, so could I.

I stepped out ahead of Grayson and landed ankle deep in water. Grayson's strong hand on my arm was all that kept me from falling completely and getting soaked. He pulled me back into the bar's doorway, his arm now around my waist, anchoring me. We watched the water lapping against the stoop.

"Wow." I thought about wiggling free of his arm, then decided not to. "When did that happen?"

"The waters must've shifted. Or maybe they're rising." Grayson searched the area. "It looks like it's dry over there. Ready to try it?"

"What else can we do?" I straightened my shoulders.

I knew what else I could have done. I could have gone back inside and tried again to get Dad out of there, or resigned myself to spending the night in the bar, hoping the floodwaters receded.

But I didn't do that. Instead, I sloshed along in my high heels, Grayson's hand tight over mine.

The spot where he'd parked his old, beat-up car was still dry, luckily. I hesitated for a moment. I knew I should go back into the bar.

But I couldn't deal with Dad. I got into the passenger seat and told Grayson how to get me home.

The morning of the flood, my little sister, Abby, had woken me up by poking me in the eye. "Opey eye."

"Okay, okay." I opened my eyes and reached for the alarm clock.

It was off.

"What the?" I looked out the window and realized the sky was starting to brighten. That meant it was already seven-thirty. I was late for school.

I tried to turn on the light. It didn't work.

Power outage. The rainstorm the night before must have knocked down trees and wires. Had the school lost power too? I let my head fall back onto the pillow.

"I'm hungry!" Abby crawled up and plopped her fat bottom onto my stomach.

"How can you be hungry when you're such a fat little bumblebee?" I tickled her with one hand while I reached for my phone with the other. My battery was nearly dead. I'd been up late, comparing pictures of outfits with my friends, all of us looking forward to the school dance.

"Okay, Abby, come on, come on, let's go eat!"

We tiptoed quietly past Dad's room, then sprinted to the kitchen. I pulled on my clothes as I made toast, sliced up bananas, peeled oranges, whatever would keep Abby from wailing that she was hungry and wake up Dad in the process.

Finally, she was in her clothes and her jacket and had her lunch in her little backpack and we were out the door.

"Up, up," Abby begged.

Normally I would say no to that. She was getting too heavy. And I wanted her to walk.

But today I figured it would get us there quicker, so I heaved her up and off we went to Mrs. Clarinda's. Abby sat on my shoulders and sang while eating her PB&J.

"Abby, gimme that. I don't want peanut butter all in my hair."

Too late. Glop.

I would have yelled at her but there was Mrs. Clarinda standing in her doorway, receiving the babies as they were dropped off.

"Well, if it isn't the Abby and Zoey show," she said to me.

"I was hoping you would have power. Ours is out."

I lifted Abby off my shoulders and put her on the ground, gratefully. "Go inside, see your friends," I told her.

Abby ran in.

"Generator. Hold still a moment." Mrs. Clarinda tried to get the glop of peanut butter out of my hair. "Did you hear that wind last night? I couldn't believe it."

"Yeah, that was something. Do you know if school is open, or delayed, or what?"

"You haven't heard, have you?" Mrs. Clarinda gave up on the peanut butter. "Come inside and I'll get that out for you."

"I'll take care of it. Heard what?"

"The Barlow is flooded."

"What? Everything?"

Mrs. Clarinda shrugged. "That's what I heard. You might want to go check yourself." She turned to a parent carrying in a wailing child.

I waved and dashed off.

It seemed to take forever for the bus to come, and when it came, it was packed. That was unusual. I managed to squeeze in. Everyone was talking about how the rains had swelled the Laguna de Santa Rosa, and how the Russian River had overrun its banks. Now people were canoeing up and down Main Street.

A block from the Barlow, the Sebastopol shopping district, the bus stopped.

"Road's flooded. Can't go any further," said the bus driver.

I got up and followed everyone else out. I had to squeeze my way through a crowd of people just standing there. I ducked down and forced my way past their elbows and knees.

Two women in kayaks paddled up to us, one carrying a bird in a cage. I helped steady her boat while she got out. She handed me the paddle. "You have the ice cream store, right?"

I nodded dumbly.

"Check it out. Then bring it back and let someone else use it."

I didn't wait for her to change her mind. I clambered into the kayak, grabbed the paddle, and pushed off.

The cars parked in front of the Barlow shops were up to their hood ornaments in water. A low building up ahead had water up to the eaves. Trees were so deep in water they looked like bushes. Here and there an old tree listed to the side, close to toppling over. I could only see the top of signposts.

As I paddled further into the Barlow's market district the water seemed to get deeper. There were other people in kayaks and some in rowboats. A few brave souls were trying to walk through the waist-deep water. All the fancy edible plantings, a nod to the agricultural history of the area, were completely submerged. Everything looked so different I had trouble knowing which way to turn. No matter where I went, one thing was clear: the entire shopping district was flooded.

At last, I paddled up to our shop. Water up to the doorknob.

"Awesome."

"Not so awesome. Our business is surely ruined." That was Mr. Shivantha, standing in the door of his clothing boutique, thigh deep in water. "Have you been to look?"

"Not yet." I paddled up to the door, pulled out my keys, and tried to unlock it, but I was too unstable.

"Stop, stop, you don't want to drop your keys. You need galoshes."

I realized he had tall waders on, the kind people used for fly fishing.

"I don't have anything like that."

"Wait. Wait. Don't move."

He splashed back into his own store, then returned carrying a pair of galoshes. "My wife's," he said. He held the kayak steady while I dropped them into the water, then stepped into them. "Thank you," I said.

I always figured we were the bane of Mr. Shiv's existence because our customers kept wandering into his store while still eating our ice cream cones. But here he was, making sure the kayak didn't float off, helping me open the door to the ice cream store.

Right away I could tell everything was ruined: the calendars, the stuffed animals, the tourist souvenirs, the candy, and of course, the ice cream.

Amazingly, our huge industrial freezer had fallen over onto its side. "How could just two feet of water do that?"

Mr. Shiv shrugged. "That's the power of Nature."

"Well, Nature has left me with a huge cleanup job."

Mr. Shiv shook his head. "What's worse is the damage you don't see. Water damage. Mold. We can't just clean this up. We're going to have to gut our stores completely. Otherwise, everything will just rot."

We went into his store. No question, all his stock was ruined. All the beautiful clothes I'd often longed for and could never afford, now soaked with gray water.

We sloshed around.

"Mr. Shiv, there's a shelf here of things that are still dry." I lifted a tank top decorated with sequins.

Mr. Shiv waved me away. "Doesn't matter. We're out of business."

While his back was turned, I slipped the tank top into the pocket of my raincoat.

I paddled back to the waiting crowd and handed the kayak over to someone else who needed to check out the damage.

I tried waiting for a bus back, but there didn't seem to be one, so I walked all the way home.

Our power was still out, but Dad was prepared. He'd crafted a cute little holder out of a wire hanger, put his camping percolator on it, and slid the steno can underneath, and was making himself coffee.

"Can you make me one while I change?"

"Why aren't you in school?"

So, he hadn't heard.

I didn't answer until I was in dry clothes and back in the kitchen with a warm mug of coffee between my hands.

Then I told him.

41

Dad had always seemed solid to me. Or stolid. When Mom died, he buried her, made a schedule that divided the chores and taking care of Abby between us, and trudged on. He never smiled again, but I never saw him cry, either.

Until now. He went to look at our ice cream store himself, then came back, went into his room, and shut the door. I could hear him weeping long into the night.

I went and got Abby. Mrs. Clarinda let me charge my cell phone on an outlet powered by her generator.

Dad came out of his room long enough to eat with me and Abby. Abby chatted at him nonstop, and he would sort of listen, then settle back into his gloom.

As soon as Abby was asleep, I called my best friend, Isabella.

"The dance is still happening," she said. "They think it will cheer us up. You'll come, right?"

At breakfast the next morning I asked Dad about going to the dance. He just grunted and nodded.

I was so excited. Isabella lent me some black slacks, and I had the gold-sequined top from Mr. Shiv's store, which shook and shimmered when I moved, and my mom's earrings and bangles. I took a bus, then walked the last few blocks. I could hear the music and see the bright lights through the gym windows when I got the call.

It was Mrs. Clarinda. I could hear Abby crying in the background. "When are you coming to pick up your sister? You should have been here hours ago!"

"My dad was going to get her today." I stared at the gym, the lights and music fading away even though I was standing still.

"Something must have happened. I have to go look for him. Can you keep her just a little longer? I'm so sorry."

I knew Dad wasn't at home because I had just left there. Maybe he was working at the store, trying to clean it up in spite of what Mr. Shiv had said, and lost track of time.

But when I got to Main Street, the area was dark, all the stores shuttered.

The only place open was a bar. A cruddy place, just as water stained and moldy as all the other businesses that had been flooded, but I guess no one cared.

Sure enough, Dad was in there, sitting in a dark booth by himself, completely wasted.

"Dad, you were supposed to get Abby."

"Damn women," muttered Dad. "Always needing something, never contributing anything."

"How can you say that, Dad? I work with you, and I take care of Abby. I barely have time for school."

"Worthless, all of you." He took a swig of beer. "Should've had sons."

"Dad, this isn't like you. We'll do what you said. We'll get the insurance, and we'll rebuild."

"Couldn't pay the insurance," Dad said. "Too many mouths to feed."

A chill traveled through me. Up until then I'd trusted him, trusted he would stay on the wagon, trusted that I could follow his advice, and everything would be okay.

And just like that, everything I thought I knew was proved wrong.

"Well, whatever, let's go get Abby, go home, and tomorrow we will figure it out." I tried to pull the bottle away from him.

"Get the hell away from me." He swung the bottle at me. I managed to duck before he could hit me.

"Fine." I stood up.

Dad didn't react.

I walked away from him.

He still didn't react.

He really didn't care.

And that's when I heard the guys screaming at the game. That's when I sat at the bar and screamed along with them, and that's where Grayson found me.

"There's no way to get there," Grayson was saying. "Every way I try is flooded."

I sat silently in the car for a moment, staring at the water.

"Want to come to my place?" Grayson asked without taking his eyes off the water.

I'd fooled around with boys at school, of course, but it was nothing like this. Grayson was a real man. Being with him was overwhelming. The sensation took me over. It lifted me out of myself. And that was exactly what I needed.

We stayed in his motel room for three days. Not leaving except for food now and then. Booze.

Then one day I came out of the shower and found him dressed.

"Where are you going?"

"Can't stay here forever, hotness."

"Why not?" I was toweling myself dry as fast as I could.

He didn't look at me when I dropped the towel.

What had mattered so much to him just that morning bored him now.

"We've run out of money. Gotta go get some more."

"You have a job?" I pulled on my underwear and my sequined tank top. "What kind of job?"

"I can't tell you. If I did, I'd have to kill you."

I stared at him. Then I burst out laughing. "Okay, okay, what if I guess?"

He shrugged.

"Uhm. You're an axe murderer?"

He shook his head.

"Any kind of murderer?"

He shook his head again.

I had to admit I was kind of relieved. "A professional gambler, then?"

He shook his head.

"A bank robber."

He almost nodded, then shook his head.

"I know. A robber. But not banks. Just plain . . . robbery."

He nodded.

"Good," I said. "Then you need an assistant. Just give me a sec." I pulled on my tight black jeans and my spiky heels. "Why don't we start with robbing me some new clothes?"

We started small. He'd gas up the car while I shoplifted candy, a flashlight, a pack of Bic classic lighters. As I sashayed out past the gas station cashier, Grayson would come in and hold him up.

Grayson taught me change-making and similar cons.

After we'd done a few of those I asked him why we couldn't rest for a few days at a motel.

"They'd find us. We're criminals now. Both of us. Anyway, we gotta save the money, not spend it."

"What for?" I wanted to know. The only clothes he'd gotten me were a big, oversize T-shirt from a gas station store and a big hat that covered my hair with flaps that covered my ears. And a pair of oversized sunglasses. "You won't let me go buy proper clothes, like you said you would."

"Car's no good. We need something better. Faster. Easier to get lost with. We need a motorcycle."

We went into this motorcycle place in Santa Rosa, me in the sequin tank top and heels, Grayson all business. The sales guy was all over me, flirting with me, while Grayson checked out different bikes.

At one point, while Grayson was sitting on a bike to see how it felt, the sales guy whispered to me, "Hey, aren't you that girl? The one on TV? That's supposed to be missing?"

"How could I be missing?" I giggled. "I'm right in front of you!"

I turned to Grayson. "You hear that, baby? This guy says I'm missing."

"She's missing a couple screws, all right," Grayson shouted to the guy.

"Ha, ha." I turned back to the salesman.

"I'm serious, miss," the guy whispered. "If you need help, you just say so."

I practically poked him in the eye with my finger. "Stop saying that! I told you, I'm not!" I turned to Grayson. "Baby, let's get out of here; this guy is annoying me."

"Fine with me." Grayson got off the bike and we left.

But later, once he was sleeping, I thought about it. The guy said he'd seen me on TV. Did that mean Dad was looking for me?

I thought he would be happy to be rid of me. But what if he wasn't?

Probably he just wanted me back so I would take care of Abby.

Let him take care of her for once. I was having fun, and I wanted to keep having fun. I spooned up to Grayson's back and went to sleep.

Grayson had finally bought me new, sexy clothes. Tight leather pants and my own denim jacket for riding the bike. A silk blouse and a pair of blue capris. Cute little white tennies. And most importantly, some sexy lacy stuff to wear in bed.

Not that I wore it long.

As a precaution, I stopped wearing the red shirt with gold sequins, but I kept it in the bottom of my new backpack.

We found another motorcycle shop, with an even more distractible salesman. They had the bike Grayson wanted. I worked up the salesman, got him into a bit of a lather. Then Grayson said he wanted to take the bike for a test drive. 'Course the guy said yes.

Grayson put on a helmet, got on the bike, revved her up.

I got on right behind him. No helmet, but who cared?

Grayson drove us right out of there and we didn't come back.

We were free.

Now life was just like Grayson said it would be. I leaned on his strong back with my arms around his waist. We kept going the way we'd been. Spending money, getting money, spending it again. Never staying anywhere long. Movin' on, movin' on.

I got good at it. Got good at all the little cons, got better at the big ones. Most times I was the distraction while Grayson did the action.

We headed out of Santa Rosa and went north. We found more little places to hold up, riding past vineyards, little shopping centers, little kid play parks as we made our escape. I was driving the bike this time. I'd gotten good at it.

None of it seemed real to me. I was like a girl in a movie, a robber girl in a ballad, a maiden in a fairy tale.

And like two kids in a fairy tale, we rode into a deep forest. The forest trees were so tall and so thick the sun seemed to dim when we went through them. Like we were leaving the light behind and entering a kind of tunnel. The trees whizzed past us, fast, then faster as the road cleared and I put on speed.

I let out a yee-haw and held out my arms, letting the wind blow through my hair.

Grayson muttered something, but I didn't pay attention to him.

"What's that?" he yelled louder.

"What's what?" I peered ahead. It looked really smoggy up there.

As we got closer, I realized it was smoke.

The forest was burning.

"We better go back," said Grayson.

"There's no going back," I answered. And I sped up.

The smoke got thicker and thicker, and then we saw trucks and people standing next to their cars on the side of the road.

"Should we stop?" Grayson yelled.

I didn't answer. I didn't stop either. I just slid on through the barriers, wove through cars and emergency vehicles, until we were driving through the fire itself, the flames burning hot on both sides of the road, people yelling at us to stop, turn around.

But I kept going. When I saw the flames ready to leap from one side of the road to the other, I just sped up, riding right through the fire. We went through so fast, it was like we were water flowing through a hot oven.

My hat had come off and my hair got singed.

The holy water of the flood had led me here, and now I was hellfire.

Finally, I rode up a hill and stopped at a scenic rest stop.

Grayson jumped off the bike. "That was awesome! Woo hoo!"

That night we slept by the edge of a lake. Well, I thought it was a lake, but Grayson said it was a reservoir. We found a spot to ourselves and when it was dark ran into the water naked, splashing each other.

Then while he slept, I embroidered some colors on the back of his jacket. A cocktail glass and a $50 bill like a banner around the stem, flames bursting in its wake. And underneath, the words "Hellfire & Holywater." That was us. Hellfire & Holywater.

I worked on that embroidery all night. I thought Grayson would like it, but when he woke up the next morning and saw it, he slapped me.

"Are you stupid? That's the only jacket I have. And you want to put something on it that every witness will notice? That anyone could recognize? You want me to get caught? Huh? Is that what you want?"

I hung my head, my chin quivering, trying not to cry.

"I'll steal you another one."

"Don't you get it, you stupid—I need to wear a jacket when I ride the bike. And I can't wear something that any witness could easily describe."

"I'll pull all the threads out. I promise."

So I did, but I was so sleepy by then it took me forever. Grayson would go out and walk around and come back and I still wouldn't be done, and he'd say things about how useless women were and how all I did was weigh him down and cost him money.

He sounded so much like Dad I wanted to scream.

Thinking about Dad made me think about Abby. I'd managed not to think about her all that time. I'd put her out of my mind. This was my time, after all.

When Grayson hit me, something changed in me.

And thinking about Abby changed something in me.

I stopped just living in the moment and I started thinking about what I was doing.

And once I started, I couldn't stop. When I closed my eyes to sleep, I could feel her poking them.

We held up bigger stores. Bars. Even a grocery store.

I would be the lookout, keep the bike running and ready, while he ran in, got the money, and ran out again.

What finished us wasn't one of the big jobs. It wasn't the cops catching us. It wasn't one of us making a mistake. It wasn't even bad luck, like running out of gas, like they show in the movies.

What finished us was me.

The plan was to hold up a gas station, just like our first job. I went in first, got the clerk all distracted, then Grayson went in and held him up.

It was only after Grayson had yelled "Put your hands in the air. This is a robbery!" that I realized we weren't alone in the store. There was a little girl in the back corner, and her dad was down on one knee next to her, helping her tie her shoe.

The little girl looked so much like Abby it made my heart ache.

When she saw me, she giggled.

And Grayson whirled around, his gun in his hand. He pointed it at the dad.

"No! No!" I gave Grayson a shove. The gun went off.

"Run!" I said to the dad and the little girl.

The dad reached his arm out for me. "Come with us!"

But I couldn't run.

I couldn't move.

I was falling, falling, until I slammed onto the ground.

"Zoey," yelled Grayson, and dropped down next to me.

"You shot me," I whispered.

And that's how they caught us.

They had a doctor at the trial who said I had something called Stockholm Syndrome. That wasn't true, but I could see Dad and Mrs. Clarinda and most of all Abby in the gallery. To get out of the glass cage I was in and past the wooden barriers between me and them, I had to lie.

So I did.

When Grayson heard I was only sixteen he gave me a look of pure fury. "You lied to me," he said. "You made me think you were all grown up. Instead, you are just a stupid kid."

Not that stupid. They let me off with mandated counseling and community service.

I wasn't allowed to go see Grayson in jail, but Dad said he was away for a long, long time.

And I was back in Sebastopol, back on the Barlow.

Mr. Shiv and his wife had given up and gone.

After I got out, the first thing we did was take Abby out for ice cream.

Then we went to the store.

The flood waters had receded, of course. "They're talking about a new water mitigation plan," Dad said as he unlocked the front door. "They're saying they'll install interlocking aluminum flood logs between brackets in each roll-up storefront. Sump pumps located inside each leased space and hooked up to generators."

The only part of that I understood was "sump pumps" and "generator." I was too taken aback by the sight of the store to ask questions.

Everything was gone. The ruined industrial freezer, the counters, all the merchandise. The stools, the booths, the walls.

"What happened to the walls?"

"I took 'em down during your trial. Didn't have nuthin' else to do."

He stood next to me, his arm tight around my shoulder, as if he was afraid I would run away again. "So, now we start over. New store, new life."

I pulled away from him. "With what?" I said. "You told me you didn't have any insurance. Where is the money going to come from?"

Dad looked at the floor.

"You don't have an answer for that, do you?" I spoke sternly, like the matron at the prison had always spoken to me.

It worked. His shoulders slumped just like mine did the first time I heard the matron's sour, bossy voice.

I'd learned to stand up to matron. I couldn't bear to see Dad like that. "But guess what," I punched him in the arm playfully. "I do."

Starting the day Grayson hit me, I'd taken to keeping a bit of the cash we'd stolen, a little bit each time, little enough he didn't miss it. I preferred hundred-dollar bills. I folded each bill up real small and then I sewed it to my tank top, lifting the rows of sequins and fitting the bill under there so you'd hardly notice. Dad watched me, mesmerized, as I carefully pulled the threads on each one.

It wasn't enough, but it was enough to get started.

We started selling ice cream out the front of the store with the back still unfinished. Then we bought Mr. Shiv's store and expanded, Dad doing the demolition at night after I'd taken Abby home and he'd closed the store.

See, everyone wants to see the Hellfire & Holywater girl.

I hated being called that at first. But now I roll with it. I embroidered the cocktail glass and the fifty-dollar bill in flames on all our aprons. And if you order six ice cream cones, I'll give you a postcard with my mug shot on it and my autograph. So, what'll it be? ❖

Gonna Be the Heck of a Band

Sarah Smith

On the very eve of his death, Mozart had the score of the *Requiem* brought to his bed, and himself (it was two o'clock in the afternoon) sang the alto part; Schack sang the soprano line, as he had always previously done. Hofer, Mozart's brother-in-law, took the tenor, Gerl, later a bass singer at the Mannheim Theater, the bass. They were at the first bars of the *Lacrimosa* when Mozart began to weep bitterly, laid the score aside, and eleven hours later, at one o'clock in the morning, departed this life. He never finished the *Lacrimosa*.

It's 1:35 in the morning before his wife leaves the room. She pauses at the door, sobs once, wipes her eyes. Then she's gone and we're alone with the body.

"And a three, two, one. Okay, here we go."

Zoe pushes the button. All the sounds we've stopped noticing go silent—a late horse's hoofs against stone, the creak of frost on the window, the hiss of the sickroom fire. Rix goes first with the body double. I take pictures. The contemps are okay with the double not looking quite right, but it's not so good if he's changed position.

"Undress him." The body double needs his clothes.

"You do it," Zoe says. "He must have been wearing that nightshirt two weeks."

I do it. Zoe loads the real guy onto the gurney, plugs him in, inserts needles, starts her magic infusions. Rix and I dress the body substitute, lay him in the bed, and compare him with the pictures.

"Okay."

"Take the other end of the gurney."

"And a one, two, three."

We clump down the time tunnel, and it *zoops* into nonexistence behind us. We can just hear the fire begin to crackle again, the horse's hoof hit stone.

We're back in our apartment. We can hear the traffic on Mem Drive.

"Whoa. We did it."

And Mozart begins to breathe.

We weren't actually supposed to do this.

"Where is here?" he says.

According to Zoe, when we got him he had tonsillitis, bronchitis, pneumonia; he could have had strep; his kidneys were failing; he could have been poisoning himself with a patent medicine he liked to take. And, thanks to eighteenth-century doctors, he'd had so much blood drawn he could have died from just that. Nothing beyond what Zoe can fix with her bots. But for a couple of scary days we have this guy zonked out on our sofa, and Zoe's cat-sized medical bots are going *neep neep neep* around him, and we're getting up in the middle of the night checking on whether he's still alive.

"When he wakes up," Zoe says, "don't tell him right away. He could explode. That's a medical term, *explode*."

And then he's okay enough to sit up, and we've got to tell him something.

He looks around our living room. Computers scattered everywhere, crumpled up or rolled up. Zoe's violin. Zoe's packed away her bots. Still, not a single thing here is going to be familiar to him except the violin.

"My friends were singing with me," he says shakily. "Constanze was with me. I have begun to cry because I could not provide for my children. Then I don't remember. Now I am here. Where is here?"

Rix starts to explain, I kick him in the ankle.

"Am I in Heaven?" he asks. "That would be *ein Spass*."

He's speaking mostly English at least.

"It is not Hell," he says. He gestures at Zoe's violin. He's wearing Rix's old MIT Crew T-shirt and a pair of my sweat pants, and his arms are still bruised from IVs, but the gesture is like he's shaking back ruffles. "There are no violins in Hell."

He's made a joke. It doesn't reach his eyes, though. He's figuring out he's not in Kansas anymore.

"I am alive?"

He gets up, shaky; I help him. He goes across the room and picks up the violin. He looks around for the bow; Zoe hands it to him. He looks at it curiously. He sits in a chair, tucks the violin under his chin, and begins to play.

And that's when I get what we've done. We've unofficially resuscitated this guy who's a musical genius; he wakes up from being dead and the first thing he reaches for is Zoe's violin. And he can *play*. Zoe's mouth opens, O, and she shivers. My drug of choice is classic rock, and even I can tell.

He's going to be able to do what we need him to do.

Then he breaks off. From where he's sitting, he can see out the window. He puts down the violin, groping for the edge of the table to keep himself upright. I stand by him, ready to catch him.

Outside, floors below us, runs the shallow river that used to be Mem Drive. A little red carboat drives down Fowler Street, splashes into the Drive, and takes a left turn into the river.

"Where is here?" he says again. "Where is Constanze? Where are my children?"

"This is Cambridge, Massachusetts," I say. "United States of America. But, dude, you don't mean where. You mean when."

We call them the Grave Robbers Agency. The GRA. We call them things we try to make funny, because we don't know who they are. They recruited Zoe first. Zoe recruited Rix and me.

"That much money?" Rix said. "For kidnapping corpses? For that money, I'd *eat* corpses."

"Are you both in?" Zoe asked. "Because I can't do it alone. I need help."

"These gray guys. They're sending us out to pick up random people," I said, "and we're random people. Techie, but random. What does that sound like to you?"

"Sounds like money," Rix said.

"Sounds like experimenting. And we're the lab rats."

Zoe put her head in her hands.

I've got scholarships. Doesn't mean I don't eat ramen. Zoe's doing medical research. She needs the money, needs it so bad she said yes to them.

"What happens to us when we time travel?" I asked her. "Do we explode? Get cancer? Or weird diseases?"

"They say not."

"But they don't know. And what happens to the ones who come here?"

"That I know," Zoe said. She looked miserable. "The GRA gives them a new identity. But a lot of them commit suicide."

"Suicide. And we're supposed to hang around with them, talk with them, introduce them to the world? The gray guys aren't paying us enough."

"They're paying me enough," Rix said. "I'm in."

"And I'm already in," Zoe said. "If we gave them a reason for living, maybe they'd live. Bobby?"

"I'm in," I said. Because my friends were.

Of course we don't get away with it.

It's all the medical supplies Zoe uses. We'd been supposed to pick up some J. Random Plumber from Nebraska in 1935. He'd died from anesthesia while getting his tonsils extracted, and he'd have been fine once Zoe got him breathing.

A Gray Guy comes to visit. He's one of those carefully anonymous white men, sandy-haired, fortyish, business casual. He looks like government.

"Huh," Gray Guy says. "Mozart."

Our man's asleep on the couch, curled up, face to the wall. Gray Guy peers over his shoulder and takes a long look.

"Mozart."

"Yeah."

"Whose idea?"

"Mine," I say quickly, because I'm not going to rat out Zoe.

"We thought," Zoe says in a small voice, "somebody who had a reason for living would live. He died in the middle of writing a really big piece. His *Requiem*."

"Music for his funeral," Gray Guy says. "Don't look surprised. I sing in my church choir."

Huh, I think.

Gray Guy considers. "It's almost a good idea."

We look at each other, hoping.

"Except," he continues. "This is a *secret* project. You were thinking you'd tell the world, here's Mozart, we've got Mozart, maybe have him finish the *Requiem* and get it performed, and no one would ask you how you got him?"

He looks at us. We look at him.

"You're not surprised," I say.

"You're not the first people who tried this. People want to meet their great-grandmother who died of COVID." He turns to me. "I'm surprised you didn't want to meet your father."

"Yeah, no." I have one good memory of my dad. I don't want to spoil it with the actual man.

"So what happens now?" Zoe asks.

"What usually happens. We watch him for a while, give him a cover identity, park him in the Midwest somewhere. Keep watching him. And then," Gray Guy lifts one shoulder. "At least maybe he'll finish the *Requiem* first."

"What happens to us, she means?" Rix says.

"I don't mean," Zoe says.

"Same deal as before. You watch him." Gray Guy's pale eyes rest a moment on me. "Watch him while he gives up. That'll be punishment enough."

I find myself opening my mouth.

"We're going to need money," I say. "To buy him instruments, hire singers. He's going to want to put the *Requiem* on."

"And if he could, I'd come," Gray Guy says. "But here are the rules. First rule: He can't be Mozart."

When I was a kid, I wanted a dog. It was just me and Mama by then; we didn't have the cash. But one day a little black puppy followed me home.

"If you keep him, Bobby, you got to work for him."

I worked. In junior high I shoveled snow, I stocked shelves for Walmart and used my employee discount to buy dog food. I got smart and learned how to program the robots that were taking stock boy jobs away. I used my dad's old phone and took videos of Fruddy for YouGram. I talked Smiling Metal Robotics into letting me do a video of Fruddy playing with their Rover. When Fruddy died of canine COVID a couple of years ago, Smiling Metal named their next model after him.

Here I am at MIT studying robotics, on scholarships from Smiling Metal and Walmart, on a patchwork of Patreon and Kickstarter.

I don't give up easily.

And I'm not giving up on him.

It ends up me who has to tell him the rules.

"Nothing will happen to you. Or us." I'm still not entirely sure of that. "They'll take care of you. Financially, I mean."

"There is no need," he says. "I write music, I give concerts."

"You can write music," I say. "You can play it. But not with other people. Not in front of audiences."

"I am a musician," he says. "Music needs audience."

"You can finish your *Requiem*. But you can't be Mozart."

"I am Mozart," he says, sharp. "I can be no one else."

"It's a secret project," I say. "Time travel's not supposed to exist. How do we explain you?"

"Why not say, here is time travel? Look, here is Mozart?"

Good question.

"It's secret because it's the government," Zoe says.

"If I am here," he says. "I do not boast what I am, but I cannot waste what I am given. If I am here I must make music."

"Finish your *Requiem*," Zoe says. "We'll record it."

"Record?"

"On a—"

Of course he's never seen a computer. I unroll mine, plug in the keyboard, and set him up as a user. He touches a key and looks surprised at the letter on the screen.

Then smiles at us. It's the first time I've seen him smile.

"If there is this keyboard, there's *wie ein Klavier*?" He spreads his hands like he's playing a piano. Two minutes since he's seen his first computer and he's intuited digital keyboards.

I say, "We're going shopping."

It's not as though he can't go out. Who's going to recognize Mozart in a down jacket and a knit hat with a pompom? We take a carboat to Music Mall in Watertown.

He moves through the racks of guitars and saxes like he's in a cathedral. He takes them down and plays them one by one. He finds the aisle of electronic keyboards and electronic pianos. He tries them all, makes faces at most of them. Zoe shows him how to make different instrumental sounds on a keyboard.

"*Aber die Instrumente müssen alles gemischt sein*." He forgets to speak English. "Instruments must counterpoint."

"You can do that on a computer."

We go over to MicroCenter and get him his own computer and some good speakers, bring it back to the apartment, and load it up with DAWs and virtual instruments.

"You make music?" he asks me.

"Not me. My dad did." Which is a good, good reason I don't.

He goes through the learning curve like a chainsaw through cheese. When I crash at four in the morning, he's still working.

When I stagger awake at ten, he's discovered electronic music.

He finishes the *Requiem* a week later.

And it's . . . bad.

"It's good," Zoe says uncertainly.

"It's not good," he says. "The music is good. But this . . . voices." He's been using electronic voices. "They are voices of *Wilis*," he gropes. "*Unsterbliche*." Undying. "To sing death, crying, needs body, breath. The body vibrating. And also the instruments. Breath, wood, strings, reeds, fingers."

Zoe blinks and nods.

"You could sing all the parts yourself," she says in a small voice. "And change the pitch."

"I have discovered that," he snaps.

"I'm just trying to help," she says. She looks like she's going to burst into tears.

"Leave now."

"I'll go too," Rix says. "I have some work to do at the lab. C'mon, Zoe." He stops at the door. "I thought it was great," he says. He closes the door.

"You also. Leave."

"No."

So there's the two of us, left together.

"You," he says. "Tell me why I cannot."

I feel like I did when Fruddy followed me home, but no amount of shoveling snow and stocking shelves at Walmart is going to get him singers and an orchestra.

So I tell him the rest of the story of the GRA.

"We get sent to random dates, pick up random people, watch them for a couple of weeks, get to know them."

"I am random?"

"We were supposed to take someone else."

"You are in trouble for this?"

"Don't worry about it."

"Thank you," he says. "What happens to them after? To me?"

"They get taken away in a carboat."

"And then?"

I don't say anything. I look down at my shoes. We're both sitting on the sofa, one at either end. He reaches over and turns my head so I'm looking at him.

"And then?"

What Zoe heard is they kill themselves. I know they never email us again, don't thank us like he just did. Even get mad at us or tell us they're sorry. Mostly they were polite old-fashioned people. They would have sent a note.

I have to say this even though I don't want to think it, I don't want to say it, especially not to him.

"There are more stray dogs than people to adopt them," I say. "When a kid figures that out and asks what happens to the other dogs, the kid's mother says they go to a nice farm in the country. The GRA tells us the people we took go to a new home with new identities.

"I sort of wonder if they didn't go to a nice farm in the country, which," I take a deep breath. "Which means that Rix and Zoe and I are helping commit murder."

I've never said it that way, not even to myself. Because it's true.

"Rix says it doesn't matter, because the people we took were," I'm not going to say *already dead* in front of him, "but Rix is an asshole and even he doesn't believe it. The people we took had *names*, Arthur and Walter and George. They had lives they could have gone on with. And we just sent them off and said *stay well* and then we went off and took somebody else. So Zoe said, let's take someone who's important to everyone. Someone they can't get rid of."

"You think they can't get rid of me," he says flatly.

"I don't know, but when they decide this whole time travel works? They're going to start taking people *they* think are important. And none of them is going to be you. They'll go for Vlad the Impaler. Hitler."

"And you think I would change this." Zoe's violin is on the side table. He picks it up and fingers it like a guitar.

"Music—" I unroll my computer. "My dad was a musician. He was barely ever home and he died when I was five, but I can just remember going to one of his shows. People screaming, dancing in the aisles. I guess I thought it would be like that with you. You'd finish the *Requiem* and conduct it with an orchestra and the whole world would listen, and then everyone would know what was going down and they'd stop it."

"Your father was recorded?"

One live session on YouGram. Sixteen hundred plays, at least fifteen hundred of which are me. I start it up. "He was better than this. I think. The video's crap." I could have done it ten times better when I was thirteen and shooting videos of Fruddy.

Robert Boi Brown. Died of an overdose in an alley behind the Community Center in Roseville, Illinois, where the band had played a show. Nobody found him until a half hour later. Zoe could have fixed him with Narcan. He was twenty-seven years old and I was five when he left Mom and me. I listen to Boi Brown for the fifteen hundred and first time.

"It's not your kind of music."

He's listening like he's tasting some weird fruit for the first time: what is this stuff?

"It is music," he says. "It has balls. Why do you not bring him back?"

"If I wanted to hang around a crazy addict musician who's only four years older than me, I'd have the whole 27 Club to choose from."

"What is the 27 Club?" asks Mozart.

We make lists.

He listens to what feels like all of YouGram.

We make THE list. And the backup list. And the list for now. And here's who we're going to take.

LoLo Laura studied piano at Juilliard; died at twenty-seven of an overdose. Brian Jones founded the Rolling Stones, played every instrument there was, died at twenty-seven by drowning. Jimi. Janis. Jim. Amy. Klaus Nomi: he's going to be tricky but Zoe thinks the bots can do it. The bassist for Metallica; we'll have to get him alive, just before the bus lands on him. Robert Johnson, died of poisoning or an overdose; we'll find out.

And we'll go to Roseville, Illinois, to rescue a lead singer you never heard of, Robert Boi Brown.

We're going to do all this in one night, because we're time travelers. And then we'll run. I know a guy at Smiling Metal who owns an island in Canada. It's not going to be easy pulling this together. Most of these folks had serious habits, which I am not going to take well. Zoe's going to use up a barrel of Narcan.

But I can see the video I'll do. Late afternoon, on the beach at Stu's island. All the musicians you know, the ones taken too soon. They may be playing violins, maybe they're playing guitars, but they're singing with body and breath. They're singing the *Lacrimosa*, the whole *Lacrimosa*, the words Mozart never put to music.

And running in the grass, there'll be a little black dog named Fruddy, because canine COVID is curable now. And even if you don't know LoLo or Brian Jones or Robert Johnson or my dad, a lot of you knew Fruddy.

Hey, guess what? We can raise the dead. And a dog.

And then what?

I have no idea. All I know?

Gonna be the heck of a band. ❖

One Shy of a Load

Nancy Brewka-Clark

Woody's head was deep inside the dryer drum when the front door of the laundromat banged open.

"Hey, Ed. How's it hanging?"

Rubbing his scalp where he'd whacked it on the drum rim, Woody straightened all the way up. Folks in Rupert Falls didn't go in much for greetings of any kind, never mind what he thought he heard.

"Say, you aren't Ed." The old lady was jiggling an overflowing supermarket cart like she was lulling a baby to sleep. And maybe she was, because Woody certainly couldn't tell what was buried beneath the jumbled clothes, cracker boxes, and wads of plastic bags. "Where's my boy Ed?"

Woody shrugged. "He quit."

"Since when?"

"You have to ask the owner."

She snorted. "I don't care all that much."

Woody shrugged again."

"Man, that's some twitch you got there." She grinned, showing more gaps in her gums than teeth. "You should get that looked at."

"Yes, ma'am." Woody was having a brainstorm that had nothing to do with his sole customer. He could look up commercial dryer repair videos on the internet. His boss said he always left the ancient computer in the office up and running for just that sort of thing. "Have a nice day."

No sooner had he plunked himself down at the battered desk in the cluttered little office than the old lady shouted, "Hey, you, get out here."

Woody went to the door. "What's the matter now?"

"Your machine ate my money."

She gave the stainless steel side an indignant slap. Riding atop was a knockoff blue and orange box of dollar-store detergent called Tidi. From the gummy residue around the flap, it had been a while since she'd peeled away the masking tape holding it shut. "I put my load in and nothing happened. Now the door's up and locked on me."

Woody peered at the coin slot. "How much did you put in?"

"Just like that sign there says. Three bucks." She jiggled a sagging beige sock. Two black buttons were stitched onto the bulging toe. Beneath them a line of faded red embroidery curved upward. "Hard cash."

"Huh." Woody bent, cupped his hands to his face and peered in through the murky porthole. "These days everybody uses plastic."

"I ain't everybody. And like I said, I put in twelve quarters. You got a problem with that?"

He looked over his shoulder. Over the years of odd jobs in poor places Woody had encountered far more menacing weapons than a sock puppet. "Nope."

"Good. This here's Theodore. Means gift from God." When she cocked her head, she reminded him of a fat old hen, her short ginger hair streaked white like feathers. "You from around here?"

"Laconia."

"Never been there."

Woody almost shrugged. Instead, he said, "No reason to."

She laughed. "Same everywhere." She shook her head. "No reason to go, no reason to stay."

The only place Woody wanted to go was back to the computer. The longer she distracted him, the greater the chances were that Norm, the owner, would drop by to see how things were going. And just now, the answer would be, not so great.

"Hang on," he said. "Got to get me some tools."

Behind the tiny office was a great big dingy mostly empty space. At one time the building had been an A&P grocery store. The service entrance was exactly the same as when farm trucks with big broad bumpers and wide runners pulled in with local produce. Even after a hundred years, the old flooring still gave off the odors of raw fish and McIntosh apples. The double doors had been chain-locked for decades, but some enterprising soul had sawed out a normal-sized door in one of them.

Hoping Norm wasn't about to let himself in, Woody poked around in the battered tool chest, came up with two screw drivers, Phillips and flathead, and plodded back out.

"Took you long enough." The old lady eyed his finds. "You plan on taking the whole damn thing apart?"

The front door banged again. "There you are, Grandma."

Another voice, this one female, cried, "We've been so worried."

They were both wearing blue medical masks, black parkas, and blue Red Sox caps and appeared to be in their late forties, maybe even fifties. Kind of old for grandkids, Woody mused, but then again maybe they'd had hard lives. Or maybe the old lady was even older than she looked.

"Who the hell are you?" the old lady asked.

By now the pair was on her, flanking her as they each took an arm.

"Come on, Grandma," the male of the duo said. "Let's get you home."

The old lady scowled into one face and then the other. "I don't know you from Adam."

"Uh-oh, Grandma forgot to take her meds," the female cooed.

Trying to shake them off, the old lady shouted into Woody's face, "Call the cops."

Woody felt a stab of pity. Poor old girl. Gaga, all right. Lucky for her she had kin to care for her. How many times had he seen people just like her sleeping beneath the abandoned railroad bridge in town, their grocery carts pulled up all around them with all their worldly goods piled in willy-nilly.

"Help," the old lady cried as the male towed her toward the door, the female jogging behind with the cart. "Help me, Jesus."

She had religion, no question about that. But marbles? If she had any, they'd be in that cart somewhere, probably stuffed in a matching beige sock.

The cart!

Woody stopped laughing.

That overloaded grocery cart didn't look like the kind of thing a grandma would need to keep around any house where she was loved and cared for.

Tossing the screw drivers on top of the washing machine next to the abandoned box of Tidi, he ran to the front windows. It was already coming on toward dusk, the sky heavy with low gray clouds. That could mean rain, but might just as well mean snow, this being April.

Wrenching open the door, he ran out.

The lights were on in Burt's Hardware but the diner had already closed for the day, being a breakfast and lunch place. The lights were on in the library, too. The old white church, now nondenominational to catch whatever stragglers still wanted to spend Sunday mornings on their knees, lay in darkness. A small drooping evergreen still bore some strings of Christmas lights, unlit too. One of the town's two police cars was parked in front of City Hall, the station itself being a little wart of a building attached to its ancient red-brick side.

There was no sign of the old lady and her elderly grandkids. But there was the cart, tipped over on the sidewalk with its contents spilling out into the gutter.

"Grandma my ass," Woody said, and set out for the station.

He was halfway down the block when he realized two things. One, if Norm came by now, he'd find the laundromat unmanned and unlocked. Two, the less he had to do with local law enforcement, the better. Not that he had a criminal past, just a hard one. A couple of needy ex-wives, a history of garnished paychecks and hungry loan sharks, a few short stints in various town jails for drunk and disorderly in the bad old days when he tried to drown his problems, they all trailed him like tin cans on a beater at a shotgun wedding. Nope, he was in no position to play Good Samaritan.

Woody was heading for the computer when the front door banged open, propelled by the woman who'd grabbed the old lady. As she loped toward him, the big plate-glass windows behind her gave off all kinds of shiny reflections, like rays of light shooting through black water.

"I want to apologize," she began. "You must think me and my brother are horrible people, treating our grandmother that way."

"Nah." Woody was ready to fend off further apologies or any other kind of intercourse that would slow down his research. "Family's family."

"She has a habit of filling that old cart with stuff she finds on the street. But you never know what else she's got in there." She laughed again behind the blue paper mask. "What washing machine did she use? Maybe she threw in something from the house, you know, the good towels, stuff like that."

Woody was just about to point to it when he noticed the quarter on the floor. Son of a gun, he thought, thing wasn't busted after all. At the exact same moment he stooped, the woman said, "Hey, that's Grandma's quarter."

When he stood, he was laughing a little. "Now how would you know that?"

"None of your business." Her eyes and voice hardened. "Hand it over."

He'd met a lot of cheapskates in this world, but she took the cake. "Nope." This family, or whatever they claimed to be, was getting on his nerves. "Property of the laundromat."

Her eyes flicked from the machine back to the coin he was holding. "We'll see about that."

A nerve twitched somewhere deep in Woody's gut. As threats went, it was mild. But there was something in the way she said it that was far more menacing than the words themselves. Then there was the matter of the overturned cart.

"So, where's your grandma now?"

"Home, with my brother, drinking tea." She held her hand out. "Now, for the last time. Give me that quarter."

They must live pretty close by. Or she was lying.

"Sorry." Woody took his time shoving the quarter into the pocket of his jeans. "No refunds."

Glad to see the back of her, Woody dug out the quarter and sank down in the desk chair. Painfully, with one finger, he began to type in the basic information stamped on the coin.

"Holy cow."

According to the website, he was holding a 1965 PCSG Au50 silver transitional twenty-five-cent piece minted in Philadelphia worth twenty thousand dollars.

Not trusting what he'd just read, he checked a few more websites. The only change was that one dealer was asking thirty grand.

The outer door-within-a-door clicked open behind him.

Woody snatched up the quarter and dropped it into his shirt pocket. "Hey, Norm." He hit X and wiped out the website. "Looks like snow's coming."

Something hard rammed into his spine. "Don't move."

Woody froze.

"Hands up over your head."

"Look, lady—"

"Shut up. Now push back the chair, real easy, and stand up. Turn, move, fart, and you're a dead man."

Woody stood.

"Give me the quarter."

A thought jigged into Woody's brain from nowhere. "It's in the washing machine."

"Bullshit. I saw you put it in your pocket."

"But then I realized I had to use it," Woody said, "to get the machine up and running."

"So it's in the change thingy?"

"Yeah," he said.

"Let's go."

Woody went out into the empty laundromat with his hands held high and his brain working overtime. "It's that machine over there."

"So, open it."

Woody sighed. "I can't. I don't have the key."

"Bullshit."

"Look, I'm a new hire. Real new. Like first-day new."

When he got a glimpse of their reflections in the plate-glass window, his brain flew into supergear. "And speaking of bullshit." With a surprisingly neat pivot, he whacked the old laundromat broom out of her hands.

"Bastard!" She lunged at him with both bare hands bent into claws.

He tried to palm her in the face, not a slap by any means, but just a little shove against her masked nose. When that didn't work, he yanked down her mask. Reaching up with his free hand, he snatched off her cap, grabbed the box of Tidi, and dumped it over her head.

"Pffft."

Cobras probably spat out their venom like that. Feeling triumphant, he stooped to pick up her cap. When he stood, she was smiling through a speckled mask of turquoise soap granules. "Bobby, this asshole says he can't unlock the machine."

Woody turned to see her brother right behind him, holding something that looked more like a museum piece than a gun. "That thing real?"

"Want to find out?"

A wail out in the street caught them all by surprise. Wavering blue light washed up against the front windows. A smaller red light shuddered higher up on the panes. The front door burst open, shoved by the fattest cop Woody had ever seen. "Police!"

A clatter from the back room spun their heads in the other direction.

"Freddy, what the hell's going on?" Norm shouted from the office door.

Their heads swiveled in unison again as the old lady barged through the front door swinging Theodore over her head like an Argentine bolo. "You kids never learn!"

"Wait," Woody said. "These really are your grandchildren?"

"Hell, yeah. Disgusting, aren't they?" She jerked her head at Bobby. "Give that thing to Freddy before you blow your privates off." To Woody, she said, "Blunderbuss. They don't make 'em like that anymore."

Woody's knees felt like cooked pasta. Yielding to the feeling, he sank down onto the floor. "I don't get it."

Norm said, "This is the Rupert family. Betty, Barbara, and Bobby. And that big guy there is Police Chief Freddy Rupert, Ms. Barb's brother's boy. Like the name says, they've been here since Day One."

"And that was, what, almost four hundred years ago, come Tuesday," Chief Freddy said, drawing a laugh from them all.

"Pleased to meet you all," Woody lied.

"So, Auntie Barb, you want to press charges?" the cop asked.

"What, against my own kin?" the old lady asked indignantly. "Hell, no. I just want them to apologize for trying to snitch Theodore and spill his guts."

Woody felt a shudder of revulsion mixed with sorrow rise up through him, like he was coming down with a rare digestive disease with a side effect of mental disorder. Then he thought, hey, I probably am, Rupert Falls Syndrome, what doesn't kill you makes you want to kill others, but instead you move on.

"Those guts, as you call them, are made up of Grandpa's coin collection," Bobby said, breathing hard as if he'd come in from a long climb up a cold mountain. "You don't do laundry with them."

"I'll do as I damn well please," the old lady said. "You don't get one red cent until I pass. You just remember that."

"Oh, yeah," Bobby muttered. "I forgot."

"Yeah, me, too," Betty said, shooting him a look beneath green-dotted lashes.

In the meantime, Woody was calculating something so exciting he was afraid his face would broadcast it like a satellite dish.

That washing machine was a Rupert piggy bank. Eleven times twenty grand—

"So, Norm, get the key," Betty said, "and give Grandma back her quarters."

"Yes, ma'am," Norm said.

Once on his feet, it was all Woody could do to keep from bolting out the back door. "Norm, we done here for the night?"

"Yup."

"See you tomorrow then."

"Yup."

Once in his car, blue and battered like a million other beaters, Woody patted his shirt pocket and laughed like a man cured of a fatal disease. "Nope."❖

The Book Club

Leslie Wheeler

Whaddya mean, you don't have enough bars?" I complained to my GPS. Yes, I often argue with the device. So what? There was no one else in the car with me that evening in late October, when I was on my way to a book club meeting in the town of Sagfield, Massachusetts. I'd just turned onto the Sagfield Road when my GPS went blank. Oh well, I'd get there somehow. I'd been given an address on Main Street, just beyond the Sagfield Inn. Surely, that couldn't be hard to find. Yet I drove on and on down the Sagfield Road without coming to Main Street. I passed the town hall on my right, then several miles later, the police department, and more miles later, the library. Strange. What was the point of having a main street when the town buildings were so far apart?

Meanwhile, the sun, already low on the horizon when I started out, was replaced by shadowy dusk. Maybe I should call the woman who had invited me, and let her know I was running late. Except when I tried, my phone didn't have enough bars to make the call.

Darn! I had been looking forward to this event for months. I was selling my mystery novels at a craft fair when a nice middle-aged woman approached me. She had frizzy gray-streaked brown hair, kind of like how mine would look if it weren't dyed and straightened, or relaxed as my stylist calls it. And she wore tortoise shell glasses like the ones I wear when I need a break from my contacts. She seemed thrilled to meet a real, live author for the first time. I knew what that was like. I'd been a swooning fan myself long before I became an underpaid and overworked writer, who spent more time in the fictional worlds I was creating than in my everyday life.

After the nice woman and I chatted a bit, she bought a copy of the first book in my cozy mystery series: *Milk Chocolate Death*. In case the title doesn't give it away, all my books are set at a chocolate shop. There's *Dark Chocolate Death*, *Semisweet Death*, and *Bittersweet Death*. My work in progress will be titled *Unsweetened Death*, once I figure out how to end it.

The lady told me she was in a book club that might be interested in having me come to one of their meetings. As an added incentive, she mentioned that the hotshot literary agent Naomi Florvetta often attended these meetings, looking for new talent. Naomi was known for turning writers into superstars. My career would skyrocket with her as my agent.

But if I couldn't find the house where the club was meeting. I was just about to give up when my GPS suddenly sprang to life, speaking with an odd new French accent: "Turn left onto ze Main Street in a quarter mile, s'il vous plait." Maybe it was just my GPS having a little fun. Do GPS units have a sense of humor?

Instead of the club meeting house being located just past the inn, as my host had told me, I had to drive another two miles to reach it. Main Street itself was unlike any other main street I'd ever seen: there were no other structures between the inn and the meeting house, and as far as I could tell, no other houses beyond the meeting house either.

The annoyances of the trip gave way when I arrived at a big yellow house. The woman who'd invited me stood out front, illuminated by outdoor lights. "Keri, we're so glad you made it!" she said, as she hugged me. "We were afraid you'd gotten cold feet."

Cold feet? Gotten lost was more like it, given her directions, but I let it pass. She wore a yellow dress that matched the color of the house, and she was shorter than I remembered, about my height actually.

Kendra—as she reminded me her name was—ushered me inside, where about a dozen people were seated around a long dining room table. It warmed my heart to see copies of *Milk Chocolate Death* at each of their places. They were engaged in animated conversations, but fell silent when I entered the room. Kendra introduced me to everyone, but she spoke so quickly and softly that I didn't catch any names. The group was mostly women, as I had come to expect from other book clubs I'd attended, except for two men with movie-star good looks who appeared to be identical twins.

Their names were Darren and Dennis, the only names I could hear because they introduced themselves. They stood near the head of the table where Kendra instructed me to sit with one of them on either side. With such handsome guys as seat mates, I wished I'd run a comb through my hair and freshened my makeup while still in the car.

The introductions made, the other members of the group returned to their animated conversations, while Darren and Dennis spoke with me, though in an unusual manner as if they were doing a ventriloquist act. One would say something, his lips moving, but the actual sound came from the other man beside me. Strange, but I wrote it off as a silly game these twins liked to play.

Noticing that both my wine and water glasses were empty, I mentioned this to one of the Ds, as I thought of them, because of my inability to keep them straight. He said they were out of red wine, but offered to give me some of his white wine. He poured wine into my glass, even as I demurred. The other D followed suit by pouring some of his red into my glass, again before I could stop him. "And now you've got rosé!" he cried gleefully.

I would've preferred straight red or white, but I took a big drink anyway, and immediately regretted it because the alcohol went straight to my head. I knew better than to drink on an empty stomach, which mine certainly was—to the point of growling, as the tantalizing aromas of delicious dishes wafted into the dining room. That's another thing I'd learned about book clubs—they're about eating well, socializing with friends, and only then asking a few questions of the guest author.

"Will we be having dinner soon?" I asked a D.

"Not until Naomi arrives."

"Naomi Florvetta, the literary agent?"

"Yes. Do you know her?"

"Not personally, but I was hoping to meet her here. When do you expect her?"

"I really don't know, given the terrible car accident she was in. You must have seen it as you were driving here."

My heart sank. This was terrible news, assuming it was true. "I didn't see any accident."

"You're sure? It happened near the site of the fire that destroyed a huge chunk of the woods on the way here."

"I didn't see any burned-out areas either."

"Really? As a mystery author I would think you'd notice things like that."

"Well, I didn't," I said with ill-concealed annoyance. "Why is Naomi coming to dinner when she was in a bad accident? Shouldn't she be going to the hospital?"

"Naomi would never miss a book club meeting, especially this one."

A terrible car accident and a devastating fire? What on earth was going on here?

Fifteen minutes later, loud knocking sounded on the front door. "That must be Naomi," Kendra said. "Help her driver bring her in," she told the Ds. Moments later, the Ds and another man, presumably the chauffeur, wheeled in a woman bandaged from head to toe, with only her eyes visible.

I'd done a book event at an assisted living place, where a few attendees were in wheelchairs, but none of them had been so badly injured as Naomi. She belonged in the ER instead of a book club meeting. Yet no one but me seemed concerned about her appearance. Something was wrong, *very* wrong—unless the bandages were part of a Halloween costume that everyone knew about except me. Halloween *was* only a few nights away.

The Ds wheeled Naomi to a place at the table near me. Then, as if her arrival was the signal for dinner, they joined the throng of people rushing to the kitchen. Naomi gave me a penetrating look that made my heart pound. Could she tell how desperate I was to have her sign me on as a client?

"I'm delighted to finally meet you," I said, hoping I didn't sound too gushy, "but so sorry about your accident. If there's anything I can do to help you, please let me know." Silence. "Oh, I almost forgot, I brought a small present for you." I removed a nicely wrapped package from my tote bag. Inside was a hardcover edition of *Milk Chocolate Murder* I'd had made especially for her. Bound in leather with gold lettering and trim, the book had cost a small fortune, but it didn't seem right to give Naomi a mass market paperback without even a glossy cover.

I placed the package on the table in front of her, and for one thrilling moment I thought she'd open it on the spot. Instead, she pointed wordlessly toward the kitchen. Kendra, who'd remained in the dining room, smiled. "Naomi wants you to take her to get dinner," she whispered in my ear. "I can tell she likes you already!"

That settled it. Brushing aside my growing suspicions that something was off about this book club, I pushed Naomi's wheelchair toward the kitchen, no easy task, given that we had to navigate against the oncoming traffic of people returning to the dining room. When we finally made it, there was hardly any food left. Nevertheless, I dutifully filled a plate for Naomi, placed it on her lap, and wheeled her back to the dining room. When I returned for my own dinner, I saw the help had cleared the table where the food had been, and were busy loading dishes into the dishwasher. I was tempted to grab a dish that still had a little food left when Kendra called me back to the dining room. "Naomi needs to be fed, and she wants you to do it."

A hole had been cut in Naomi's bandages so her mouth was no longer covered. Seating myself beside her, I tried to spoon feed her food I would have liked to eat myself. But more of it spilled down her front than went into her mouth.

"I think you need to hand feed her," Kendra advised. This worked a bit better, although it was kind of gross, because half-eaten food landed back into my hands, and Naomi's teeth nipped my fingers when she chewed. I had to keep reminding myself that this was a small price to pay, considering what Naomi could do for me if she were my agent. Like getting me a bigger and better publisher who might actually promote my books and even pay for a book tour.

At last, we were done. Or so I thought. A rumbling noise sounded deep within Naomi. Then like an erupting volcano, everything I'd taken such pains to get into her spewed out—onto me and onto the still unwrapped book I'd brought her. Kendra brought me a roll of paper towels to clean up the mess, but neither she nor anyone else offered to help. And Naomi flashed me an annoyed look, as if the mishap were all my fault. She shooed me back to my seat between the Ds like a bored queen dismissing an unworthy supplicant.

The Ds at least seemed to realize I'd had no dinner. One of them said, "I'd offer you the remains of my kale salad, but I know you hate kale." It was true, but how the heck did he know that? The other D said, "I'd offer you some of my beef stew, but all that's left is gristle that you'd choke on. Don't worry, though. Dessert is on its way."

"And it's a special dessert in your honor," the other D said.

"Chocolate?" I guessed.

"You got it!" they cried in unison.

I could never resist chocolate under any circumstances. And in this instance, despite Naomi's regurgitated meal, I hadn't lost my appetite. I was even starting to feel faint from hunger. Chocolate might give me the boost I needed to make an intelligent decision about whether to remain in this very weird place. Kendra left the room, returning with a large basket filled with chocolate bars. To my dismay, she deposited the basket at the far end of the table from where I sat, so I had to wait until it reached me. While I was waiting, a heavily made-up woman, who reminded me of someone I'd known, bit into a chocolate bar, fell from her chair, and after writhing in agony lay still. Kendra hurried over to her, pressed a finger on her wrist, and declared her dead!

My mouth opened in a silent scream, but Kendra and the others seemed to take her death in stride.

"Take her into the sewing nook," she told the Ds, pointing in the direction of a small room I hadn't noticed before.

This was turning out to be the most terrifying book club I'd ever attended, and I'd gone to some strange ones. I'd never been at a meeting where someone arrived looking like they were at death's door, and someone else actually died. I needed to get out of here fast!

The basket with one remaining chocolate bar reached me, but instead of taking the candy I turned to one of the Ds. "Can you tell me where the bathroom is?"

"Down the hall, third door to the left."

I'd barely risen from my seat when Naomi struggled to rise also. Pushing herself up from her wheelchair, she placed one hand on a chair arm, while she aimed the other hand at me, her index finger poking through the bandages to reveal a blood red nail. "*You*," she croaked in a voice that dripped venom.

I froze. The next instant Naomi lurched forward. Her head landed smack on the table top; her empty dinner plate and the unopened book clattered to the floor. Kendra rushed over to her. She cut away the bandages on Naomi's nose, and whipping out a compact from her purse, she held the mirror up to Naomi's nostrils, and pronounced her dead. "Wheel her into the sewing room," she instructed the Ds.

I was shaking all over, but somehow I managed to get myself to the bathroom. Once inside, I locked the door behind me and flopped down on the toilet seat. Who were these people anyway? I realized that two of them, the heavily made-up woman and Naomi herself, reminded me of characters in my books. The heavily made-up woman resembled an obnoxious client, whom my main character was wrongfully accused of murdering in *Bittersweet Death*. And bandaged, now dead Naomi? She was Nancy in *Dark Chocolate Death,* where a woman dies in an awful car crash on her way to deliver a box of the shop's artisanal dark chocolate to a friend. There were probably others too; they just hadn't bared their unfriendly faces yet. I had, after all, killed at least one character in each of my books.

Before they came after me, I'd get in my car, and drive home. Jumping to my feet, I caught a quick glimpse of myself in the mirror over the sink. I recoiled in horror. Kendra stared back at me with a ferocious expression. Thinking she must be standing behind me, I spun around. No one was there! I dashed down the hall and out the back door.

My car was parked in front. Crouching low to avoid being seen, I scurried toward it—only to discover that my Honda was now a total wreck. The Ds emerged from shadows. "What happened to my car?"

"It was in the accident that killed Naomi. Don't you remember?"

"No, I wasn't in any accident."

"Don't get upset. One of us will drive you home."

They closed in on me, one in front and the other in back, and began to force-walk me toward a sleek black sedan I hadn't noticed before. A line from one of my books flashed through my brain: *When threatened, try to keep your assailant talking.*

"One of you, huh? Who are you, anyway?"

"I'm Darren," the one in front of me said.

"And I'm Dennis," the one in back said.

"So you say, but are those your real names?" I demanded.

They exchanged quick glances, then with identical smiles, they said in unison, "That's for us to know and you to find out."

"All right. Let me put it another way. If you were characters in my books, which role would each of you play?"

"I'd be the main character's romantic partner," Darren said. That worked for me, because the love interest in my series was tall, dark, and handsome.

"And I'd be the villain," Dennis said.

"Impossible!" I protested.

"Why? We're simply flip sides of the same coin. Just like you and Kendra."

"Huh?"

"C'mon now," Darren said, "you must have noticed a certain similarity between the two of you."

"A little bit maybe," I hedged.

"You even have similar names," Dennis said.

Right. Keri and Kendra.

"And look at how the two of you react to things," Darren said. "When Naomi died, you were horrified while Kendra took it in stride. Like us, you're the flipsides of the same coin."

My head was spinning with all the back-and-forth. Still, one thing was clear. "Okay, but it won't work for the love interest and the villain to be identical twins. There must be a way to tell you apart."

"And voilà, there is a way!" they cried together. "I have a scar on my right wrist." Dennis rolled up his sleeve so I could see it. While he was doing this, I seized the opportunity to try to escape through the opening he'd given me on my right. But Darren spun around and cut me off.

"And I don't." Darren revealed his scarless right wrist. "Do you want me or Dennis to drive you home?" he asked, since we were almost at the car.

They could both be bad guys. I chose Darren as the love interest and possibly the lesser of two evils. When we reached the sedan, Dennis pinned me to the door on the passenger side, while Darren ran around to the driver's side, got in, and fired up the engine. Dennis shoved me into the car and we tore down Main Street in the opposite direction from which I'd originally come.

When I pointed this out to him, Darren said, "Trust me. I know the way."

In my books, when a character tells another to trust them, it's a warning sign. Was it the same in real life? Not always. But this wasn't real life. It was some bizarre portal I'd slipped into by accident like Alice in Wonderland or Dorothy in Oz. Confirming my worst fears, a sudden streak of moonlight lit up the car, and I caught a glimpse of my reflection in the window. Except it wasn't me but Kendra with a horrified expression. Following her gaze, I saw that Darren's shirtsleeve was hiked up to reveal that a scar was now on his right wrist.

A cold sweat enveloped me. I could hurl myself from the sedan, but when I tried the door handle, I discovered Darren had locked me in. Crying out for help wouldn't work either, because no one was around to hear me. I was trapped in a car with a character from my books. A man who might be the villain or the love interest or both. And he was taking me and my double Kendra down a dark, dangerous road with no ending in sight.

No ending? Impossible. I was a writer, after all. I couldn't leave this story hanging the way I'd left *Unsweetened Death* hanging.

I had to write the ending. And if I did it right, maybe I could regain control of the narrative and transform myself from the victim in a horror story to the hero in a cozy. Or so I hoped and prayed. Yanking my phone from my pocket, I tapped furiously. Darren saw what I was doing and reached over to wrest the phone from me. In the struggle, he lost control of the car. We veered off the road, and headed straight for a large maple. Time stopped as the tree loomed before us. Closer and closer. At the last second, I shut my eyes.

When I opened my eyes again, I was unhurt and seated behind the wheel of my undamaged car in the driveway of my house. Darren was gone. Had I dreamed the whole thing? Or was I dreaming now?

My phone lay on the seat beside me. In the last rays of the setting sun, my selfie glistened in fractured sparkles through a large crack in the screen. ❖

A Christmas Cat in the Woods

Eugenia Parrish

Sergeant Mayfield, detective with the Vermont State Police, hunched his shoulders against a chill gust of wind. He could usually, and gratefully, avoid the vast forests that cloaked the mountains.

But this was where Noah Davis had found the frozen corpse.

The man lay with his face half-pressed into a snowbank, in a clearing surrounded by black tree trunks. One hand seemed to grasp at the hillside. The other lay near a knife handle sticking out of his side. Some blood had spattered the clearing, but most had pooled into a frozen dull-red flag on the ground.

There was dried blood around the man's nostrils, and deep scratches on his bare hands and wrists. Other than that, the only color came from his blue windbreaker, snow-crusted jeans, and expensive-looking athletic shoes. What Mayfield could see of his face was colorless.

Mayfield turned to the little man standing beside him. "Noah, what were you doing halfway up the mountain in the middle of December?"

Noah glanced around the clearing, at the corpse and the crime scene investigators in white coveralls, at the medical examiner crouched beside the body. He rattled keys in the pocket of his work pants and wiped his nose with the back of one gloved hand.

"I lost my job last Friday. I needed to think. The kids are makin' a racket around the house all day 'cause there's no school, it's Christmas holiday, so I thought I'd go for a walk. Get a little peace and quiet." He added sullenly, "I done it before."

Noah wasn't what Mayfield considered a criminal; he just wasn't averse to taking any shortcut the law allowed and maybe a few the law didn't allow but nobody cared enough to spend time and resources slapping his hand.

"You've been up here before, yeah," agreed Mayfield. "Usually to do a little off-season hunting. Where's your gun?"

"Didn't bring it with me. I told you, I just needed to take a walk. So, can I get back to it? I'm starting to be real sorry I called you guys. I could of just left him here."

"You move him?"

"Nossir. I know you ain't s'posed to do that. I watch TV. Besides, I don't like to touch dead bodies."

Mayfield believed him. They had found no ID, no wallet or car keys, but picking a dead man's pockets wasn't Noah's style. He studied Noah's boots, his thick coat, winter gloves, woolly scarf, and a hat with furry earflaps. At least he was dressed for a hike in mid-December. Unlike their stabbing victim.

"How'd you get here? I didn't see your truck."

"There's a spot up the road where you can pull into the trees."

"It's pretty steep up here. Not the usual place for a hike, even in summer. C'mon, Noah. You don't care about the woods except to take a leak or shoot something. What were you doing this far off the main trail?"

After a moment Noah said reluctantly, "I was following a cat."

"A cat." Mayfield kept his expression smooth. A cop for twenty years, he'd heard worse and weirder. "You mean a bobcat?"

Noah shook his head. "Naw, it wasn't no wild thing. It was this, like, little black and white kitty, somebody's pet. I mean, that's why I followed it. Figured it was real lost, being up here. You think it was his cat? The dead guy's? It led me up here."

"Noah, I've heard of dogs leading people to where their owners are. But never a cat. So where's the cat now?"

"Once I got to the dead guy, it took off." Noah's eyes slid again to the silent corpse. The crime scene crew was setting up lights. Noah hadn't found the man until midafternoon, and already the weak winter sun was sinking behind the trees, casting shadows over everything. "Man," he went on, "after I saw him, I didn't feel like chasing no cat no more."

"Did you see any other tracks?"

"Hard to say. There mighta been some on the hiking trail, but I didn't pay no attention. There's all kinds a tracks up here, though, ain't there? Looks like there was a ruckus."

Noah was right. The snow was heavily disturbed in the clearing. So far they hadn't found any tracks plainly leading away from it. The obvious conclusion was that the killer had gone back down to the trail. But with last night's snowfall and the path having been trampled, first by Noah and then by the first responders who had answered Noah's call, it was hard to be sure. And Mayfield liked to be sure.

Noah shifted from foot to foot, his breath making clouds. "It's cold, man. Okay if I go home now?"

"What time was it when you got here?" Mayfield wanted to know what Noah had been doing and why, and pinning him down to details usually got answers.

"I dunno," said Noah. "Left the house around noon, drove around, decided to get out and walk the trail a ways. Then I saw the cat sitting on a dead tree trunk."

Mayfield wondered if Noah had been drinking. Or maybe worse, but then, Noah had been raised old school. Alcohol was a man's drink, but drugs were the devil's work.

"Anyhoo," said Noah, "it hissed at me."

"Hissed at you."

"Yessir. Then it dropped down on the other side of the trunk and jumped back up. Kept doing that, looking at me the whole time. So I figured I better go grab it. Didn't want it to freeze out here." Noah went on. "Well, a cat can freeze to death, can't it?"

"Describe it."

"Y'see, that's the funny thing," Noah said earnestly. "It was the weirdest cat I ever did see. At first I thought it didn't have any ears, only then I saw they were sort of folded down flat. It was mostly white with black on top of its head, so it looked like it was wearing one a them berets them French guys wear up in Quebec. Anyhoo, I figured I'd take it to my truck to stay warm and then I'd come back up. But as soon as I moved toward it, it took off."

"So you chased it."

"Well, I went after it. Not much chasin' when it's this steep. And that's when I saw some weird tracks comin' up this way. I mean, they were shoe prints, not boots. Who'd wear shoes up here and not even stick to the trail? You think it was the dead guy's cat and he came lookin' for it?"

He looked at Mayfield as if for an answer.

"Noah, I need to know what you were doing up here in the first place."

"Just takin' a walk, man, I swear! I told you, I don't even have my rifle with me. I saw the cat and then I saw them fool tracks. Figured some tourist lost their cat and come after it." He gave a pious sniff. "I was just trying to help."

"Was there a car parked at the trailhead when you got here?"

"I didn't see one. But I had my mind on my own problems."

Mayfield gazed at the dead man. A bloody corpse in a windbreaker and sneakers, sprawled in a snowbank halfway up a mountain. And a cat.

"Noah, if you're the only one who came up here, and he's dead, it doesn't look so good for you, does it?"

Noah gaped at him. "Now you just hold on a minute! I ain't never seen that guy. I got no reason to kill somebody I don't even know!"

"How do you know you don't know him? You said you didn't move him."

"Well, hell, I can see enough, I guess. And I don't know no damn fools who'd climb up here dressed like that, and anyhoo, if I knew who he was, I'da said so when I called."

Mayfield decided that was probably true. "And you were just taking a walk. On a mountain, in December. C'mon, Noah, tell me what you were doing here, or I'll have to take you in on suspicion."

There was a silence that Mayfield allowed to stretch out. Noah's wind-burnt cheeks flushed deeper. He finally said with a sulky note, "I was looking to cut down a tree."

"In the National Forest? You got a permit for that?"

"Dammit to hell, Mayfield! What I got is kids, and they want a tree, okay? A Christmas tree. No, I ain't got no permit. You gotta go to goddamn Montpelier or something, and if I had the gas money for that, I could go buy a tree."

"You could get a permit online. They're free."

"Ain't got a computer, or the internet either."

"Where's your saw?"

Reluctantly Noah said, "I hid it down the hill when I had to go back down a ways to get a signal."

Boots crunched through the snow. Mayfield turned to see Benny Dutton coming up the path. Benny was an older trooper who was the first officer to respond to Noah's call. After seeing what Noah had found, he called the Major Crime Unit to report a homicide.

"Find anything along the road?" Mayfield asked him.

"There's a car about half a mile down that way, with its nose in the ditch and the keys still in it. Registration is Jerrold Markham, from New York."

"You see a cat anywhere?"

"A cat? No. There's bobcats and lynx all around here, but you hardly ever see one."

"No, I mean a domestic type. Maybe what they call a Scottish Fold-Ear."

Benny narrowed his eyes. "You puttin' me on?"

"I'm not, but Noah might be. He says he followed a cat, that's what made him leave the trail and find the body."

After a moment Benny said, "Well, that does kind of sound like Maudie Thompson's cat. But a cat like that, way up here, it'd be food for a coyote in no time. Maybe you saw a gray fox. They aren't much bigger than a good size cat."

"It was a cat," said Noah. "I ain't never seen Ms. Thompson's cat, but if it's hers, I'm sorry it ran away. I'd like to take it home to her."

"For a reward?" Benny asked dryly.

"For to take it home to her!" Noah flushed again but with anger this time. "She's a nice lady. Maybe after I get me a Christmas tree, I'll get one for her too."

"Not around here, you won't," said Benny. "You can cut down one Christmas tree for free, Noah, but you need a permit, and I'm guessing you haven't got one. On top of which, you can only cut in a designated area, and this doesn't happen to be one of them."

"Benny," Mayfield broke in, "right now I need you to walk Noah down and find somebody to take his statement. Then come back up here."

Noah protested, "I told you everything that happened!"

"You need to tell it to an officer who can write it out and you can sign it."

Noah groused until Benny gave him a friendly shove toward the downward trail. "C'mon, Noah, you know the drill."

Noah started down. Benny turned back to Mayfield and asked with a straight face, "We gonna go look for that cat? Sounds like it might have been first on the scene."

"I doubt it'll have much to say. Anyway, it appears to be long gone."

"Or a figment of Noah's imagination."

"Speaking of Noah, you better go after him before he decides to skip."

The ME's team had loaded the bagged corpse onto a litter. Mayfield stepped aside as they angled past trying not to slip and drop their burden in the snow.

The medical examiner was packing his kit bag. With a grunt the big man straightened up. "Not much more for me here."

"Frank, did you happen to recognize our dead guy?"

Frank Missom scratched his head under his fur-lined cap. "Now you ask, he looks kinda like that guy that's been dating Maudie Thompson's granddaughter Shirley."

"Maudie again. What's his name?"

"Jerry something. I was sitting with Maudie over at the Legion a couple weeks ago, and Maudie was telling me all about how she didn't like him at all, and he and his friends don't do much but hang out at Gorbin's bar and cause trouble. Maudie said he's been in more than one fight with Shirley's brother Paul, so you might want to talk with him."

"I will. What else can you tell me?"

Frank blew out through fat lips. "Scratches and bruises. Don't hold me to it until the autopsy, but right now I'd say there was a fight, and the other person either brought a knife or grabbed his and shoved it in him. Death by exsanguination. And cold."

"Time of death?"

Frank scowled at him. "Gimme a break. It's barely above freezing now and the sun's going down. He's nicely preserved. But I don't think he's been here longer than last night. Listen, I gotta get outa here. My toes are starting to glaze over."

Mayfield walked down a ways and called Benny Dutton on his cell. He relayed what Frank had said. "After you're done with Noah, call Maudie Thompson and find out if anybody's seen the granddaughter or her boyfriend. And send somebody to question her brother. Apparently he and the boyfriend didn't get along. Then come back up here."

"Right," came Benny's crackly answer.

Something moved in the trees. Mayfield hesitated, then stepped carefully through the snow. When he got to where he thought he had seen the movement, he felt foolish. There was nothing there. No marks in the snow, no tracks. He listened. The wind hummed in the treetops.

He jumped when Benny spoke behind him. Mayfield wondered irritably how such a big man could move so quietly.

"Find out anything?" he snapped.

"Maudie hasn't seen Shirley's boyfriend for a couple days. Shirley wasn't there, but Maudie says sometimes she spends the night at her dad's house if he's feeling bad."

"Alright. I want to look around up here some more, in case our killer took off either up and over or sideways through the woods."

Benny looked around. "They'd have to be an experienced hiker to manage that. Easier to go back down."

"But what if the only car they had for getting away was in a ditch?"

Benny shrugged. "You're the boss."

They worked their way upward, carefully stepping so as not to disturb the snow more than necessary. Mayfield followed literally in Benny's deep footsteps, peering at every tree and snowbank, looking for any sign that someone had left the clearing in that direction. To his eyes, there was nothing.

"Damn, Benny," he said after a while. "I guess you're right, this is a waste of time. Whoever stabbed this guy probably drove away in another car. Either that, or he flew away."

"Maybe the cat carried him out."

"You think I'm nuts? Thinking somebody might have come up this way?"

Benny surprised him by answering, "Nope. See over there?" He pointed. "Somebody's rucked up the snow climbing to that tree up there."

They puffed upward, their feet making post holes in the deeper snowdrifts. Mayfield's breath fogged out thick and white.

His heart stopped. A small black and white shape moved out from behind a tree and stared down at him with light eyes. Mayfield took off at an angle, pushing through the snow, climbing fiercely.

"Where the hell you going?" asked Benny.

Mayfield looked around. The snow was as smooth as milk. Nothing looked disturbed. Oh, hell, he thought. You're getting as nutty as Noah. He retraced his steps.

Benny pointed, saying, "Whoever it was crawled under these low-hanging branches, and then took off over them rocks on the other side."

Benny led the way, walking almost sideways, eyes intent on the ground. Mayfield returned to silently following him. His feet were getting cold even in his all-weather boots.

They were almost on the shed before they saw it, tucked into a copse of coniferous trees, showing only a bit of roof eave. A heavy wooden door wore a shield that identified it as a National Forest Service shed. It was barely large enough for a few shovels and other tools, but even Mayfield could see the boot prints leading up to it.

Benny hitched up his rifle to hold it in both hands. Mayfield pulled his service pistol. He motioned Benny to the rear of the shed and waited until he was out of sight.

"POLICE!" he shouted. "The shed is surrounded. Throw out any weapons and come out with your hands on your head!"

There was no answer. Mayfield crept to the door. The latch hung loose. He stood to the side and shoved the door open.

No shots. No sound. Gun leading, he peered around the door jamb. It was dark inside. There weren't many tools and nowhere to hide. But something crouched in a corner.

"Show your hands!" Nothing moved.

He approached the form slowly, reached out and pulled back the sacking that covered it. A woman lay curled up, white and still. Mayfield pressed the vein at her throat and sighed with relief.

He called Benny. "She's still alive. Go where you can call and get a rescue team up here."

Benny nodded. "Think she's our killer?"

"No idea. But she's no threat. Get moving before she's dead too."

Mayfield followed the ambulance to the hospital. Inside was a flurry of action, and he was thrust to the side and ignored. Benny brought in an older woman he introduced as Maude Thompson. A doctor came out to tell them the girl was conscious.

"Don't stay too long," he told Mayfield. "She'll recover from the hypothermia, thanks to you guys, but she's weak."

Maude Thompson sat in a chair by the bed. Faint color showed in Shirley's cheeks, but her closed eyelids looked bluish. Bruises stained her jaw. Both hands were wrapped in warming bandages, and heat pads lined her sides. Her feet looked enormous under the heavy heated blankets, and Mayfield thought they must be wrapped up too.

90

"Shirley?" he said gently.

The bluish eyelids lifted, showing soft dark eyes. They asked a question. He introduced himself. "Can you tell me what happened? How'd you end up in that shed?"

"Where's Jerry?"

"Sorry. He didn't make it."

Her eyes closed again. "I killed him." It wasn't much more than a whisper.

"Tell me what happened."

She sighed. "We went to Gorbin's and got in a big argument. He said he'd take me home. Then he drove right past Gramma's house. I got scared."

"Scared of what?"

"He said we was going back to New York right then and there, like I got no say about it. I screamed at him to take me home." She paused to clear her throat. Maude Thompson held a water cup so she could sip from the straw. Mayfield waited.

"He pulled over and started hitting me, so I brought my feet up and kicked at him like they taught us in self-defense. My boots are heavy ones—I caught him a good one on the jaw."

"How'd the car end up in the ditch?"

"It just sorta rolled forward and went down in the ditch. He hit his nose on the steering wheel. I jumped out, run up to the road and took off."

"What made you go up in the woods? Why not stay on the road?"

"I didn't see any cars at all, or houses, and I just wanted to hide. I saw that hiking trail. I know it from when me and Paul was kids. Thought maybe I could lose him, him being a city boy. Only it was steep and the snow was so damn deep. He caught me, and swear to God, I thought he was going to kill me. He hit me, then he grabbed my hair and started dragging me back down towards the road."

She coughed, a weak little sound. Maude Thompson held the straw again so she could sip.

"Then what?" Mayfield pressed, ignoring Maude's frown. "How'd you get away?"

"Well, he had ahold of my hair, real tight." One bandaged hand made a weak gesture at the scalp above her forehead. "Then all of a sudden he started swinging his other arm around his head like he was being attacked by bees."

"Bees. In December?"

"I dunno, that's what it looked like. He was hollering and cussing and waving his arm around. But he went right on yanking on my hair. God, that hurt."

"Shirley," he said, "how'd he get stabbed?"

She took a shuddering breath. "I . . . I remember grabbing his knife. I think I wanted to cut off my hair where he had ahold of it, so I could get away. But he tried to grab it and then, God, it just went in so easy. He hollered and let go and started staggering around."

"Why didn't you go back down to the road then, to find help?"

"Well, I woulda, but he was between me and the way down. I was afraid he'd grab me again. I just wanted to get away from him."

She started to weep. Maude took tissues from a box and wiped the tears. Shirley sniffed and went on. "I ducked under this one tree that had branches that came down to the ground. Like a little tent where I could hide."

"But you didn't stay there."

"I got cold. I mean real cold. I was afraid he could hear my teeth chatter. So I took off out the other side."

Maude said to Mayfield, "The girl was scared stiff. Isn't that enough?"

"I need to know why she never went down to the road for help."

"I toldja, I was scared he'd grab me! I didn't know I killed him!" The words were a mixture of defiance and fear.

Mayfield nodded to show he understood. It sounded like a good case of self-defense, but that wouldn't be up to him.

"After a while," she went on, "it was like I couldn't think real good. Couldn't feel my feet hardly either. I saw this little hut and thought at least it'd be warmer. Maybe I could hide out until he was gone. I found some old blanket or something, and then I must of went to sleep. Next thing I know, I'm here. They said my hands are all frost-bit. And I might lose some toes." Her voice started to shake. "God, I didn't mean to kill him."

She began to cry again.

Mayfield hesitated. Then he asked, "Did you and Jerry have a cat with you?"

"A cat?"

"Someone reported seeing a cat in the area. And I thought I saw something in the trees."

She and Maude both stared at him. He said, "It was described as a black and white house cat with flat ears, all black on the top of its head like it was wearing a hat."

"Detective," Maude said with a frown, "that sounds like my cat alright. But Maurice couldn't have been with them. He died over a week ago. The vet said it was some kinda cat cancer, but you ask me, that Jerry poisoned him somehow."

Shirley shuddered. "He hated Maurice. He was always sayin' I loved that cat more'n him. Gramma and me buried Maurice under a big rock in the garden." Her eyes filled with wonder. "I think maybe somebody's playing a joke on you."

Late that afternoon Mayfield saw Noah's pickup truck parked at the trailhead, with Benny's patrol car behind it, blocking it from leaving. Mayfield pulled in as Benny came down the trail.

Benny took off his hat and used it to swipe snow off his pants.

"Spotted Noah's truck and thought I better see what he's up to. Looked all up and down, but there's no sign of him." He added with disgust, "I catch that boy taking a tree without a permit, I'll have to write him up."

"It's just one little tree, Benny."

"He takes one, somebody else takes another, and pretty soon you got a bald mountain. You know it has to be regulated, and it's not hard to get a permit. Noah's just got a bug about doing things the legal way. Well, I can't sit here all day waiting to catch him."

"I'm going back up to the scene. If I see him, I'll give you a call."

"You still looking for that cat?"

Mayfield didn't answer, and Benny drove off with a grin.

In the clearing, fresh snow had nearly covered the blood. Animal tracks crisscrossed everywhere, but they were just the usual small wildlife. His eyes scanned the woods, but nothing moved.

He wondered about Maurice, and then told himself if the cat was still around, it was probably prowling the halls of Community Hospital, watching over Shirley.

On the way back down, he paused to look over at marks in the snow about twenty yards away, angling downward through the trees. Maybe the kind of marks made by dragging a small tree.

By the time he got back to the road, Noah's truck was gone. Mayfield smiled as he got into his car. He slammed the door and turned the heat on high. It looked like the kids would have their Christmas tree. ❖

Fish Eyes

Paula Messina

The morning had been uneventful, if not quiet, allowing Donatello Laguardia to study for his ancient Greek history exam. A radio across from the stall where Donatello worked interrupted the music of the Glenn Miller Orchestra, Dinah Shore, and the Mills Brothers to report on the Allies' advance in Italy. Donatello slapped his book shut when he saw Mrs. Davoli headed his way.

"How may I help you, Mrs. Davoli? The cod is particularly nice today, and the smelts are excellent."

"Mr. Clemente is here, no?"

Donatello smiled, hoping to put her at ease. "I'm the only one here."

Her large hazel eyes studied the curtain behind Donatello. "You have the mackerel?"

"The mackerel went early." He knew she wasn't there for the fish, but he played along and held up a haddock. "I can fillet this for you, if you'd like."

She shook her head.

He couldn't interest her in haddock, cod, or swordfish. This was Donatello's third day on the job, the third day Mrs. Davoli came to Boston's Quincy Market looking for Mr. Clemente, and the third day the fishmonger bolted into the small, curtained space behind his stall when he saw her coming.

Donatello wasn't there to sell fish or run interference between Mrs. Davoli and Mr. Clemente. Someone wanted to destroy Mr. Clemente's business. He'd begged Donatello to find the villain, and Donatello agreed to try. Only Mr. Clemente, normally a fun loving person, had been less than cooperative, insisting no one wanted to hurt him. When Donatello suggested there might be a connection between his troubles and Mrs. Davoli's visits, Mr. Clemente snapped his mouth shut faster than an outraged clam.

The trouble began when Mr. Clemente's ice delivery was canceled. No ice in the dog days of August. No fish. No sales. The trouble increased when a pile of horse manure greeted Mr. Clemente when he arrived one morning.

After working for him for three days, the only thing out of the ordinary that Donatello had detected was Mr. Clemente's frantic disappearances at the sight of Mrs. Davoli.

Mr. Clemente insisted Mrs. Davoli was not behind the efforts to hurt him. Donatello knew the fishmonger, who was happily married to a beautiful, sweet woman, adored the opposite sex. He reveled in their company but was faithful to his vow "till death do us part." Maybe Mrs. Davoli had mistaken his flirting for something more amorous. Or maybe she had a problem only Mr. Clemente could fix. Donatello couldn't imagine what that would be, and he couldn't connect the dots between her visits and the ice cancellation.

Donatello thought if he could interest her in buying something, he might learn what she really wanted.

"The snails are delicious, and the quahogs are nice and plump."

Seafood was of no interest. She scanned the area behind Donatello. She wanted Mr. Clemente and only Mr. Clemente.

Donatello squatted low so he could look Mrs. Davoli in the eye. "Is everything all right? Is there anything I can do for you?"

Mrs. Davoli shook her head and turned to leave. She looked dejected, all alone, and he felt sorry for her. He didn't know her well, but she and Donatello's mother belonged to the women's group at St. Leonard of Port Maurice Church.

"I'd like to help you. I don't want you to keep coming here and missing Mr. Clemente."

She looked all around, leaned toward Donatello, and let out a stream of Sardinian. She spoke so fast he couldn't make out even one word that might be similar to Italian. He had no idea what she'd said.

Grabbing Donatello's arms and pulling him close, Mrs. Davoli said, "I want to warm him."

Warm? Her hands were blazing hot. Donatello's face burned scarlet. He rose to his full height and stepped back. He didn't want any more misunderstandings.

Her voice was a soft coo. "I want to warm him."

Warm him? Good grief. What else could go wrong?

Donatello finally understood. Mr. Clemente had two gigantic problems. Someone wanted to destroy his business, and Mrs. Davoli wanted to destroy his marriage. No wonder Mr. Clemente fled every time he saw her.

A dead rat was propped up on the counter, its arms wrapped around an equally dead mouse. Donatello swore the rat looked as if he'd died happy.

"Donatello, what am I to do?" Mr. Clemente pointed at the rat. "I teach you how to fillet fish, but you don't find the person who wants to ruin me."

"I never promised I'd find him. I said I'd try. This is only my fourth day. I need more time."

"Time I no have. Who buys fish with dead rats and bad smells? Tell me this?"

"Mr. Clemente, I know baseball and the classics. If you want me to translate The Odyssey into Italian, I'm your man. I don't know how to find someone who doesn't want to be found."

"I don't need L'Odissea." Mr. Clemente waved his hands at him. "Don't joke. You solved that murder better than the police. You find the person who does this."

Donatello thought finding the man who'd murdered his sister involved more luck than skill, but now everyone expected him to be another C. Auguste Dupin. Or maybe the Oracle of Delphi. He had learned nothing useful during the last three days. He was reluctant to bring up Mrs. Davoli's amorous intentions. He knew it would only result in Mr. Clemente clamming up before Donatello finished asking a question, but he also wanted to get back to his own life so he could study for his final exams.

He took a deep breath and tried again.

"Mr. Clemente, I can't help you unless you're honest with me. There's something you're not telling me. Do you know anyone who bears a grudge against you? Anyone you crossed lately?"

"You mean I lie to you? Donatello, I know you since you were a bambino. I tell the truth to you. No. No. I no cross anyone. Never."

"You have no idea who might be doing this?"

"I tell you again and again." He slapped his chest. "No one who knows me, Napoleone Clemente, would do this."

Donatello tried asking about enemies, outstanding bills, the resurrected Black Hand, unpaid taxes, a jealous husband, a rival fishmonger, an angry father-in-law, a vindictive bocci player. For his efforts, Donatello earned a string of nos. He knew no more than when he began.

"The stupid questions you ask. The taxes I pay. Mio Suocero, he loves me, and I love his daughter. Only his daughter. She has the most beautiful eyes, like the soft fur of a baby doe. Everybody likes Napoleone Clemente."

He was right. Donatello had asked everyone who worked at Quincy Market if they'd noticed anything unusual. No one had seen anything. Did Mr. Clemente have any enemies, any angry customers, or disgruntled suppliers? Absolutely not.

Everyone enjoyed dealing with him. To a man, even his rival fish peddlers all said Mr. Clemente was a good man, always with the kind word, always helpful.

Each time Donatello started to ask the men about a possible jealous husband, he was cut off. Everyone knew Mr. Clemente enjoyed women, but he adored his wife.

Donatello was in over his head. This was no practical joke. Mr. Clemente's business was suffering. So far, he hadn't lost any customers, but he'd definitely lost income. He was out of pocket for the spoiled fish.

It had taken hours to clean up the messes, long hours when Mr. Clemente couldn't sell anything. Donatello knew from his father's bakery that turning away customers for any reason meant risking that their business would walk out the door and never come back.

Donatello tried to imagine what Sherlock Holmes would do and decided to eliminate every possible explanation.

"Mr. Clemente, I have nothing to go on, but I think this has something to do with Mrs. Davoli."

"You think she dumped manure here?" He touched Donatello's forehead. "Use your head. You're a bright boy. Mrs. Davoli didn't do this."

"I didn't blame her. I said I think she's connected somehow. Why does she come here every day, and why won't you speak to her?"

Mr. Clemente turned his back on Donatello.

"Please tell me why are you afraid of Mrs. Davoli. I think it's important."

Mr. Clemente spun around and placed his hands on his hips. His face was crimson. "Afraid of Mrs. Davoli. Who says this? Me? Napoleone Clemente? Afraid of a woman? Bah. Don't joke with me."

"I'm not joking. Whenever she comes, you run away."

Mr. Clemente started to protest, then he turned white. Mrs. Davoli made a beeline for his stall.

"I have work to do. Important work. Tell her I no here," he said as he disappeared behind the curtain to his tiny office.

"Mrs. Davoli, how are you today? What can I do for you?"

"Mr. Clemente? He no here?"

"He was called away, but I can help you with whatever you need. The sole is fresh. Caught this morning."

She looked as if she were about to burst into tears.

Donatello pointed to the clams on ice. "They're Ipswich clams. The best."

"I don't want the fish."

"Mrs. Davoli, is there anything else I can do for you? Anything at all?"

"Tell Mr. Clemente I ask for him. I want to warm him."

Donatello groaned. It would be easier to find another murderer than solve Mrs. Davoli's carnal desires.

"How is my son the pescivendolo doing?"

"Papa, if I don't pass my exams, I can become a fishmonger. I'm the maestro of filleting, and I can shuck oysters faster than Mr. Clemente. But he isn't paying me to sell fish. Someone wants to destroy him. There was a dead rat waiting for us this morning. Mr. Clemente is worried he'll lose his business."

Mrs. Laguardia smiled as she passed Donatello a plate of peas and macaroni. She was one of the women in the North End who enjoyed Mr. Clemente's harmless attention. "Such a nice man with those big, beautiful brown eyes. Who would want to hurt him?"

"I'm supposed to find out, but I haven't a clue."

"You'll figure it out," she said as she passed the grater and pecorino. "You know how to solve puzzles."

Donatello didn't point out that Mr. Clemente's problem wasn't a crossword puzzle. If it were only that easy.

When Mrs. Laguardia served fruit salad, Donatello asked, "Mamma, what do you know about Mrs. Davoli?"

"She's nice but sometimes she seems sad. She said we should pray for her. When I asked if anything was wrong, she said, 'Nothing you can make good.' "

"You're right. She seems sad."

Mr. Laguardia asked, "Do you think she has something to do with Mr. Clemente's problem?"

"I'm not sure. Maybe."

"Mrs. Davoli wouldn't do those bad things," Mrs. Laguardia said. "She's a good woman."

Donatello nodded. He didn't think Mrs. Davoli was responsible for what had happened, but he was worried she had misunderstood Mr. Clemente's flirting for something more involved.

"Mamma, does Mrs. Davoli have a good marriage? I mean would she ever . . . Is she faithful?"

"Certo. How can you ask such a question? She's a good woman and a good wife, and she'll make a good mother."

"I think she wants to tell Mr. Clemente something important. Only Mr. Clemente is too scared to listen. He won't tell me what's going on. And she won't either." He turned to his father. "Papa, I'm spending the night at Mr. Clemente's stall. I think it's the only way I'll find the culprit."

"By yourself? What if this person is dangerous?"

"I'll be safe. Whoever's doing this doesn't want to hurt Mr. Clemente. He wants to humiliate him. Besides, if he shows up, he'll never see me. I'll hide in the cubbyhole Mr. Clemente calls an office."

"How can you be so sure?"

Donatello looked at his father, then his mother. "I can't explain how I know. I just do. And if I go tonight, I think I'll solve Mr. Clemente's problem. Filleting haddock is easier than translating Homer, but Homer doesn't leave me smelling like low tide."

Donatello sat in the space that served as Mr. Clemente's office and nibbled on the sandwich his mother had made. In the dim light, he read *Not Quite Dead Enough*. So far, Archie Goodwin was the only one experiencing any excitement, if being arrested for murder while serving Uncle Sam qualified as excitement.

Donatello hoped to solve Mr. Clemente's problem before the night was over. There was nothing wrong with filleting fish, but he had other things to do besides study for his exams. He'd agreed to help his father write a cookbook, and tomorrow he had plans to take his gal to watch Red Barrett pitch for the Boston Braves.

He was almost asleep when footsteps jolted him awake. He set his book down and peered out from behind the curtain into the dim light.

Donatello wasn't the least bit surprised when Mr. Davoli came into view. He'd been expecting him. Mr. Davoli had a can of paint in one hand and a screwdriver in the other.

Donatello reached into his pocket for his baseball. He let it roll across the floor and bang against an empty barrel.

Mr. Davoli dropped the paint can and ran toward the exit.

Mrs. Davoli was surprised when she opened the door and saw Donatello.

"May I come in? If it's all right, I'd like to ask you a few questions."

She waved him into a parlor filled with bric-a-brac and velvet maroon overstuffed furniture. They sat at opposite ends of the sofa.

"Did something happen between you and Mr. Clemente?"

She looked shocked, then she shook her head. "Nothing."

"Does your husband believe something happened?"

"Yes, but I am a faithful wife, and Mr. Clemente only said I have beautiful eyes. Nothing else."

"Have you been trying to tell Mr. Clemente that Mr. Davoli is jealous?"

"Yes. I want to warm Mr. Clemente, but he won't listen."

Donatello bit his lip to stop from laughing out loud. He felt like an idiot for misunderstanding her. "You were trying to warn him?"

"That's what I said. I try to warm him. Mr. Davoli thinks we still live in the Old Country. I tell him things are different in America. A man can tell a woman she has beautiful eyes. It doesn't mean he wants more."

Her voice was tiny. Donatello had to lean close to hear her.

"I told Mr. Davoli, but he didn't listen. I'm afraid for Mr. Clemente and his beautiful wife. My husband is a good man, but sometimes his temper is too hot."

Donatello was relieved. He could have cracked the case faster than shucking an oyster if Mr. Clemente had told him the truth on day one.

"Don't be afraid. I'll take care of everything. I recommend the fishmonger on North Street near my father's bakery. Two sisters are working there while their husbands are fighting in the Pacific. Their fish is as good as Mr. Clemente's. I think Mr. Davoli will approve."

Donatello finished reading *Not Quite Dead Enough* just as Mr. Davoli, a beefy man with a thick head of dark brown hair, turned onto Salem Street. He called out to Mr. Davoli and asked if he could have a moment of his time.

"Yes? What is it?"

"Mr. Davoli, you're new to the neighborhood. You might not know that rumors have a way of racing up and down Hanover Street. Rumors can ruin a person's good name. They might even cost him his job. Someone is trying to destroy Napoleone Cle—"

"Why bring him up?"

"As I was saying, someone is trying to destroy his business. I know who canceled Mr. Clemente's ice delivery and spread manure in his stall. If this person doesn't stop, I'll make sure everyone in the North End knows what he did."

"You wouldn't."

Donatello swiped his fingers across his lips. "If it stops, I won't say anything. If anything else happens to Mr. Clemente, I'll sing like a bird."

Mr. Davoli became all flustered and unable to speak.

"Mr. Clemente is happily married—"

"This Clemente is no concern of mine."

"I think he is. I want you to understand that he's happily married with five beautiful sons. Mr. Clemente enjoys the company of women, but he is faithful to his wife. Sometimes husbands misunderstand him and think he's up to no good."

Mr. Davoli stared at Donatello with eyes as round and wide as the fish Mr. Clemente sold. "I don't know what you're talking about."

"My father has known Mr. Clemente since they were children. They're from the same Calabrian village. I've known him all my life. He's a good man, a good husband and father. He loves his wife—"

"Why are you wasting my time."

"You have a wife who loves you and is devoted to you."

"My wife is not your concern."

"She's a good woman. I hate to think of the terrible shame she'd suffer if everyone in the North End knew who left the dead rat in Mr. Clemente's stall. I hope I've made myself clear."

Donatello walked away without waiting for a response.

"You no come yesterday. How come?"

"I was working on your problem. You no longer need me. I took care of everything. No one will bother you again. I promise."

"You sure? You arrest this man?"

"I'm not a police officer. I can't arrest anyone, but I made sure no one will bother you."

Mr. Clemente looked all around him. "And Mrs. Davoli? She stops hunting me?"

"Yes, I even took care of that. From now on, she'll buy her fish from a different pescivendolo.

"Mille grazie. You're the genius. I knew you'd solve the crime."

Mr. Clemente took two large mackerels and wrapped them in newspaper, then he filled a paper bag with mussels.

"Your mother, she's a beautiful woman. Her eyes are like sparkling black diamonds. You give these to her and tell her I soon look forward to seeing her."

"I promise."

Donatello laughed as he walked away. Nothing, no one would ever stop Mr. Clemente from reveling in a beautiful woman's eyes.❖

The Princess and the Corpse

Stephen D. Rogers

It was a school night when I discovered the body. After I checked for a pulse, I called 911 and waited with my back turned until the police arrived.

Of course that's what my folks fixated on. I called the authorities first. Then, while I waited for them, I didn't immediately call my mommy and daddy in a panic as though I were still a little girl.

They didn't even know I was out! I'm supposed to call and wake them up, listen to all that, when the police might be trying to get through to me?

Meanwhile, how about some respect? Tripping over a dead body in the middle of the night, I kept my head and acted responsibly. My folks should have been proud. Instead, they were furious.

But that was after the police escorted me home. Before that, I protected the body, wondering what I would do if he came back to life, if all of a sudden his cold fingers landed on my shoulder.

Better to think about the hours before discovering the body.

On full moons, Ella would meet me on the path that cut through the woods connecting (or maybe separating) our two properties. At table rock, glowing in the moonlight, we would kiss and stuff.

My folks were horrified to learn I climbed through my window after dark, as if they would have preferred I woke them up and told them why. As if I would ask for PERMISSION.

Let's just say it was a good thing the officer was still there when my folks came out of their bedroom.

They got to ground me and impose a curfew; I got to cry and act traumatized; the officer got to calm everybody down.

What I wanted to know was, if my folks were going to ground me, why did I need a curfew? I wasn't going anywhere. I was grounded!

Anyway, it wouldn't matter that I was right and they were wrong. That's not how things worked in that house. In that house, they were always right, no questions asked.

I know, right? How messed up is that? They never heard of debate? They never heard of democracy?

No, the evil overlords have spoken. Everybody else bow and scrape. Everybody else, straight to the dungeon!

I don't know how the officer, who must hear this kind of nonsense all the time, managed to keep a straight face.

Especially as, guess what folks? Your daughter needs to come down to the station first thing tomorrow morning. Even if she's grounded.

Even though it's a school day.

Even though I have a quiz in history.

Even though I wasn't going to have anything to add to my story. My "story," as if I was making it up. I'd never seen the man before. He wasn't there the first time I went by. I didn't hear anything unusual. I didn't see anybody else.

Question me in the woods. Question me in the living room. Question me at the station.

I only know what I know.

Don't you people have someone who can test for DNA?

Meanwhile, my folks are freaked because I'm an actual person with my own life, which apparently is news to them. If ignorance is bliss, they must be the happiest people on the planet.

I guess for all these years they must have believed I was a performing animatronic. They were probably very confused when I kept outgrowing my clothes, but perhaps they thought it an advanced feature of my particular model.

She grows so that you can keep shopping!

Meanwhile, my folks keep pestering the officer about the victim, asking who he was, why he was in their woods, whether they were in any danger.

Not from him, obviously!

Seriously, could you just go back to bed?

So annoying.

I'm the one who discovered a dead body, and they're acting like they're going to need years of counseling to deal with their PTSD.

Self-centered much?

The officer who brought me home, who kept my folks from exploding, needed to go.

Once that happened, more screaming, more yelling, more recriminations.

Finally, I couldn't take any more. "I'm going to bed. I just had a horrible experience, I have a history test tomorrow, and now I have to go to the police station in the morning for questioning. If I don't get some sleep, I'm going to have a nervous breakdown!"

My show of drama apparently sufficient, I was left alone long enough to do my business without my parents banging on the bathroom door, long enough to sneak across the hall to my bedroom where I pulled the covers over my head.

A dead body.

I would be forever known as the young woman who discovered a dead body. For years, my parents would harp on that, would trace every unfortunate event back to what happened tonight. That's just how they are.

Give them an inch, and they'd drag it out until the apocalypse.

I would never live it down.

Rolling onto my side, I tucked in my knees.

How do I explain being grounded to Ella?

My folks will probably install bars over my windows, put up an electric fence, dig a moat. Security guards will follow me to and from school, stand behind me during every class.

And where does it end?

When do I stop being held prisoner as if I did something wrong?

A flood of tears dampened my pillow.

Ella wouldn't be able to wait. She would find someone else. Yes, I wanted her to be happy, but she was my world. Life without Ella wouldn't be worth living.

My folks would be wringing their hands, watching me waste away, unable to admit the part they played.

Ella would be the only mourner at my funeral, my folks too bereft to attend, too ashamed, too, too late finally taking responsibility for what they did.

I pulled my phone from the charger, checking to see what people were saying. ❖

By the Light of the Silvery Moon

Ang Pompano

Officer Sheila Wright glanced at her watch as she stifled a yawn; two hours left in her double shift. She wondered if Jamie was driving her mother crazy and if Mom had remembered to give him his meds. As soon as she wrapped up here she'd call to make sure her well-meaning mother wasn't allowing her son to tear the house apart. She willed herself to focus on the task at hand.

"Please step back, Mrs. Blake. There may be footprints," Sheila told the old lady who was about to step off the garden path.

Mrs. Blake made a quick, almost comical, sidestep back onto the flagstones.

"Oh, of course. I'm so sorry. Nothing like this has ever happened before. I'll just stand here by Mr. Riley. Is that okay?"

The woman's voice was almost a tweet, which went right along with her birdlike appearance. She stood next to Riley, a shadow of a man with a blank stare that reminded Sheila of how her son gazed into space when he was in quiet mode, which wasn't often.

"That will be fine," Sheila said.

Sheila bent down to examine the ground. No footprints were discernable in the trampled ground cover beneath the jimmied window. It reminded her of the pathetic flower bed outside Jamie's bedroom that she had long ago given up on, beaten into the ground from his comings and goings.

Turning her attention to the broken window, she recognized marks on the wooden sill indicating that it had been forced open with a flat object. A metal crowbar maybe?

"You don't have an alarm system?"

"No, I never thought we needed one. It's always been a safe neighborhood."

"I see. Now, Mrs. Blake, tell me again what happened," Sheila said.

"I returned home about an hour ago after spending the night at my daughter's place in Manhattan."

The widow, who Sheila guessed to be about eighty, dabbed her eyes with a hankie.

"She was helping me make decorations for a dinner party tomorrow evening."

"You were giving," Riley muttered, snapping out of his daze.

Sheila glanced at the man.

"So, you arrived home about noon?" she asked.

Mrs. Blake stopped to think for a moment. Dabbed her eyes once more and then answered.

"Yes, that's correct. I took the train in from the city and then a cab brought me home. When I got here I discovered that Bonnie was missing from the living room."

"Bonnie?"

"A painting my late husband, Herbert, bought me on our honeymoon in Paris. It was of a young girl that he fancied looked like me. I nicknamed it Bonnie. She's been a part of our family for years."

"Go on."

"I noticed the open window and I ran to my neighbor's house. That's when Mr. Riley here," she pointed to her elderly neighbor, "told me he thought he heard someone in my moon garden last night."

Sheila wrote something on a pad. "Did you investigate, Mr. Riley?"

"No, I didn't know Emma had been out of town. I thought she was in her garden."

"At night?" Sheila looked doubtful.

"It's a moon garden," Mrs. Blake explained. "The flowers bloom at night and close during the day. I sit out there almost every night. The white flowers look beautiful in the moonlight, and the fragrance is so relaxing. I planted it just this summer."

Again, Sheila wrote on her pad.

"Was anything else missing?"

"No, just the painting."

"I take it the painting was valuable."

"I had it appraised recently—$125,000. I decided to donate it to the museum, but first I wanted to have a dinner party to raise some money. Bonnie was going to be the guest of honor. Some friends and family haven't seen her in a while and I thought they'd want to say goodbye."

"She invited half of Connecticut," Riley said. "No point in having the party now, I'll come over and help you get rid of the food. Don't want to waste it. Food costs money. Reminds me of when I was a kid—"

"Any idea who might have taken it?" Sheila interrupted, keen to move things along. She still had to write the report back at the station, and she was exhausted.

Mrs. Blake was hesitant. "I wouldn't want to accuse anyone."

Sheila nodded. "Understood. Have any strangers entered your home recently?"

"I had two visitors the day before I left for my daughter's. One was the man who came to appraise the painting before I send it to the museum next month."

"Is he the one who told you the painting was worth $125,000?"

"Yes, his name is Woods, if I recall; somebody or another Woods. If we can go inside I can find you his card."

The three of them retreated into the house to retrieve the business card from Mrs. Blake's writing desk in the living room. Sheila noticed an empty artist's easel in the middle of the floor.

"Is this where you kept the painting?"

"Usually it hangs on the wall in the den, but it was on the easel for display at the dinner party. As I told you, Bonnie was going to be the guest of honor." Mrs. Blake sighed. "This is the appraiser's card."

She handed Sheila a business card for Nutmeg State Art Appraisal LLC, Edward Woods proprietor.

"You said you had two visitors?"

"Yes. The other was a young fellow who installed a new carpet in my living room. Now that I think of it, he did comment on the painting. Oh dear!"

A look of severe regret passed over the woman's face and she put her hand to her mouth.

"What is it, Mrs. Blake?"

"I foolishly told him the painting was very valuable when we moved the easel so he could install the carpet."

"Do you have his name?"

"Roger. I didn't get his last name. He works for Treasures of the Orient, the carpet shop here in town."

Sheila knew the store, too rich for her blood. Instead, she'd gotten her industrial grade carpet at Home Depot. She duly noted the store and the first name of the installer on her pad.

Mr. Riley piped in. "It was one of them. Take my word for it. Me, I'm putting my money on the young guy. You should go and arrest him." He was waving his arms as he spoke. Riley was definitely hyper, kind of an eighty-year-old Jamie.

"That would be premature, Mr. Riley. We're still in the investigation stage. But thank you for your suggestion."

Mrs. Blake looked thoughtful. "I guess I should get busy and make calls to cancel tomorrow's dinner party."

"I wish you wouldn't, Mrs. Blake. Why don't you hold your fund-raiser anyway?"

"Without the painting? That's crazy!" Riley said. He was so wired now that he was hopping around like a kid who had to go to the bathroom.

Sheila ignored the old man's remark. "Make the best of it. Tell your guests that the police are on the case. If anything, the mystery should generate interest. The museum needs the money whether they get the painting or not. In fact, I'd love to donate."

"Why, thank you! And I insist you come to the party," the old lady said.

I was hoping you'd say that, Sheila thought.

"That's about all I can do here for now, Mrs. Blake. I'll talk to the two men you mentioned and get back to you."

It was two o'clock and with only an hour left until the end of her double shift, Sheila called her mother from the car to check on Jamie and say that she had to make a couple of stops on the way home.

"Jamie's not having a good day," her mom reported. "He had a fit when I told him he couldn't wear his new school sneakers to play in outside."

"Is he all right?"

"Fine."

"Did he break anything?"

There wasn't much left to break. Almost everything she wanted to preserve she had put away in storage long ago. There was an uneasy silence on the other end of the phone.

"What did he do, Mom?"

"It wasn't his fault. He was in such a frenzy that he crashed into the grandfather clock. It went over."

The clock. The last thing she and her husband bought together before he left, abandoning her to care for their autistic son alone. It was just as well; she didn't need a reminder of the scoundrel.

With her son heavy on her mind, Sheila returned to the station and wrote her report. It was three-thirty when she left the station. She was on her own time now, but on the way home she dropped in on Edward Woods at Nutmeg State Art Appraisal.

Woods was a stocky middle-aged man with a bald pate, dressed in a rumpled brown suit.

"I'm a reputable appraiser, not a thief. And even if I were, why would I steal a painting I just appraised?"

"I'm not accusing you, Mr. Woods. I'm only here to gather information. Mrs. Blake tells me the painting was very valuable," Sheila said.

"Yes, an Eva Gonzales."

"I never heard of her."

"She was Manet's only formal student. She never exhibited with the Impressionists but her style is definitely of that school."

"I take it that Mrs. Blake was very happy with your appraisal."

"I should say so. She had already arranged to have the painting donated to the museum, but didn't realize it was that valuable."

"Do you find it unusual that she didn't know its value?"

"Not at all. The painting was unsigned. That happens sometimes, especially if the work is a study. She assumed it was the work of an unknown street artist."

"But you recognized the work right away?"

"I knew of a similar work by Gonzales and suspected it to be hers. Of course, I had to do research before I knew for sure. Now I'm quite positive.

"Research? I thought you met Mrs. Blake for the first time the day before yesterday. Doesn't research take time?"

"Of course it does! What a foolish question."

"I'm sorry. I'm just trying to understand how you could take one look at a painting and decide who the painter was and how valuable it is on the spot. Especially if it is unsigned."

"For one thing the formal appraisal was not done. The client wanted a rough idea before her party. The only time we could meet was two days ago. But I had detailed pictures of the painting from a year ago. When I saw the painting in person it confirmed my research and I told her it most likely was a Gonzales. I have more work to do of course."

A year ago, Sheila thought. Mrs. Blake had said she only decided to donate the painting two weeks before.

"Again, I'm sorry. I didn't realize you had met Mrs. Blake before."

"I didn't. A young man brought me the pictures a year ago. He wanted me to tell him what I could about the painting. He said he was a courier for a client who wanted to remain anonymous for the time being."

"You would take a job for an anonymous client?"

"Many collectors wish to remain anonymous for obvious reasons. There is nothing that prohibits me from giving my professional opinion about photographs of a painting. I gave my conclusions to the client, but I made it clear that I would have to see the painting in person before I would give a written appraisal. I checked to see if a painting of that description was stolen and there was none. And in case you are wondering, I was paid cash, and, I must emphasize, I declared the fee on my taxes."

"Your bookkeeping is not my bailiwick, Mr. Woods. But one more thing, could you tell me what the young man looked like?"

"It was a year ago, but as I recall, he was tall and thin, brown, no, light hair. As I said, it was a while ago."

Next, she stopped at Treasures of the Orient, where the young carpet installer, who she learned was named Roger Bailey, had just returned from an installation. He was sitting in the employees' kitchen drinking a Coke. He was wearing a cap, but she could see he had brown hair. She explained she was there concerning a missing painting.

"Sure, I asked about the painting," the young man said. "I only install carpet part time. I'm also an art student so I was interested."

"Interested?"

"Well yeah, it was unsigned but I thought maybe it could be a Manet. There was that obvious transition from Realism to Impressionism right on the canvas."

"So, you realized it was valuable?"

"I thought it might be and she said she had just learned that it was. I told her she shouldn't have it sitting around in her living room. I hadn't noticed it there last time."

"You've been to Mrs. Blake's before."

"Yeah, a year or so ago. I delivered a carpet for her bedroom. Look, if you're finished I have to make one more delivery before I go home." He threw his Coke can in the basket and stood. He towered over Sheila.

"Did you return to the house at any point?" she asked.

"No. I installed the new carpet and left. Listen, why would I draw attention to myself by asking about the painting if I was going to steal it?"

He removed his cap and ran his fingers through a mess of curls, obviously dyed blond since they didn't match the sides of his hair.

Sheila informed Roger Bailey that she'd keep in touch. Enough for today. Sheila rushed home and tried to have some quality time with Jamie, but she didn't have the energy. She'd make it up to him tomorrow, her day off.

Sheila spent her day off with Jamie, who had a pretty good day until she caught him in a lie. He had denied breaking a mirror in her bedroom, swearing he hadn't been in there, but he gave himself away when he asked for a basketball that she was going to surprise him with and had hidden in her closet. Maybe he would earn the basketball in a week or two she thought as she headed to Mrs. Blake's party that evening. She hoped so.

She looked forward to relaxing a bit at the party, but in the back of her mind she knew she would be working, keeping her eyes and ears open.

The minute she walked through the door Mrs. Blake greeted her. Mr. Riley approached her and spoke in a conspiratorial tone.

"I told Emma not to tell anyone that you were a police officer. I figured you'd want to work under the covers."

She couldn't help smiling.

"That's fine." She turned to Mrs. Blake.

"What did you tell them about the painting not being here?"

"I told them it was missing and the police were working on the case. You were correct. That stirred up quite an interest and has increased donations. This is going to be quite a successful fund-raiser. But I do hope you find Bonnie soon."

"I will, trust me. You know, Mrs. Blake, when you learned it was valuable, you really should have had it locked away."

"Oh, I was going to. I called my daughter to ask her what I should do. She suggested, since it had been in the house all of these years without a problem, that to keep it here for one more day until the party was over wouldn't hurt."

"Is she here tonight?"

"Why, yes. She is." She pointed to a tall blond woman across the room who was wearing a dress that brought prison stripes to mind.

"Amy, come here, please. I want you to meet my new friend, Mrs. Sheila Wright," Mrs. Blake said.

After introductions, Sheila cut right to the chase. "You must be very proud that your mother wanted to give such a beautiful painting to the museum."

At first Amy looked taken aback. Then she looked as if she were about to tell Sheila to go to hell. Finally, she looked calm and collected.

"Not only beautiful, but valuable, apparently. You don't need to be coy, Officer Wright. My mother told me you're with the police." Amy let out a long sigh. "And for the record, Officer, my father left me quite well off. I don't need any money from the painting." She grabbed a drink from a tray as a server came by. Then she turned on her heel and walked away.

Sheila was talking to a small group of guests when she glanced out of the living room window to see a young man with shaggy blond hair come up the sidewalk.

Mrs. Blake grew very excited.

"Oh, that's my nephew, Jack! I haven't seen or heard from him since he went off to California a year ago. I'm so happy he received the invitation to the party."

She threw open the door.

"Oh Jack, the most terrible thing has happened. Someone stole Bonnie."

"No way!" Jack exclaimed.

"When did you get into town?" Sheila asked.

"This morning. I came straight here, but Aunt Emma wasn't home. So, I sat in the garden for a while. The white flowers are beautiful. When she didn't show up, I grabbed lunch and then went back to my hotel." He turned to Mrs. Blake.

"Auntie, I'm so sorry about the painting. Anything I can do?"

"What you can do is answer a few questions for me," Sheila said.

"I didn't do anything," said Jack.

"Surely you don't think he did it. The painting was taken last night," Mrs. Blake protested. "He told you he got here this morning."

"I'm sorry Mrs. Blake. Your nephew was here last night."

Amy came over. "You have no evidence of that! Leave my cousin alone."

"But I do have evidence. If Jack's last visit was a year ago, he wouldn't have seen the new moon garden. Since the flowers bloom at night, he couldn't have known they were white."

Jack made a run for the front door when he went flying after tripping over Mr. Riley's outstretched foot.

"Gotcha!" Riley cried.

"I'm sure Mr. Woods will identify you as the one who brought the pictures to his office," Officer Wright said as she helped Jack up.

"No, it's not what you think!"

"Cuff him before he escapes," Riley demanded.

"I don't think so, Mr. Riley. Amy, you were quick to defend your cousin, and I know why. Jack didn't take the painting."

"I told you I didn't steal it," Jack insisted.

"Of course, Jack didn't do it," Amy said. "I've been saying that all along."

"Yes, because you were behind the whole plot."

Mrs. Blake gasped.

"Hear me out, Mrs. Blake," Sheila said. "Your husband left Amy well off, but it wasn't enough, right, Amy?"

Tears came to Amy's eyes. "My father left me money, but also sad memories of him going on business trips when I was a little girl. When I'd worry he wouldn't come home, I'd confide in Bonnie and feel better. That painting became my best friend. I know it sounds crazy."

"It doesn't," Sheila said, remembering her son and his imaginary friend. "Do you want to tell us the rest?"

"Last year, when my mother mentioned giving the painting away, I asked Jack to take photos to an appraiser in case she was serious. When she did give it to the museum, I asked Jack to help again. While my mother and I were in the city, he broke in last night, but it was my idea, not his."

"I knew it! Take them both away!" Riley shouted, practically hopping with excitement.

"Mr. Riley, stop!" Mrs. Blake shouted.

"It's true," Jack said. "But I didn't take the painting. When I got here, it was gone. I thought my aunt had already given it to the museum."

"Of course it was gone—Mr. Riley had already stolen it. Hands behind your back, sir."

"This is insane!" Riley protested.

"Is it? For the painting to disappear before Jack could get to it, someone with access and knowledge of the house had to be involved." She turned to Mrs. Blake. "Does he have a key?"

"Yes, in case of emergency."

"And your comments about waste suggest financial troubles, which I'm sure we can confirm." Sheila took him by the arm.

"Let go of me. I know my rights!"

"Let me read them to you just the same," she said, snapping the cuffs on him. ❖

The Cottage

Christine Bagley

Grief is harsh and anger is ugly, but fear is what consumes me. Winter in Cornwall is not helping, with a dark gray sky that feels too close. Behind the cottage, a row of skeletal trees reminds me of the walking dead about to charge down the hill.

Six months ago, my husband, Julian, drowned while sailing alone on the English Channel. The weather had turned nasty with strong winds and pelting rain. I stood at the window, tears pouring down my face as I watched branches snap in the air. I knew then he was never coming home. The next day, I learned his boat had flipped over and his body had washed up on Polkerris Beach. That's the grief.

The anger is toward my stepdaughter, Tessa, who's contesting Julian's will. Dividing the estate does not appeal to the little princess. She wants it all. I'd be much more magnanimous had she not been such an insufferable brat to me for the nine years I was married to her father.

I first met Tessa at Julian's home in Connecticut. She looked me straight in the eye and said, "I don't like your *art*," using air quotes to emphasize the word *art*. Sitting in the living room while Julian made drinks in the kitchen, she flipped her auburn hair over her shoulder and added, "There's no depth or promise of something more."

My eyes widened as I forced myself to stay calm. "I had no idea you were such a connoisseur of the arts, Tessa. How interesting."

Whenever she called and Julian wasn't home, she hung up on me. I felt the heat of her contempt, but I never told Julian. What I wanted to do was yell over the phone, "Grow the hell up."

Bodinnick, Cornwall, the riverside village where I live, faces the town of Fowey with the River Fowey flowing between the two. A ferry runs daily for residents and tourists. At the top of a hill behind a barrier of hedgerows sits the cottage of my dreams. When I first saw it four years ago, I felt like I was falling in love for the first time; my heart beat a little faster, and I felt a painful yearning because I thought it was unattainable.

"I'm going to assume you like it, Eve," said Julian, smiling when he saw my expression.

"It's perfect," I said.

A white stucco structure, it has a dark thatched roof, black wooden door, and black-framed windows with window boxes I fill each spring with trailing vinca and colorful impatiens. Living high on the hill allows me a stunning view of the river and the boats in the harbor.

The inside has been renovated over time yet still retains its ambiance from the past. Three enormous rooms include a kitchen with a marble island, a living room with an open fireplace and wood beams, and a master bedroom suite with a shower and clawfoot tub that I relish. At the back of the living room are French doors that open to a stone patio and a field of wildflowers beyond.

I've never been so enamored of anything in my life. Not my pets. Not the little red sports car I once owned. Not even Julian, if I'm honest. Should Tessa win the court battle, I won't be able to afford to stay in the cottage. That is the fear that consumes me.

As a painter I've become immensely attached to the area and its history. I often walk the same footpath where King Charles I survived an assassination attempt. After hearing that I painted him on his horse on the same path and sold it at the local gallery.

Elowyn Sumner, the curator who sells my paintings, is a good friend. Until Julian passed, I used her back room for art lessons twice a week where I met Tristan Whiting, another good friend and an older man who attended my classes.

I also have a quirky neighbor, Gladys Usher, who is ninety-four years old and reminds me of a scarecrow—straw hat, flannel shirts, overalls, and wild white hair. Two years ago, I found Gladys on the side of the road where she'd fallen on the ice.

"Oh my God, are you okay?" I asked.

"No, I am not okay. I've landed on my bloody arse!"

"Let me help you. I'm your neighbor, Eve Blakely."

I picked her up and helped her to the cottage, where I bandaged the cut on her hand, iced her knee, and made her tea. She told me her name and said most people call her Glad-ass because she's so happy all the time.

Now I ask if she needs anything in town whenever I go to Fowey. After Julian died, she started leaving food on my doorstep. Cornish pasties, the most delicious shepherd's pie in Cornwall, and bread and butter puddings are delivered in a picnic basket covered with a dishtowel. In the past six months, I've lost twenty-eight pounds. If not for Gladys, I would have starved.

Today, I sit in a chair gazing through the French doors at wildflowers waving in the wind. The gloomy day darkens the room but rather than get up and put a lamp on I sit there in a daze. My attorney, Mark Trevethan, rings, jarring me from nothingness. His agreeable voice is difficult for me to match in my current state of mind.

"Good morning, Eve. How are you today?"

"I'm okay."

"Just, okay?"

I don't answer.

He clears his throat. "Apologies for the intrusion."

"It's fine."

"We need to crack on is all."

I've been avoiding Mark, afraid to learn that Tessa was still holding out. "Are there any new developments?"

I hear him sigh.

"Why don't I take you to lunch at the Lighthouse tomorrow, get you out and about. What do you say? We can talk then."

I stand up and look in the mirror over the chair, noticing the blue grooves under my eyes and long black hair hanging in strings like a homeless person. I smell the armpit of my NYU sweatshirt and wince.

Mark has been patient, waiting for me to get on my feet. Even now he gives me time to respond.

"Alright," I say before I change my mind. "I'll meet you there."

The next day, I shower and shampoo, blow my hair dry, then toss it in a pony tail wondering if, at forty-four, I'm too old for a ponytail. I peek at the black mole beside my mouth to see if it's grown. With gray wool pants I wear a white turtleneck and a navy blazer. Then apply red lipstick to add color to my face.

Grabbing my winter coat, I knock on Gladys's door to return the empty basket she'd left days ago. She peeks through the crack and opens the door when she recognizes me. I smell the warm aroma of baked goods. She's wearing a stained apron over a flannel shirt and baggy jeans.

"You look spiffy. Where you goin'?"

"Fowey, to meet my lawyer. Need anything at the store?"

"No. Bloody lawyers. They're all pirates. Careful what you sign."

I half smile at the BEWARE OF DOG sign sticking in the grass. Gladys doesn't have a dog.

I take the ferry and pull up the collar of my coat as a brisk wind makes me feel more alert than I've felt in months.

For the ten minutes it takes to cross over, herring gulls, crows, and cormorants screech overhead and follow like my personal entourage. The holiday season is under way and people are milling about. I step off the dock and join the throng.

The pungent smell of garlic and steamed mussels greets me in front of the restaurant. Mark stands as I enter. "Eve," he says, eyes sweeping over me in a quick glance.

"Hi, Mark."

After we sit, he asks, "Are you still walking the footpath?"

Embarrassed to admit I've hardly been out I lie and say, "Once in a while."

"Good. Now. Will you join me in a glass of wine?" he asks, signaling the waitress.

Mark is tall with dark brown hair and crystal blue eyes.

"I saw your paintings in Fowey River Gallery recently. They're quite good, Eve. I'd not realized you're an impressionist. Monet is a favorite of mine and you use colors he used in his Giverny paintings. Have you been to Giverny?"

"I have. It's beautiful. Too bad these great artists die never knowing how extraordinary they were."

"Sad but true." Then he adds, "Are you painting at all?"

My shoulders slump but I don't want to lie again. "I'm not really in the mood for soft colors and serene landscapes."

We order wine and while we wait he says, "I'm sorry to report Tessa is continuing to challenge the will with no compromises."

This does not surprise me. But Mark is adamant about fighting the contestation.

"Half the estate is what you're entitled to and any court would agree."

I close my eyes and slowly shake my head. "The home in Connecticut is on the market for nearly three million dollars, to be split between the two of us. All I need is a minute portion to renew my lease until I can sell more paintings or get a job. You think she'd agree to that instead of going to court?"

"From my dealings with her lawyer, I doubt it. The law is on your side, Eve. I strongly advise you to stay the course a bit longer."

"Mark, you must know Julian and I made a terrible investment last year and lost everything but the home in Connecticut. His consulting business kept us very comfortable but since his death there's nothing coming in."

Mark looks troubled. "Eve, if you need money, I'd be happy to float you a loan. Your husband was a good man and we always enjoyed a nice round of golf at Carlyon Bay. I'm sure he'd want me to help you."

"No."

"It would be a loan, Eve, not a handout. And when this case is settled, we'll discuss paying me back."

"Are you so sure we're going to win?"

"I don't see how we can't. The fact that Tessa is even contesting the will is ludicrous."

"Thank you for the offer. It's kind of you but I can't do that."

I feel queasy, picking at my food and pushing the scallops around on my plate. Mark watches me with a helpless look, and I try not to tear up. After lunch, he holds my arm as we walk along the river to the ferry landing. Before I board, his hand cups my shoulder.

"Please call if you need anything, Eve. And do think about the loan. It's not that much to renew your lease and I know how much you love that cottage. Right now, the best thing for you is to stay put and not make any premature decisions."

"You're a good friend, Mark, and I appreciate your thoughtfulness."

"I'll be in touch. But I have every intention of standing firm."

I nod. "Thank you for lunch. It was good to get out."

On the boat back to Bodinnick, I stare at Ferryside, the chaletlike home where Daphne du Maurier once lived and wrote her first novel. With inherited wealth, she wrote the rest of her life without having to worry about money. Lucky Daphne.

At home, I go over my financials. My bank account is embarrassing, and with less than three weeks left to renew the lease, the idea of not living here makes me want to throw up. I need to sell more paintings. If Elowyn lets me teach classes again, and I work in one of the book shops in Fowey, I might be able to make ends meet. Slouching at Julian's desk, I start to cry. But the tears are not for Julian. They're for the cottage I may have to vacate.

Three days later, Mark phones that Tessa is not budging.

"I'm sorry, Eve. Even her lawyer agrees with us."

My face flushes with anger.

"She's still holding a grudge ever since Julian divorced her mother twelve years ago, despite the whopping amount of child support and alimony he gave them. Never mind the exorbitant amounts he gave Tessa over the years."

After the call, my hands clench and I can feel my blood pressure rising. I pace the room. I throw a book against the wall. I swipe a hummingbird figurine off the table, and yell, "You little bitch!"

Then I turn to my easel to vent my anger and fear, splashing red, black, and dark purple paint in furious whips and harsh strokes, the colors splattering my smock and the floor. All my pent-up emotions are released on the canvas. When I step back—the result is compelling. My arm aches and I fall into bed still in my clothes.

The next afternoon Elowyn's bright green eyes open wide when she sees the painting at the gallery. It is stark, apoplectic, and she stares at it for a long time with her hand across her heart. Finally, she says, "It's powerful and I feel your fury and passion. It's not your normal style, but Monet also painted during a dark time in his life. Remember *Camille on Her Deathbed*?" she asks, turning to look at me.

"I'm glad you like it."

"I love it. I'm putting it in the front window and charging more than your other paintings. Congratulations. Do you have a title for it?"

"*Trepidation.*"

"Brilliant."

When I return home, there's a basket of ginger biscuits from Gladys, and an invitation from Tristan Whiting for tea at his home. Tristan never progressed beyond sketches, but came to my class every week. He often stayed after the other students left, and I suspect he has a bit of a crush on me. A widower, in his late seventies, he is alert and fit with a shock of white hair. I put off responding to Tristan unsure I'm ready for casual banter.

But the very next day Elowyn phones and I can tell by the excitement in her voice she's sold one of my paintings.

"Eve! *Trepidation* just sold for seven thousand pounds sterling!"

Elowyn knows I need the money and lowers her commission, which will more than cover my lease renewal. I am thrilled beyond words. But the buyer remains anonymous.

"Why anonymous?" I ask.

"Many buyers do that. They don't want anyone to know their financial status or that they have an expensive painting in their home."

I immediately think of Mark. It's just like him to buy a painting rather than make me uncomfortable with a personal loan.

I take Elowyn to dinner at Fowey Hall to celebrate. "Cheers and thank you," I say over a bottle of Hambledon Classic wine. "I've been so worried about not being able to stay in the cottage."

"I'm absolutely over the moon for you," she says, lifting her glass. Slender fingers are adorned with an assortment of silver rings and her nails are painted a bright blue.

"Now I can be assured you'll be around a while longer. I would have missed you terribly, my friend."

"I feel the same. But I'm still curious about the buyer. Do I know him?"

Elowyn smiles coyly. "You might."

Excited about selling the painting at such a high price, I contact Tristan the next morning and reply to his invitation for tea. My whole life has suddenly turned around, and Tessa can go to hell in a handbasket.

But my relief over not losing the cottage is short-lived. The property owner informs me that I can only have the lease for six more months, after which he is putting the cottage up for sale. I am dumbfounded when he says he's asking eight hundred and fifty thousand pounds for it. Six months. That's all I have.

I'm hardly in the mood for tea with Tristan, but I take the ferry, then a taxi to his home. I've never been to Cliffcombe and had no idea how wealthy he is. A nice man answers the door and leads me through the great hall to the library on the right.

"Eve! It's so good to see you. How are you, my dear?"

"I'm alright. Thank you for the beautiful card and flowers."

"You're quite welcome. Come sit down," he says, gesturing to a leather wing chair.

The room is paneled in intricately carved wood, and I try not to be too wowed by my surroundings. But they are sumptuous: antique lamps, pastoral paintings of fox hunts and pastures, and a thick oriental rug. I could buy my cottage outright for the price of the rug alone.

Once we sit down, I say, "Your home is beautiful, Tristan. You have exceptional taste."

"You mustn't compliment me. It's all due to my wife, Maggie. God rest her soul."

He tells me about Maggie, how she could be mad as hell, smashing an empty plastic bottle on the counter, then pick up the cat and gently pat her. How she hated his business partner and said he looked like a mob boss. He laughs softly. "We had a great marriage and I loved her dearly."

He tells me he was relentless as a business man. "Maggie was right, I did deal with some unsavory characters along the way."

I admire Tristan's honesty and tell him how I met Julian at the Museum of Modern Art in New York. I was on a blind date and he was the blind date's friend. My date never worked out but Julian and I did. I speak of his sense of humor and his recklessness when it came to sports: car racing, parachute jumping, and rock climbing. "I always had a feeling he would die young."

Tristan is a good listener as I talk about Julian for the first time since his death.

"I'm so sorry. It's been such a dreadful time for you."

"I'm okay. It's good for me to be out and I appreciate your invitation."

"It's my pleasure. I'd do anything to erase the grief you're feeling. It took me a long time to heal, but as they say, life goes on."

"I suppose. But I'm afraid of what the future holds. It's all so uncertain now."

"What do you mean?"

I hesitate, not sure of how personal I should be. "I don't want to burden you with my problems, Tristan."

"That's what friends are for, Eve. This is a traumatic time in your life. And I've been through exactly what you're going through now."

I pause. "I'm very angry."

"Anger is part of grief, dear."

"The anger's not at my husband. It's toward my stepdaughter, Tessa, who's contesting the will."

"*That* is another matter. Why do relatives persist in adding to one's grief with their greed? What does she want?"

"All of it. The will states we each get half the proceeds of the home in Connecticut. I can only stay in the cottage for six more months because the owner is selling it for much more than I can pay. If my stepdaughter wins the case, I'll lose my home." I look down at my lap and close my eyes, trying not to cry.

"I remember the cottage. The painting was at the gallery. A perfect place for you, especially now."

My eyes well up and I take a handkerchief from my purse.

Tristan looks at me thoughtfully. "Perhaps a G&T rather than a cup of tea?"

I remain in constant fear of what lies ahead. I don't know what to do or who to turn to. I invite Mark for dinner, hoping he might have some suggestions. It's also a silent thank you. I make my signature dish: eggplant parmigiana with pasta, Caesar salad, and Italian bread. Because Gladys is such a great baker, I recruit her for dessert. She comes through with sticky toffee pudding and a bowl of whipped cream.

"You're having the pirate over?" Gladys asks when she drops off the goods.

"He's not a pirate. In fact, I'm pretty sure he's the one who bought my painting."

She strokes her chin. "Shoulda made a pan of shortbread just for him."

Mark brings a lovely bouquet of winter burgundy peonies. It's strange to have him at the cottage without Julian, who normally brought him home for hamburgers after golf. I tell him I'm trying to get out more, and that I had tea with Tristan Whiting.

"Tristan Whiting? How did that happen?"

"He was an art student of mine. He's wonderful company and I think he's lonely."

"Really." Mark looks at me with an unreadable expression. "I didn't realize you knew him."

"Do you know him?"

"I've had a few dealings with him," he says offhandedly. But I can tell he's uncomfortable and wonder if he's jealous. After an awkward pause, he looks around the room and changes the subject. "This cottage is a wonderful home for you."

"The good thing is," I say, watching for any clue he bought *Trepidation*, "Elowyn sold one of my paintings, so I can at least stay another six months. Unfortunately, it doesn't matter now because after that the owner is selling the cottage for way more than I can afford."

"I thought your lease allowed more time than that." It's obvious he's shocked—his eyes telling me more than his words. There's a pause as he considers this new development. "Well, things will be settled by then and you'll be able to buy this cottage outright. I'm sure of it."

"I'm not as sure as you are, Mark. In the meantime, do you know of any studio apartments in Fowey or Bodinnick I could rent if the court case is delayed?"

The rest of the evening is spent discussing the Fowey Christmas Market festivities. But I keep thinking about Tessa dragging out the court proceedings and that someone else will buy the cottage.

Tristan and I take a walk along the cliffs near his house one afternoon.

"I've been thinking, Eve. I have plenty of room at Cliffcombe. You can live here free for as long as you want and paint your heart away!"

"Thank you but I love my cottage. It's where I want to stay. But it may take a long time before Julian's estate is settled, and I don't want the owner to sell the cottage in the meantime."

We don't talk as we walk back to Tristan's home though I stay for a while as we discuss my situation at length.

One night after Tristan's maid serves dinner and leaves the room, my cell begins to play "Clair de lune." Tristan hears and asks, "Do you have to get that?"

I hold up my forefinger and look at the caller. It's Mark. The message reads, "Urgent—please call back as soon as possible. M."

"Excuse me, Tristan. It's a message from my lawyer."

"Of course," he says, standing until I leave the room. "Wait here," he tells the maid who enters the room again.

"Mark, what's going on?"

"Eve, I have bad news. Tessa's lawyer just called. She died in a car accident this afternoon. Apparently, it was a hit-and-run."

Immediately I sit down on the stairs.

"Eve, are you there?"

"Yes, I'm here. I'm just in shock. A hit-and-run you say?"

"Yes."

"I hope it was quick and she didn't suffer." He doesn't respond.

Finally, he says, "As I recall there are no other living relatives on Julian's side, correct?"

"Yes. Julian was an only child. His parents passed away years ago. Do you think I should fly back?"

"That's up to you."

"There'll only be Tessa's mother's side of the family at the wake, and I'm sure they don't want to see me. Maybe I'll just send flowers."

"That sounds appropriate."

I walk back to Tristan.

"My stepdaughter was killed in a car accident this morning."

"How awful!" He hurries over and clasps both my arms. "I'm so sorry. What can I do to help?"

"Nothing. There's nothing anyone can do," I say, turning to the maid with a sorrowful look. "Can you please call me a taxi? I need to go home. This is terrible news."

On the ferry back to Bodinnick, my hands are shaking—but I am also wearing an assassin's smile. During dinner, when the maid was out of the room, Tristan showed me the photo on his cell of Tessa lying on a stretcher, her auburn hair half-covered by a white sheet. He'd been true to his word. The hit-and-run had been done by an unsavory associate from his past.

I now sit in the cottage I will soon own, looking out the front window and watching the boats sway on their anchors. There are five messages on my cell from Mark, but it's too soon to call him back. My voice would not convey the appropriate regret. Far from it.

I will always feel the grief of losing Julian, yet my anger is gone, and fear no longer consumes me. I never wanted to have Tessa killed. But she was cruel in many ways and left me no choice. It was her or the cottage.

A loud rap on the door abruptly interrupts my newfound contentment. A FedEx package arrives and inside is a letter from Tessa. As I read the letter my heart starts pounding like a battle drum. Tessa has withdrawn her objection and the estate will now be divided according to Julian's will. I look at the date. She relented on the very day she was killed. The papers slide off my lap and scatter to the floor as a horrifying numbness engulfs me."❖

Novem Vitae

Bruce Robert Coffin

B arry Ginsburg knelt on the floor at the far side of the bed, arms fully extended as he steadied the butt of the semiauto atop the mattress. The sound of the stairs creaking had been unmistakable, tugging him from his shallow slumber like the electric touch of a lover.

Barry was intimately familiar with every single squeak and groan of the hundred-year-old farmhouse. Five steps up the staircase to the second floor, where his bedroom was located, a tread had curled slightly, separating from the corresponding riser, causing it to creak no matter how little weight was placed upon it. The only way to avoid the noise was to avoid the step altogether.

He kept the front sight of his Sig Sauer trained on the darkened doorway. Years of training had taught him to snug his index finger against the outside of the trigger guard until he was sure of his target and ready to fire. But on this night his finger was positioned inside the guard, curled firmly around the handgun's trigger. No slack. He would not risk even the slightest hesitation.

Having severed all ties to the agency months prior, he knew they would come; it was only a matter of time. In his business loose ends were a problem that needed solving. By quitting he had become a loose end. The hunter had become the hunted. Barry did not know who they would send, or even when, only that they would come for him. Of that there was no doubt. His former employers, the ones he had crossed, were as patient as they were ruthless. Like time and tide, he knew they would never stop searching.

A bead of moisture trickled down Barry's temple past his unshaven face. He caught a whiff of his own sweat, a pungent mixture of fear and excitement. Every one of his senses was on high alert. He lived for these moments. A game of cat and mouse played to its deadly conclusion.

Usually, it was Barry who assumed the role of the feline. The predator, stealthy and deadly. He had lost count of the number of contracts filled during the past fifteen years. How many times had he traded his soul for—what? Gold? Truthfully, it had never been about the money for him. Much like the allure of sex, it was the thrill of the hunt that had kept him in the game. He fed on the exhilaration that came from taking a life. Reason never factored into it. He did it because he loved it and excelled at it. And until the last contract, he had never deviated from the plan, executing to perfection every time. Until the last job when something drastically changed.

The hit had gone off without a hitch. He had stalked and studied his prey for weeks, learning the mark's schedule and habits, waiting for precisely the right moment to snuff out another meaningless life. Barry had killed the man as he lay in bed—making his current situation no less ironic. Three bullets, at close range. Two to the chest and one to the head. This method had always seemed like overkill to Barry, considering a single shot to the head was more than sufficient, but his employers always insisted on that little detail. He supposed it was more about the effect than anything. Delivering a "don't fuck with us" message to any others dumb enough to consider crossing the agency. Barry had always blamed Hollywood for the unrealistic expectation. Several generations of uninformed screenwriters had conditioned society to expect professional hits to be carried out in this prescribed manner. And silencers, which Barry took considerable pride in constructing himself, though not actually silent, did help to mask the extra rounds.

Immediately following his last kill, Barry discovered a suitcase full of cash tucked under the bed. Calmly and methodically, he sat at the edge of the mattress, next to the dead man, and counted each banded stack of bills. He knew such a large amount had to have been earmarked for something untoward. Regardless, the man he killed wouldn't be needing it, not unless cash was an accepted form of payment in the afterlife. Barry didn't imagine it was. After removing any trace of his involvement, Barry strolled from the dead man's residence, suitcase in hand, and never looked back.

Gradually, his eyes grew accustomed to the gloom of the landing beyond the open bedroom door. Dim moonlight spilled through the window at the far end of the hall, projecting the shadows of swaying treetops across the peeling wallpaper. Aside from the low mechanical whir of the ancient icebox running in the downstairs kitchen, the house was devoid of further sounds. Despite the late summer heat, Barry never availed himself of the comfort an air conditioner would've provided. Though tempting, the white noise of an AC could easily mask a killer's approach, as he knew too well.

He wondered if the agency had dispatched a solo contractor, or—due to his proficiency—a pair had been assigned. If there were only one, was the killer now standing motionless on the stairwell? Was the contractor wired too? Perspiring? Exhilarated over the prospect of moving up on the agency's go-to list? Perhaps there were a pair of contractors, even now continuing their advance to the second floor, the backup hitter merely stepping over the troublesome stair tread. No matter. There was more than enough ammunition in Barry's gun to take out a pair.

Seconds ticked by like minutes. All his senses were on high alert. Barry was in the moment. He felt the hardness of the wood floor through the worn remnant beneath his bare knees, and the twinge in his lower back from an old combat injury. Readjusting the gun in his sweaty grip, he focused his attention on the right side of the doorway, the top of the landing a mere six feet down the hall to the right.

Only one question niggled him. How had they located him? He had been hypervigilant about not leaving a trail for them to follow. And yet here he was, half-naked, in the middle of a sweltering night, waiting to snuff out the life of at least one fellow assassin. True, this had been his childhood home, but he had been known by a completely different name then. In fact, he had changed his identity not once but twice prior to being recruited by the agency.

He was careful to avoid all forms of electronic communication. Paid cash for every purchase. Changed his appearance regularly. Flew below the radar. He was the consummate professional. He had never brought home a lover, preferring one-night stands at cheap motels—the kind that accepted cash, and never asked for identification. Barry had only allowed one living creature inside his home. A stray cat he had named Ginger. She had greeted him atop the back steps one night when he had arrived home late. Ginger, also a night owl, enjoyed hunting in the overgrown meadow beside the house. Barry would occasionally treat her to a can of tuna, but Ginger preferred fresher kill. One more thing that bonded them, he supposed.

Something brushed against his leg, startling him, nearly causing him to jerk the trigger. He tore his eyes from the doorway and glanced down to find Ginger affectionately rubbing the side of her face against his bare skin.

"Damn, girl," he said, feeling foolish. "You scared the hell out of me."

The cat responded with a soft mew, looking up at him through half-closed eyes.

He lowered the gun to his side and scratched behind her ears. Ginger purred loudly before hopping up onto the bed.

He froze. How did you get inside?

Another floorboard creaked, this one just outside the bedroom door. With practiced quickness and deadly precision, Barry swung the handgun in a wide arc, aiming above the cat toward the doorway. He fired two rounds into the plaster six inches to the right of the door frame. The bullets punched through the wall, kicking up a cloud of dust. Ginger darted under the bed. Barry maintained cover while keeping the gun trained on the empty doorway, waiting to see if he had successfully neutralized the threat. After several seconds, a figure dressed in dark clothing collapsed onto the hallway floor. He kept his gun trained on the figure as he rose and slowly skirted the bed.

The would-be assassin lay face up, his eyes wide and lifeless. Barry studied the dark-haired stranger for a moment before firing an additional round into the man's forehead. Carefully, he stepped over the body, then bent down to retrieve the man's gun.

Starting with the second floor Barry began a tactical sweep of the entire house, one room at a time until he was confident that the corpse decorating the upstairs hall had come alone.

As he ascended the steps, Barry found Ginger staring at him from atop the landing. Her tail swished back and forth, telegraphing her agitation.

"You just saved my life, little lady," he said softly as he bent and lifted her into his arms.

Ginger rubbed the side of her face against his while purring contentedly.

Barry glanced at the body lying in the hall and let out a long sigh. Unlike his usual kills this one would need to be cleaned up and disposed of properly. And, of course, he and Ginger would need to vacate the premises immediately. Others would soon follow.

As he leaned over to put the cat down, a creak came from the stairwell directly below him. The fifth step. In one fluid motion, he spun on the balls of his feet while raising the gun, but he was much too late.

The last thing Barry's eyes registered was the muzzle flash from an assassin's gun. ❖

The Shorty Beat

Clea Simon

L ooking at me now, you wouldn't believe it, but I was as bright and shiny as a new penny the day I started work at the *Sun*. Naïve, no, but full of hope. Ambition, too. Fresh out of college, I'd landed a reporter job at a big-city morning paper, and I was raring to break big stories. To topple the powerful and bring about change.

It took all of twenty minutes for those aspirations to be brought to earth.

"Let's all welcome the new girl, Emily Kelton." The Metro editor, a bone-thin scarecrow named Ted, gestured in my direction. I smiled and nodded, willing myself not to react to that "girl." I'd been hired after the paper had been sued for gender discrimination, and I figured I should let the dude hang himself rather than make waves the first day. There were a couple of other women at the morning meeting. Three, if you counted the wizened thing in the corner, her nicotine-stained fingers already itching for a smoke break. But I was the youngest by decades, and I was sure everyone there could make the connection.

"Em." I said reflexively. Suddenly, all eyes were on me. "I go by Em or Kelton. Glad to be here."

"Hi, Em." One of the younger reporters—an Ivy League, clean-cut-looking boy—smiled. The rest grunted. And that was it for the next forty minutes, as Teddo listened to progress reports on ongoing investigations, his head bobbing on that ridiculously skinny neck. As he began handing out assignments to the few who hadn't spoken, a rustling of paper and some shifting of butts signaled the upcoming end of the meeting. I was wondering how to break in and get myself a story when the Tedster turned to me.

"Kelton." He said it like it hurt his mouth. "Why don't you cover the city licensing board meeting tonight? See if there's anything interesting going on. We'll talk inches in the morning."

"On it," I replied, and the meeting was over. My first assignment didn't sound like much, but I was eager to make a start.

"The licensing board?" After the meeting, I cornered the lanky editor before he could make his escape. "Anything in particular I should be aware of."

"It's an open meeting." He looked at me with dead eyes. "If they get any business done, write it up. You know how many words in an inch, right?"

I nodded, embarrassed by what felt like a rookie move, and went to look up the when and where on the city website. The meeting would take place in the City Hall annex, which, according to Google maps, wasn't that far from my apartment. It didn't start until seven, though, which meant I had a day to kill—or to dig up another story.

"Hey." My Ivy League was hanging out by the city editor's desk. "I don't think we've met. Neil." He held out a hand, Oxford cloth shirt pushed up to his elbow. "Neil Protter, courts and crime."

"Lucky you," I said, and I meant it, looking over at the police scanner that was rattling out static on the desk in front of him. "You ever hand over smaller stories? Routine police calls?"

"Sometimes." He smiled at me like I was a child. "But a lot of my stories come out of meetings like the one you're going to cover tonight."

Yeah, right, I thought. Well, if he wasn't going to help me, I wasn't going to waste any more time on him. "Thanks," I said, not meaning it, and walked off.

It wasn't that I didn't get it. I did. I was the new kid. Worse, I was probably only hired because of that suit. Nobody was going to give me anything. But I'd done hard news reporting on my college paper, contributing pieces to the local weekly the last two years. I could handle more than discussions about water monitoring and petitions for sidewalk cut-throughs.

I also had the better part of a day, and while HR had encouraged me to spend my time getting accustomed to the *Sun*'s interface, I wasn't here to play around on a computer. No, I wanted a story. Even someone's reject—just something to prove myself.

The trick, I thought, would be to ingratiate myself with some of the older reporters. Neil might be protective of his beat; a quick look back showed him hunched over the scanner. He was still young enough to worry about his territory, but older guys, in my experience, were happy not to work. Over by the coffee machine, I saw my chance. Three of his—our—colleagues were chatting over their mugs, so I headed their way. One of them must have seen me, because the lumpiest of the three glanced over. I managed a smile, raising my own mug. I'd flirt if I had to, and besides I could use more caffeine.

They fell silent as I approached, stepping back to give me access to the machine. But by then I'd heard enough. The one who'd pointed me out had been saying something about the "charity beat"— or, no, the "shorty beat," as in "a girl's job"—before they'd moved aside. I wasn't sure which was worse, and let them know, baring my teeth in what only the most naïve would call a smile.

It wasn't that I had anything to prove. I knew I was good, so I did my homework, reading up on the last bunch of board meetings. As I'd thought, they were dull as dirt, but the intern covering them had dutifully written up the requests for variances and title changes that kept city employees busy. The last piece had covered a meeting a month before, when some new construction permit had been debated. Even in the dry-as-dust write-up, I could sense the tensions between the board members, and I found myself growing excited. Maybe a fist fight would break out tonight.

Those hopes were dashed as soon as the meeting started, a little after seven. The six men seated at the front of the cavernous hall all looked about as aggressive as teddy bears, with four of them sporting the girth to match. One of them, an older dude with wild gray hair, even wore a pocket protector, as if his tubby torso needed anything more to distinguish it.

I topped off my travel mug at the meeting's old-style coffee urn, determined not to doze off during what I was sure was going to be a thrilling evening, and took a seat. Surveying the rest of the room I counted a dozen men, all more or less what I'd call middle-aged, all more or less boring, and two equally nondescript women, sitting in their coats, as if ready to make a quick exit once their own business was concluded. My own eyes were wandering when I spotted an outlier: Tall and dark, with thick black hair that hung over what promised to be an interesting face, he stood poised by the exit, clearly wondering if he could make his own escape.

Well, this is promising. I started to stand, readying a bystander question as a pretense, when the vibe in the room changed. The men all turned, as another door opened in the front of the hall, over where a tray of sweaty pastries sat by the samovar. Even the smell of burned coffee seemed to momentarily evaporate as I turned with them to see a blousy blonde in four-inch heels and a tawny suit, the jacket open on rose silk that caught the light. Nancy Cartwright, the city council chairperson. It had to be, I realized as she paused by the pastry tray, picking a pink-lacquered one and placing it on a paper napkin, before click-clacking in, her ample hips riding the beat of those shoes.

"Madam Chair." The baldest of the men confirmed, his face reflecting the pink of that blouse.

"Gentlemen." She accepted her due as I thought once again, this might have some promise. But as the men began to lay out the pros and cons of a zoning plan, she looked as bored as I was, picking at the pastry, her eyes straying to the back corner where that rakish stranger now slumped against the wall. At one point, she even left the dais, picking up a brown paper baggie that had been left by the tureen before returning to her seat and slipping the rest of her soggy-looking treat inside.

The meeting ended at nine without anything being resolved. "We'll meet again next week," Cartwright announced. "And then we will be bringing this matter to a vote."

I bolted from my seat, determined to introduce myself to that sexy stranger, when I felt a hand on my arm.

"Hang on." I turned and found myself face to face with Pocket Protector. "I saw you taking notes. Are you writing up the meeting for someone?"

"The *Sun*." I tried to pull away. "Not that there's anything happening here," I said, my irritation growing as I took in his haggard face, the strangely light blue-gray eyes under his unruly gray mop.

"Why don't you do some actual reporting then?" Those eyes seemed to bore into me. "See where the money is going to go if this thing passes?"

"I know how to do my job," I said, as I jerked my arm free. But it was too late. The dark-haired man was gone.

That night I wrote up what I had, double-checking the names and addresses with public records and those previous articles. What I brought in for the Tedster would be too long, but I figured I could mine it once I knew the length he wanted.

"No fist fights?" Was he serious? I didn't know, but I shook my head. "Okay, three inches then."

"There seems to be some trouble brewing over this zoning bill." I tried to muster a little enthusiasm. At least enough for another inch of space. "They're going to vote on it next week."

"Business as usual, Kelton." He was already looking past me.

"You don't think there's something else going on?"

He shook me off. "Your job is to report what the board does. Don't try to reinvent the wheel."

The rest of the week followed suit. Teddo gave me two more stories, both of which had me back at City Hall. I saw no further sign of that sexy stranger, though, and had pretty much given up hope of running into him again when the time for the next board meeting rolled around.

I got there a few minutes early, telling myself I was being careful because of the job. But when I saw that dark stranger laying out sad Danishes and stale turnovers by the coffee urn, my heart sped up.

"You work for the baker?" I sidled up to him, leaning against the table. His smile told me he recognized me too.

"Me? No. These are from Pain Douce, down the block. I'm just helping out." His dark eyes took me in. "You were here last week."

"I was." I took his hand. It was warm and a little sticky from the pastries. "Em Kelton," I told him. "I'm with the *Sun*."

"I'm Ray Barillo," he said. "Maybe I'll catch you after the meeting." He had a grin like a shark, but I consider myself an apex predator as well.

"Maybe," I said. Which was how, twenty minutes after the meeting ended, still without any resolution, we found ourselves entwined in the back booth of Just Us Served, a particularly dark bar next door.

"You shouldn't be here with me, you know." His breath was warm on my neck. "I'm a bad boy."

"How do you know I'm not a bad girl?" He started laughing, and I soon put an end to that.

I filed the next day, telling Teddo first that it was business as usual. The board hadn't even managed a vote, the ongoing discussion—the board members were too old to make it a proper argument—moving everything off for yet another week.

The next week, rather than duck the assignment, I asked about covering the vote, a move that sent my editor's eyebrows toward his rapidly receding hairline.

"I thought you'd want the shooting in the warehouse district." He said it like it was a test. "It just came in, and Neil's out."

"I can do both." I smiled at the thought of two bylines. The fact that I'd impressed the boss didn't hurt either.

I used my new press pass to get past the uniform guarding the scene and ducked under the tape like a vet. I'd covered crime scenes before, for that local weekly, but never a shooting. What I hadn't counted on was the condition of the body. I don't think of myself as squeamish, but what the gun had left of his face was a mess, a smattering of matted gray hair the only thing vaguely identifiable as human. But as the techs began to load him up, angling the corpse to slip him into the waiting body bag, his jacket fell open, and I reached for the coroner.

"Wait." I caught my breath.

"If you're going to be sick, do it over there." Both hands on the corpse, he gestured over to the bare ground behind me.

"No, I know this guy." It was Pocket Protector.

The coroner sighed. "We have the ID," he said. "Whoever did this took his wallet, but he had a clip-on from the small-business group."

I nodded, my mouth suddenly sour, and began scribbling in my pad.

With the ID—Laurence Ligett—and a statement from the detective on duty, I had enough to file. For some reason, though, the words came slowly, even after I got to the *Sun*, and I had to rush to get over to the City Hall annex in time for the meeting.

My mood sank further when I didn't see Ray. It wasn't that I thought we had anything serious, just that I could have used the distraction. In lieu of that, I could at least splash some cold water on my face, I decided. Anything to get the sight of the dead man out of my mind.

Exiting the board room, I went searching for the ladies and, turning into a back hallway, saw Nancy Cartwright, dressed today in bright green silk, and—right past her—Ray.

I stopped short, frozen as she leaned in toward my onetime beau, close enough so that the silk of her shirt pressed against his arm, shadow darkening the bright green. Darkening my thoughts, as well, as I saw him lean closer, almost whispering in her ear before his face opened in surprise. He'd seen me, and then she had too, and she turned to give me her own shark's grin. I spun on my heel and stomped back to the meeting room. That woman was old enough to be my mother. But what's a few years when you've got tits like that?

"Babe." Ray found me in my seat. "What did you run off for?"

"I'm not here to break you up with cozy Cartwright." I was staring straight ahead.

He did his best to sound hurt, and out of the corner of my eye I could see his brows twisting up to disappear under that long mop of hair "What are you talking about? She's ancient—and fat, too. You're my girl."

"I don't belong to you, and I'm not a girl." My voice held steady, but I wasn't. Inexplicably, I found myself blinking back tears as the meeting began—and he walked away.

Pocket Protector's—Ligett's—murder wasn't noted that night. Of course, I realized: It wouldn't yet be public knowledge. But Cartwright did mark his absence, as well as the scheduled vote. "I move we proceed," she said, sounding both level and calm.

"I object." One of the other board members—the one who had been the strongest supporter of Ligett's arguments—leaned forward to face the seated chair.

"We have a quorum," Cartwright continued, the voice of reason. "It's not our fault Mr. Ligett decided not to attend. Haven't we delayed on this bill long enough?"

There was some token discussion following that, but no one could argue with her point, and I didn't see it as my place to let them know what had happened. By the meeting's end, the bill had passed, and I took off, too unsettled by the day's events to even want to see if Ray was around.

I'd thought it was the scene with Nancy Cartwright that had got to me. But by the time I got home, I found my thoughts going back to that poor old fool with the pocket protector. Why don't you do some actual reporting then? See where the money is going to go?

I was just going to clear my head, that was all. But once I started searching for the properties in the rezoned area, I couldn't help noticing an odd coincidence. Most of them were owned by one company. The rest—yes, a few clicks proved my hunch—were owned by a firm with a different name but the same ownership as the first. That second parcel housed a string of warehouses that had been penciled in for mixed-use housing. Which meant—I looked it up—a multi-billion-dollar development with an affordable housing component that was going to be underwritten by the state.

I was mulling this over when my phone pinged.

You up? It was Ray.

I paused, recalling my earlier shock. *Miss Top-heavy too busy?* That only got me a laughing emoji.

Guess you're just her errand boy.

Hardly. Another emoji. Laughing till he cried.

He couldn't have known the day I'd had. The way my head was aching. Then again, that was one of the things I liked about him. We had no context. I looked around my apartment, which was as messy as it was cramped.

I'll be over in 20. Where are you?

A pin dropped, not ten minutes away. The address strangely familiar. Perhaps in another life, I thought, and headed out. As I walked, I noticed the neighborhood changing. Becoming nicer, with more late-model cars. Certainly a step up from my starter-level digs, which made me glad I hadn't invited him over. And yet . . .

My steps slowed and finally stopped. I reached for my phone.

I'm not coming up.

Is this because of Nancy what's-her-name? BC she's nothing to me.

I know, I replied, because I did.

Reporters aren't cops. We aren't even private detectives. So all I could write up the next day was the kind of analysis that usually bores me to tears. What was at stake with this bill. Who would stand to benefit. But when I explained what I knew to Ted, he excused me from the morning meeting.

Down at police headquarters, I was shuttled from cop to cop before I finally sat down with the detective in charge, an older man with a face like a basset hound.

"I know who shot Laurence Ligett, or at any rate, why. It has to do with a zoning bill the city council passed. It's about money, and I know how they're moving it." I explained about the pastry delivery, about a plain brown bag handed over to the board chair and the sad tray of treats nobody would ever really want to eat.

The detective's brows went up at this, and I realized I had to give him more.

"Look, I've seen the messenger. He's not a source for me, so I'll give you his name and where he lives. But in exchange I want access. I want this to be my story."

"You drive a hard bargain." His face cracked with the slightest of smiles. Ted had smiled too, his eyes lighting up as I'd outlined my plan.

I was no longer as shiny as a new penny, but I knew what I was worth. ❖

Chinese Exclusion

Michael Ditchfield

I'd been stewing on an upcoming execution at San Quentin when Gladys set a plate of hash and eggs under my nose. She sat down opposite me nursing a cup of coffee.

I smiled. "PI Abraham 'Jolly' Lucky says thank you, ma'am."

"Don't think that smile gets you off the hook, Mr. Lucky."

I was confused. "What hook?"

"You expect every meal delivered, and you're pushing me to quit my job."

We'd been married three months. It hadn't been a smooth sail.

"In the year nineteen hundred and fifty-eight a man should be able to support his wife," I said.

"Maybe Mrs. Lucky doesn't want to be supported. How did you eat before I came on the scene?"

I heard my mother's voice: *You should have married a nice Jewish girl.*

"How about I take the weekends, Gladys?"

"It's a start. Now, spill it. What's got you tied in knots?"

"The death penalty," I said. "Jack Gilfoy."

Her hands gripped the cup tighter. "Gilfoy killed a cop."

"His wife came by the office. She says he's innocent."

The story had been all over the papers. A year ago.

Silence hung between us.

Gladys's brother had been killed during a gas station stickup. Catch the perp and she'd volunteer as executioner. My father had been falsely fingered as a snitch and whacked in prison. Fellow mobsters killed him, but the criminal justice system wasn't fair either.

I let truth break through the shadows. "I think Mrs. Gilfoy is a prostitute."

Gladys began to breathe again. "A streetwalker tells you her husband is innocent of murder, and you believe it?"

"He denies ever using a gun," I said. "He put a pack of smokes in his jacket and stuck the pocket out to make it appear like a weapon."

"Gilfoy had an accomplice," Gladys said. "Maybe he had the gun."

I set down my fork. "Megan said that—"

"Megan!"

"Mrs. Gilfoy said—"

"The streetwalker said. Was she cute?"

"She's a hollow-eyed waif with stringy blonde hair."

"What are her assets?"

"Gladys, seriously."

"Why pay for her services. Come on?"

I scratched my head. "She's large in the chest department."

Gladys unbuttoned her blouse. "You haven't glanced my way for days. Probably since Megan with the large assets showed up, so how about these?"

I blew a kiss. Brought the temperature down. "Very appealing, Mrs. Lucky."

Gladys buttoned up her blouse. "Does Megan the Streetwalker have a theory about who killed the cop?"

I forked a bit of hash. "She said a Chinese man must have done it, only she didn't put it that nicely."

Gladys stood up. "Do you think a Chinese man did it?"

"Probably not, but that isn't the point. The state should not be killing people. I could give a hundred examples of wrongful executions."

She put her coffee cup in the sink. "Do what you have to do and get this out of your system."

The central library was my mother's home away from home. Ma was my research department. There wasn't much she couldn't find, and it didn't take her long to turn up newspaper reports. Jack Gilfoy and his accomplice, who was only fifteen years old—I liked Gilfoy less by the minute—robbed a malt shop of twenty bucks, jacked a Cadillac from an old man, and took the cops on a chase into Chinatown. A gun battle ensued. An officer and Gilfoy's kid accomplice were killed; Gilfoy was wounded. The jury took an hour to convict.

"Capitalism drives the poor to desperation," Ma said.

I drummed my fingers on the table. "It doesn't require that they be idiots."

"The bosses need the uneducated, Abraham. They use the lumpen as thugs when they want union busters."

I let her have the last word. Like always. I'd spent enough summers in Communist party youth camps to know the lingo and learn that there were many shades of gray where my counselors and my mother saw black and white.

In the public defender's office, I sat next to a potted geranium. The red of the plant was the only color in the place. On the wall opposite hung a new picture. The plaque announced Clara Shortridge Foltz. I was about to read the inscription when Blake Smith invited me into his office. If he'd looked any younger, I'd have been handing him a lollipop.

I told him Gilfoy's wife had visited me.

Blake hesitated. "He abandoned his wife and kids in Omaha. The woman you met is his girlfriend."

"Does this guy have any redeeming qualities?" I asked.

Blake gave a world-weary smile. After idealism gets its brains kicked out, reality arrives on the scene. It's a hard lesson.

"The stickup Gilfoy did," Blake said. "Making a cigarette pack appear to be a gun. He'd pulled that stunt in neighborhoods where cops don't spend time investigating."

"So why rob a store downtown?"

"Trying to impress the hobo kid. He feels bad about getting the boy killed."

"Does he feel bad about the cop?"

"The cops came in with guns blazing."

"Maybe the cop was killed by another cop," I said.

"The officer was shot in the chest. Gilfoy's prints and blood were on the murder weapon."

"What about the idea that a Chinese man did it?"

Blake appeared pained. "He was in Chinatown. Fill in the rest."

I got up. "Last question: In your heart of hearts do you think Gilfoy is guilty?"

His eyes narrowed. "The soda jerk and the old man they dragged from the Cadi both testified. But they didn't see a gun. Only the cops saw the gun."

"What kind of gun was it?"

"A Colt Python."

"Six-inch barrel or four?"

"Six," he said.

"Keep up the good work," I said.

The phone kept ringing. I dragged myself from the bed to the living room and picked up.

"*China Times*," my mother said.

I glanced at the window. "It's barely light, Ma."

"We didn't think about Chinatown newspapers. I'm going to find someone who reads Chinese."

"There's no reason to go this early."

I heard roosters. Poultry being sold on the street. Guaranteed fresh if it was still clucking. You didn't hear roosters in Ma's neighborhood. She'd already arrived in Chinatown.

"Be useful and make your wife some coffee," she said.

At least that made me smile. I brewed coffee and took it to Gladys. We sat in bed together.

"Are you going to make breakfast too?" she asked.

"Sure, why not."

151

She set her cup down and rolled toward me. "Show me how a chef does it first."

A while later, quite a while, I was cooking waffles. Gladys sat in the breakfast nook working on a glass of orange juice.

"What are your plans today?" she asked.

"A woman thinks her cat has been kidnapped by a neighbor."

"You're kidding."

"Such is the life of a private detective."

"And Gilfoy?"

Gilfoy. There was the rub. "In ten days, the man will be executed. Nothing short of a miracle will stop that. And I'm not god."

"We all die," she said.

I opened the waffle iron. "Yes, but it bugs me when other people decide the date."

She hugged me. She knew I cared. I appreciated that.

After getting nowhere on the cat case, I called the answering service. One message. Mrs. Gilfoy. Not the real Mrs. Gilfoy with kids in Omaha, but the pretend Mrs. Gilfoy. She left the number for a pay phone in a rooming house. An inebriate answered, but he went to get her.

"I got to go to San Quentin," Megan said. "I need you to come and give Jack some hope."

"There isn't any hope," I said.

"Tell him there is. He feels real low."

I felt low too. Only I wasn't scheduled to die. An hour later I showed up at the flophouse Megan called home. She cracked the door, closed it again, and slid the chain. I went inside. A negligee, transparent as they come, displayed her wares.

"I owe you," she said. "Nobody works for free."

My head swam a little. "I'm married, Megan."

Her smile was sincere. "Everyone needs some fun without attitude. My regulars are married. Give it a try."

"Let's go to San Quentin," I said.

She perched on the arm of the couch and parted the negligee.

I told her to get dressed.

Her lips formed into a pout. "You don't like me."

My hands went up. "Megan, you're a beautiful woman. I'm a square."

She discarded the negligee and got dressed in front of me.

The colors over the Richmond Bridge accentuated a descent into the hell of concrete sameness called San Quentin. Gilfoy arrived in chains. Despite the restraints, he lit a smoke. He winked at Megan, as though this little maneuver would impress her.

"This is the man I been telling you about, sweetie," Megan said.

Despite the bravado, fear came over him in waves. He took a pull on his cigarette. His hands shook. "They're going to have to drag me to the gas." His eyes went to the guards. "They say to take deep breaths, makes it quicker." His eyes settled on mine. "When she told me she got a Jew lawyer, I figured you had to be smart. Any hope?"

I pushed my feelings about one deeply flawed individual aside and swallowed the bile coming up in my throat. The State of California used the gas chamber. Hydrogen cyanide. Same gas the Nazis used. "I'm not a lawyer, Jack. Your appeals have run out. I'm a private investigator. The hope is that I turn up new evidence. Give me something."

He glanced toward the guards again.

"You've been sentenced to death," I said. "Nothing you say can make it worse."

His shoulders sagged. "How are my prints on a gun I never had?"

"What about your partner?"

His eyes filled. "His folks were chicken farmers. He deserved better."

"Did he have a gun?"

The chains rattled as Gilfoy wiped his eye. "He couldn't even kill a chicken. That's why he left." His eyes became frantic. "I stole twenty bucks and they're going to murder me. Get me out of here."

The guards tensed at his agitation; I threw him a curve. "Down by five, bottom of the ninth, two outs, and a full count."

"What's that mean?"

"Bunt single. Next guy hits a double, and the next a home run. Down by two. Single, single, walk-off homer. Let's start with the bunt single."

"Nobody bunts with two strikes on 'em," he said.

"That's the surprise, Jack. You say you never had a gun."

"I never had a gun. Ever."

"Let's go from there."

Outside, the fog had rolled in. It felt like we'd been talking in a sepulcher covered by a shroud.

By the time we got back to the city it was too late to be looking for a cat. I waited out front of the Pacific Telephone & Telegraph Building for Gladys. She'd appreciate the ride home to Berkeley. Only first, we took a drive up to Pacific Heights to check on Ma.

She wasn't home.

"Want to eat Chinese?" Gladys asked.

"She couldn't still be there."

Gladys gave a wry look. "It's your mother."

Chinatown had recently become a place for white America to discover all that was supposedly exotic. The streets were crowded. The exploitive mixed with the authentic.

"Let's try the Six Companies Building," Gladys said. "It's on Stockton."

"And you know this how?" I asked.

"Chinatown doesn't have its own phone service, Jolly. PT&T knows all. Your mother has a nose for power."

Power on the losing side, I thought. The Lincoln Brigades. The Rosenbergs. Stalin's Russia. Defeat seemed to make her stronger. Or at least more resolute.

As we approached a three-story building, painted green, with a fire-engine-red door, Gladys shouted, "There she is."

My mother was arm in arm with an old Chinese gentleman who walked with a cane. We caught up with them in a restaurant no bigger than a storefront. The menu, written on a chalkboard, had nothing in English. Ma didn't seem surprised to see us. Just introduced us to her companion, Jo. What little hair he had was snow white.

"We haven't ordered yet," Ma said. "Join us."

"There's no place to sit," I said.

Jo smiled. He had one front tooth. He spoke to the waitress. We followed her into a back room with a round table. A pot of tea arrived.

"Jo was in a tong," Ma said. Brightly.

Didn't matter if the word was in Chinese, Italian, or Hebrew, it meant the same thing: organized crime.

"Hatchet man?" I asked. Hoping not.

"Hatchet man," he said. "Som Yop Tong. Little Pete."

I turned to Gladys. "Little Pete wore chainmail to protect against hatchet men from other tongs. He was gunned down in a barber shop."

"I was a teenager," Jo said. "When Pete died my life ended. For a year I smoked opium. Then a woman saved me."

"She died six years ago," Ma said.

"Do you have children?" Gladys asked.

"No children. But we were happy."

"How did you and Ma get talking?" I asked.

They glanced at each other. "Jo knew your father," Ma said.

"On politics we don't agree," Jo said. Laughing. Deftly changing the subject from my gangster father.

Ma laughed too. "I'm trying to broaden my views."

"Good luck with that, Jo," I said.

The food arrived. We settled into squab, sea cucumber, hundred-day egg, seabass, and lotus root soup. Jo took pains to explain each item, along with how to use chopsticks.

"We spent the day reviewing the *China Times*," Ma said. "An old lady died on the same day as the shootout."

"She lived in the building where it happened," Jo said. "Yet they say she died three blocks away with her son's family."

"The police shot a bystander. That's the rumor," Ma added.

"What happened to her body?" I asked. "Was there an inquest?"

Jo raised his chopsticks. "In Chinatown many deaths are not even reported."

"Gilfoy was shot in a doorway," I said. "Maybe she was behind the door."

Gladys, who'd been quiet, had heard enough. "If an old lady died, that's on him too."

She was right, but I couldn't shake the questions: If Gilfoy carried a Colt, why not pull it when they robbed the malt shop and wave it in the old man's face when they heisted his Cadillac? And if the gun had a six-inch barrel, that wouldn't have fit in a pocket. And if the cops planted the piece, as Gilfoy suggested, where did they get it?

I kept my mouth shut. About other things too. Like this thing Ma had for gangsters, even retired gangsters. The two of them had made a date to speak with the family of the dead woman. More to see each other, I guessed. Later, in bed, Gladys called it cute. Nothing about it struck me as cute.

The next morning, after I found the cat—a man down the block had been putting out treats—I drove into Chinatown. Pockmarks scarred the wall of the building where the shootout occurred. A few folks went by. All Chinese. I wasn't going to learn much by watching. The place was a three-story walk-up. Four rooms a floor. I began at the top. Of the people that opened the door, none admitted to speaking English. Back on the ground floor, a Chinese woman, about thirty years old, well dressed, wearing makeup, and carrying a grocery bag, came in from the street.

She frowned when she saw me. "Who are you?"

"Private investigator. Trying to save a guy from the gas chamber. They say he killed a cop outside this building."

Her face was beautiful, yet hard. "Sorry, nobody was home that day."

I laughed. "The whole building was empty?"

That brought a smile. "You bet."

"Do you live in the building?"

She glanced at her grocery bag. "Uncle does. A lot of old men live alone. The Chinese Exclusion Act."

I wanted to tell her that even during the Holocaust Jews weren't allowed in but sometimes the chip on my shoulder annoyed even me.

"The Chinese Exclusion Act was repealed in 1943," I said.

She raised an eyebrow. "Yes, now they allow in one hundred and five Chinese people a year."

"None of it's fair," I said. "Neither is a guy being gassed. Could we talk to your uncle? He must have known the old lady."

Her head swayed as she weighed the options. "Okay, come on up."

Uncle lived on the top floor, behind one of the doors that hadn't opened. He bowed. I bowed back. It felt awkward. His place was packed with bric-a-brac. Incense burned. His wispy beard stretched into a point from his chin, like my stereotype of a sage. He insisted on getting us tea.

"He's your uncle on which side of the family?" I asked while the man fussed over a hot plate.

She slipped off her shoes. "Uncle is a term of affection. I'm a social worker. My name's Li Hua."

"Jolly Lucky," I said. "Tell me more about Chinese Exclusion."

My credo is to open doors not close them. I learned that after the Chinese built the railroad, organized labor shut them out because they lowered wages. The public was easily convinced that these lonely men only wanted to visit prostitutes, gamble, and smoke opium. So, they shut out Chinese women, which guaranteed the former would be true.

Li was nothing if not articulate.

Uncle shuffled over with the teapot set on a tray. We sipped from tiny cups. Li said something in Chinese. "He speaks Mandarin," she said. "I told him you wanted to know about the lady who died."

"Is that really what you said?"

Her eyes were playful. "You'll have to learn Mandarin to know."

Uncle sat quietly and then began to speak. He went on a while. When he was done, he looked to Li.

"Uncle said Changying—it means flourishing and shining—was born in California. At age seven her father was killed during a riot against Chinese people. That made her afraid of whites. Always. For the last year her mind was failing. She kept remembering bad things. Her family wanted her to live with them, but she said her husband was coming back. Only he was dead. Long ago."

Uncle said something else. She listened respectfully. Her shoulders rose slightly. "He wants to understand why you need to know."

I explained that a man was going to die.

Uncle opened a box decorated with painted dragons, took out three coins, and handed them to me.

Li said, "Shake the coins and drop them on the table." I did. Uncle looked at them. Picked them up and handed them back to me. "Throw them down again," Li instructed. "Five more times."

Her tone had a slight edge.

"I'm happy to ride along," I told her.

"This is the kind of superstition we Chinese need to get beyond," she said.

I tossed the coins. Five more times. Uncle opened a book, read the text, and then shook his head. He looked to Li and spoke a while.

"Uncle says the man you ask about is to be presented before God. Ten pairs of tortoises cannot stop this."

"He thinks I should give up then?"

She spoke with him some more. Uncle picked up the coins and went through the same routine.

"Be glad he's not using yarrow stalks," Li said. "We'd be here till midnight."

Uncle finished throwing the coins and consulted the book. His face became serious. He spoke intently.

Li turned to me. "You must shoot a hawk on a high wall. You kill it with a single arrow. Afterwards, proceed like an old fox crossing a river on thin ice."

"Why would I shoot this hawk?" I asked.

Uncle listened to Li like it was the most important question in the world. His hands folded in his lap. He spoke. It was short.

"For the truth," Li said.

"And the fox on thin ice?"

Li smiled. "That means to be cautious."

"Thank him for me."

I guess she thanked him. It took a long time.

"I need to go out for a drink," she said after. "It's been a long week."

For the second time in as many days I had to say I was married.

That amused her. "I didn't ask you to go to bed."

"I guess you didn't."

She put on her shoes. "I can't go in a bar alone. I'd be arrested for soliciting."

"What about a Chinese bar?"

She stood up. "Worse. Look, this man being executed. Something Uncle told me is important."

"You'll tell me if we go to the bar."

"I'll tell you if we don't go to the bar."

"Let's get you a drink," I said. "Even though Uncle says there's nothing I can do."

Her face became taut. "Uncle believes in karma. This man did something in his past lives that led to his fate now. I just can't accept that."

Gladys gave me a kiss and whispered, "Your mother's here."

Ma came through from the living room. "You smell of cigarettes, Abraham."

I hung up my coat. "I'm surprised I don't smell of gin."

"While your wife is cooking dinner, you're in a bar?" Ma said.

"I learned that the Chinese people have stood up. Or so Chairman Mao says. I also got an earful about the Chinese Exclusion Act."

Ma beamed. "The Wobblies were the only labor group that opposed Chinese Exclusion. I was a Wobbly."

"As I've been told a hundred times."

"Your mother found something interesting today," Gladys said. She was learning to cut through our squabbles.

When she was good and ready, Ma said, "The old lady died in the doorway. The police told her son he could claim the body and cremate her. No questions asked. They made it clear there were plenty of questions that could be asked."

"I learned something too," I said. "She was afraid of white people. She bought a gun at a bar that's a known hangout for gangsters. But nobody can prove the old lady's fingerprints were on the gun because she doesn't have fingerprints. She's been cremated."

"Time to eat," Gladys said.

I'd failed to notice her setting the table. We all sat down for meatloaf, mashed potatoes, gravy, and green beans. Ma chatted about nothing all through dinner, which was never a good sign. She was holding something back. Gladys cleared the dishes, but I did get out bowls for ice cream.

"I heard a new expression today," I said. "Women hold up half the sky."

"Chairman Mao again," Ma said.

Gladys dropped spoons on the table. "There's a famine in China. They tried to kill all the sparrows to save grain, but sparrows eat bugs and now they have a plague of locusts."

Ma harrumphed about us both being brainwashed by capitalist propaganda.

"You never liked Chairman Mao," I said.

"He's a revisionist," she said. "That doesn't mean you're getting the truth from the nightly news."

I picked up a spoon. "More truth than from the Chinese Communist party."

"Enough," Gladys said. "Let's enjoy our ice cream."

When I drove Ma home, she told me she was going to see more of Jo. That's what she'd been holding back. "I'm lonely, Abraham," she said. "So is he."

My reticence hung a fraction too long. I was about to get the guilt, but then I asked what she knew about Clara Shortridge Foltz, the woman whose portrait I'd seen in the public defender's office.

Ma gripped my arm. Which didn't help my steering.

"Clara was the first female attorney in California. They wouldn't allow her into law school, and she still passed the bar. When they refused to let her practice, she worked for years on legislation that authorized female attorneys. The powerful oppose anything that supports the powerless. You should know that by now." She let go of my arm. Then she added, "Jo did what he needed to do to make it in this country. Just like your father."

Did I object to her relationship with Jo because he'd been a gangster, or because he was Chinese? Would I feel this way about an old Jewish mobster? Ma could hardly blame me. She was still struggling with my marriage to Gladys, who'd grown up Catholic. Life could get complicated.

The San Francisco Police Department was my hawk on a high wall. Hopefully someone who liked me was on duty. The desk sergeant called upstairs. Tubby Jones came down. Tubby viewed all PIs as failed cops. Aside from that, he respected my profession. We went to the cafeteria.

"I'll put my cards on the table," I said. "In the shootout with Jack Gilfoy, an old lady was killed."

Tubby eyed me the way cops do. "Who told you that?"

"I'm an investigator, I figured it out."

He lit up a smoke. "How about the men in blue were being nice? The family didn't want her name used. They wanted her body."

"Why not charge Gilfoy with manslaughter along with the homicide? It was his fault she died."

"You got that right."

"So, why not charge him?"

Smoke streamed from Tubby's nose. Reminded me of a dragon. "No reason to complicate things."

"How about the old lady had a gun?"

He took another draw on his smoke. "You ever see an old Chinese broad packing heat?"

I leaned towards him. "Here's what I believe. A senile old lady saw armed white people outside her building. She didn't see cops, she saw guns and white faces. She opened the door and fired. Set off a fusillade. Now Gilfoy's going to be executed."

Tubby gave me a hard look. "Men in blue get unforgiving when one of their own goes down. Gilfoy started this mess. Three people died. He's going to pay."

"And an old Chinese lady doesn't nearly pay the price," I said.

My livelihood depended on a decent relationship with San Francisco's finest. That fox crossing the icy river came to mind, but the decision wasn't hard. I found a pay phone and called Blake at the public defender's office. Told him the cops covered up a death. The old lady had a gun. The gun landed in Gilfoy's hands after he'd been shot. Blake was realistic: no way would the court consider new evidence. The only chance was a clemency plea. The governor might be swayed. I couldn't help but think about what Uncle had said about an appointment with god. Ten pairs of tortoises could not oppose it.

Megan told me if I didn't go to the execution, she'd be alone. So, I went. The family of the dead officer, cops, journalists, and politicians who feasted on blood votes attended. We were seated on folding chairs. There was a telephone, so the governor could call with a stay.

The curtain opened to Gilfoy strapped in a chair behind the glass. No defiance. Just beat. His last meal had been three hotdogs with mustard, ketchup, and relish. He winked at Megan. Her nails dug hard into my arm. He had no final statement, just shook his head when they asked.

The moment hung like a drip suspended at the edge of tap. The phone did not ring. Potassium cyanide pellets dropped into sulfuric acid below the chair. Hydrogen cyanide floated up, like a thin white cloud. Gilfoy took deep breaths, just like they'd told him. His body shuddered, pulled against the restraints, his head went back, and then dropped forward. His jaw went slack. Didn't take too long.

Only it did.

A detective named McCready sat on the other side of me. An old nemesis. His excitement was palpable. After Gilfoy's head fell forward McCready slapped his knee.

"Want to know what sucks, Lucky?" he said.

"Yes," I said. "Gilfoy didn't do it."

McCready grinned. "What sucks is all the scumbags that get away with it."

He disappeared to mingle with his fellow devotees of state killing. I turned to Megan and gave her a hug. I would have told the officer's family that I was sorry for their loss, but the glance I got from his widow told me to stay away.

I've always had a hard time accepting the suffering people impose on each other. I used to see it as a weakness, but Gladys says it's one of the things she loves about me. That evening she made lamb chops and roast potatoes and peas. Followed by apple pie. Afterwards, we cuddled on the couch. We were in a little cocoon that kept the rest of the world out. The next morning, she went off to the PT&T building, while I staked out a middle-aged insurance agent whose wife suspected infidelity. Turned out he did have a lover, half his age, and a man. The paycheck came with a bonus and a note: They were having a threesome. The world was turning toward equality in ways my communist mother never would have suspected. That was okay by me. We needed more justice. Like Jim Crow laws ending in the South, or homosexuals being allowed to live without fear of being arrested. Or the death penalty ending. Then I got off my internal soapbox and surprised Gladys: I put in the laundry.❖

Widow's Walk

Kate Flora

It's an ugly word, *widow*, with all its connotations of mourning and black clothes and ancient, feeble women tottering toward the end on their own. Carla was thirty-five, hardly ancient, and she wore black only because it was expected. Everything else in her closet was colorful. She enjoyed colorful clothes and Bradley had liked her in colors. Liked her to be noticed. It wouldn't have done, though, to appear at his funeral in a bright tropical print, or red, which went so well with her black hair, or even her favorite pale greens and blues. So today she was standing in a cold drizzle wearing a borrowed black trench coat over a black sheath and a cashmere cardigan, while around her Bradley's friends, colleagues, and family shifted and murmured like cattle waiting to be allowed into the barn. His sudden death at forty had been a shock to everyone.

Bradley, bless his organized and frugal heart, had left her well provided for, a retro-sounding phrase, but true. The house and cars were paid for. He'd been well insured. His papers were in impeccable order. Everything maintained and in tiptop shape. Almost everything. With an old house, there were always problems.

Last night Carla had sat in his cushy leather chair at the big desk in his study and thought about how odd it would feel with this room now perpetually empty, the place where he most often was when he was at home. Bradley had loved this room. He'd been very particular about how it was furnished, although finding the pieces he wanted had fallen to her. He'd loved the richness of the plush oriental rug. The jade-green vintage tile around the fireplace. The dark bookshelves that held his law books. The buttery softness of his chair.

Sitting at that desk, he'd looked like the master of all he surveyed. Always tanned despite so many hours at his work, with those faraway blue eyes and that rebellious shock of mahogany hair, he'd looked like he belonged on the deck of a sailing ship, waiting for someone to call out that a whale had been spotted and he would respond with "Lower the boats!" He had the old New England lineage, too. Descended from the *Mayflower*. Ancestors fought in the American Revolution and on the right side of the Civil War. He was proud of his heritage as well as what he, himself, had built—a firm of more than forty lawyers that he'd cofounded.

Bradley had loved this house. It had suited him. It had gravitas. It was a venerable house, nearly two hundred years old, with a large ocean-front lot and a cupola and widow's walk on the roof. He'd bought the house just for that, he'd said when he called her to say he'd found his house. His house. They were married, living in a cramped apartment, and had been house hunting together, but he'd gone on his own, found this house, and made an offer without consulting her.

Carla tried not to be a resentful person. She'd wanted modern and bright, open and easy to care for. Over time, though, she'd come to love the house, just as Bradley assured her she would.

The minister mumbled on. The drizzle changed to heavy rain, battering the canvas covering over their heads, making the mumble impossible to hear. The edges of the open grave turned to mud as runnels of water poured in. Raindrops glistened on the shiny wood of the coffin. Carla half expected the lid to pop open and Bradley sit up and command the minister to hurry it up, he was getting cold and wet, and people were being kept waiting. He had not tolerated discomfort well, nor had much patience with delays. Always a mover and shaker. Carla had read that sometimes the spirit hangs around for a while after death. If that was true of Bradley, having his funeral rained on was making him a very unhappy spirit.

165

At last the mumble stopped and one by one they filed forward and shoveled a bit of dirt into the hole. It was a dreadful ritual, especially since everyone was in their best clothes. At least women no longer wore white gloves. That would have been an awful mess.

Carla dabbed at her eyes with a lacy handkerchief as Bradley's partner, Scott Tremblay, took her elbow and led her to a waiting limo. Scott was a take charge guy and right now she must look like she needed taking charge of. Carla was slender and petite and now, red nosed and dwarfed by the too large black coat, she did look pretty pathetic. Actually, she felt pathetic. The rhythms of her life had been dictated by Bradley's wants and needs for so long she wasn't sure what this new phase, this widowhood, would feel like.

The last time she'd ridden in a limo was on their wedding day. She'd needed the space for her voluminous dress, a dress so bedecked with lace and beading she'd felt more like a wedding cake than a bride. The folly of having taken Bradley's mother and sister with her when she went to choose a dress. Her mother was long gone and her sister, the miserable mother of three small children, wasn't speaking to her. At first, she'd been grateful to have some women with her, until she'd come out of the dressing room in her dream dress, a slender column of silk the warm ivory of heavy cream, utterly plain and perfect, and they'd both shaken their heads.

"Not fancy enough," his mother said. "Not for Bradley's wedding."

"Makes you look too small," the sister had said, as though a small bride wasn't adequate for their beloved son and brother.

So Carla had gone with the gaudy, full-skirted number they'd gushed over, and felt more like the dress was wearing her than she was wearing it. Bradley had loved it, though. Mother and sister had been right. It fit his image of how his bride should look.

Scott and his wife, Anna, joined her in the car and it took off, smooth and silent, to the nearby restaurant where they'd booked a room for an after-funeral gathering. Actually, Bradley's mother had booked it without consulting Carla, as though she, despite being the wife—the widow—didn't have a say in things. Booked the room and ordered the food. Frankly, she was grateful. She'd been too stunned by what had happened to function well, even though normally she was an excellent organizer. She'd had to be. Bradley was very exacting.

Carla had never ridden in a funeral procession, either. Her mother's funeral had been in the local church with coffee and sandwiches in the church basement after. Carla didn't remember much of it. Too young. Too stunned. Too terrified about what was coming next: having to go and live with her grandmother. Her grandmother, who had never let a day pass when she didn't tell Carla and her sister, Nora, what a saint she was to have taken them in and what a burden they were. She'd gotten out of there, leaving for college, as soon as she could.

After college, she'd gotten a job as a paralegal at a law firm, which turned out to be Bradley's. Almost as soon as she'd begun to relish the freedom of having an apartment and a salary and was making friends, he'd asked her out. She'd been flattered that a lawyer, a partner at his own firm, was interested in her. Dating was fun. He was very sweet to her, courting her in ways she'd only read about in books. Flowers, gifts, fancy dinners, lots of phone calls between dates because he just wanted to hear her voice. Agitated calls if she was busy and didn't answer.

Despite her protests that she was too young and it was too soon, telling him she wanted to enjoy her post-college single life a while longer, Bradley overrode her wishes. Ignored her objections. He declared that now that he'd found her, he couldn't live without her. She must marry him.

She managed to put him off a while until the pressure got too great. His mother was dying to plan a wedding. His sister wanted him to have children quickly so they could play with hers and the cousins could grow up together. It all seemed so appealing—a family that wanted her to be a part of it instead of one that was indifferent or hostile. So Carla had let herself be persuaded. She was twenty-four when she and Bradley were married, and for a while, it had been almost blissful.

Not a very long while.

Their first apartment was small and with both their things there, hard to keep tidy. The mess made Bradley angry even though she explained that the problem was not having any space. He somehow managed to break or discard several things that were important to her. At the time, Carla had accepted it as his reaction to stress. Practicing law was hard. Being responsible for the whole firm and bringing in enough business to pay salaries even harder. She tried her best to please him but often sobbed into her pillow because she kept getting things wrong.

Finally there came the day when he said they needed to look for a house. He wanted to start a family and wasn't bringing his child home to their crummy apartment. For several Saturdays they'd trailed around after realtors, looking at one disappointing place after another. Then they'd seen exactly what Carla wanted. She was thrilled until Bradley had shaken his head and said absolutely not. He wasn't going to live in a glass box.

That was the week he'd taken time off from work and, without consulting her, found their house and bought it. It was lovely. She'd admit that. It was also huge, and cold and drafty and impossible to keep clean. While he extolled the virtues of the built-in cupboards, the butler's pantry, and the size of the rooms, she was imagining trying to cook in a kitchen without counters, very few cupboards, and a stove that must have come with his ancestors on that *Mayflower*. When he found her weeping in the dismal room, he assured her they could have it all redone. Briefly, she'd been comforted. But it had taken second place to rebuilding the garage, refinishing the floors in the game room, and a fancy fence to enhance the curb appeal. Then there was fixing and furnishing his office.

She'd labored to make decent meals in that nightmare room for five years before it was her turn.

When it all got to be too much, and he was in his dream office sipping Scotch and immersed in his reading, she'd steal away to the cupola, a small, sweet room with windows on all four sides and a widow's walk where she could look out to sea. She'd kept the windows shining and made floral cushions for the window seats. She could sit there and read and imagine a different life. Her grandma would have said she was ungrateful. She had a wonderful life. A beautiful house. Nice vacations. A handsome husband who adored her.

What she didn't have was happiness. Close friends. A life without the constant criticism that she was getting it wrong. The child she longed for.

Despite Bradley's assertion that he'd wanted the house so they could start a family, he'd balked every time she suggested it. He was too busy. He needed more time to get the firm established. This year wasn't good because they were moving offices and that needed all his attention. Once they'd been careless and she'd gotten pregnant. She'd expected he'd be pleased even though it wasn't planned. Instead, he'd lost his temper and shoved her, yelling that it was all her fault.

She could have told him it took two people to make a baby but by then she didn't bother to argue with him. His anger and his sulks were too difficult to bear. His shove sent her tumbling down the stairs and then to the hospital with broken ribs. They both told the police she'd tripped. The baby didn't survive her fall. She didn't pressure him again. By then she understood he'd likely be as cruel to a child as he was to her.

The rest of the world thought they had a wonderful marriage. They were lively at parties. At his parents' house, he was as good to her as he'd been when they were courting. She gave lovely dinner parties for his partners and their wives or husbands. She stopped going out with her friends because he didn't like it.

She hadn't realized his behaviors were the classic signs of an abuser until she read an article in a woman's magazine and wondered how she could have been so stupid and naive. Every behavior described fit Bradley to a tee. That was when she started squirreling away money, little bits at a time, for when she'd have enough to leave. She figured she'd be an old lady before she was ready, but the act gave her hope. She knew people might ask why didn't she just leave? Any abused wife could tell them why. Because they believed in their marriage vows. Because men like Bradley followed their violent outbursts with apologies and flowers and expressions of love. With "I couldn't live without you" that always created hope things would get better.

They also didn't leave because their years of isolation meant they lacked the skills to make a good living. Because they were physically and financially isolated, everything was in their spouse's name. Most important? Because even if the spouses demeaned and abused them, they were still property, and property didn't get to decide to leave. Property was either killed in a rage or, if the abuser was clever, died in some unfortunate accident.

Carla usually arranged for repairs around the house—after all, she was home and could supervise—though he had to approve them first. When it came to the railing on the widow's walk around the cupola, it had been rotting and unstable for months, yet when she mentioned it to Bradley, he kept putting her off, saying he'd get to it, he'd check it out, don't bother him, he was busy. Because she loved being out on the balcony, looking over their yard to the sea, smelling the salt air and listening to the birds, she'd gotten an estimate for the repairs. He'd ignored it.

It was around then she realized he was staying at the office more, coming home later, demanding sex less often. Classic signs of a man who was having an affair. Something inside her exploded as she considered the possibility. All this time she'd let him tyrannize her, trying to be the perfect, most agreeable wife. She can't have friends. Can't own anything. Can't have a life. And now this? She needed to know for sure.

She found a private investigator specializing in cheating spouses, who cleverly disguised his bills as from a doctor or a dentist. He quickly confirmed her suspicions, along with plenty of photographs. It looked to Carla like Bradley was trading her in on a newer model—the woman he was seeing was small and pretty and raven-haired. Still glowing with youth, not jumpy and worn down by a decade with Bradley.

It was on a Wednesday. She'd made dinner even though she didn't expect him to come home. She'd left it warming in the oven and gone up to her hideaway in the cupola. She was reading when Bradley suddenly appeared in the doorway.

She jumped and tried not to cringe.

"Did you forget to make dinner?" he snapped.

"It's downstairs. In the oven. Ready. I didn't know if you were coming home."

He turned toward the door that led outside. "Show me that rot on the railing again. I want to see how bad it is."

She was cautious out there now that the railing was insecure. Recently, she'd noticed strips of blue tape on the railing, marking the place where it was unsafe. It had given her hope that he meant to fix it soon, but since she liked to go out there, she'd moved the tape to mark the area that was still sturdy. She felt safer that way.

He stepped through the door and she edged out behind him, keeping her back against the wall. Edging toward the spot where the railing was safe, a place where she could still stand and look at the sea.

Something about all this felt off.

As she waited for his attention, to show him the rot, he suddenly grabbed her arm and threw her against the railing.

Carla didn't weigh much, but the floor up there was slippery, and the shove threw him off balance, too. He put a hand out to catch himself and the railing crumbled. As she watched, stunned, the rotten section of the railing gave way and cascaded three stories to the patio below, taking Bradley with it.

Her thoughts warring between "I told you that railing wasn't safe" and knowing where he'd marked the railing, Carla got out her phone and called for help.

Cautiously, using her nails so she wouldn't leave fingerprints, she removed one of the strips of blue tape and moved it to the other side of the broken section so they again marked the place that Bradley had identified. The scary empty space through which he'd tumbled. Then she rushed downstairs to check on her husband.

His eyes were open. He tried to tell her something but the words were only a faint jumble, even when she leaned in.

"Oh! Bradley. What have you done? I told you that railing was rotten," she said. "I begged you to fix it."

Even as she held him and murmured entreaties that he should stay with her, Carla understood she was the one who was supposed to be lying here, broken and dying. Why else would his shove have aimed her at the space it had? Why else shove her at all? They hadn't been fighting.

She heard sirens and car doors slamming, followed by the thudding of heavy feet. She rested her head on Bradley's chest, hearing his breathing slowly stop. A police officer gently took her arm and said, in a soothing voice, "Come away, now, ma'am, and let the medics work."

So she did. Bradley's widow let herself be led away. Stammered through an interview with the police. Sobbed into a kitchen towel as she turned off the oven on the no longer needed dinner. Sobbed as she showed them the estimate to repair the railing. As she said, "He didn't believe me. He had to check for himself. Bradley was a very hands-on man. He was strong. He liked to be in charge. He just grabbed that railing and gave it a shake. And then . . ." She had to stop. She couldn't say it. Forced herself to finish. " . . . it gave way and he fell."

She hadn't planned this but she knew how it would look. They couldn't know about the private detective. About the escape money she'd squirreled away. That these were tears of relief. ❖

Peregrine Point

Christine Eskilson

A ll happy families are alike: each unhappy family is fighting over real estate. Melinda mentally revised Tolstoy's famous quote while she watched Luke measure out coffee. His stiff shoulders and deliberate movements signaled he remained angry from last night. He came up late to their small room under the eaves and didn't respond to her murmured greeting, instead angling his body on the lumpy double mattress as far away as possible. When she woke to sun streaming through the white gauze curtains, he practically lay on the floor. She considered nudging his shoulder to complete his trajectory but decided such a move would hardly promote marital harmony. She slid off the foot of the bed to slip on a tank top and shorts, then tiptoed downstairs.

Neither of her brothers could provide a helpful buffer when Luke joined her later in the kitchen. Peter, the oldest sibling, most likely was taking a morning dip in the cove below the house, as he did on every visit to Peregrine Point. He boasted frigid water inspired his best entrepreneurial brainstorms, of which there'd been plenty over the years. Paul, probably still on LA time, might be asleep for hours. He rarely came back to coastal Maine after moving west to pursue a film career. It took their father's death and distribution of his estate to bring them all together at the rambling green shingled "cottage" that held so many happy childhood memories for Melinda.

"Do you want to talk?" Melinda ventured from her seat at the scarred wooden table in the middle of the room. She poured herself coffee from a percolator her father always used, wincing when a few drops of hot liquid dribbled on her wrist.

Luke pushed the French press plunger he insisted on bringing from their apartment and turned to face her. "About your snoring? You almost outdid yourself last night."

"Come on, Luke."

He leaned against the speckled vinyl counter, crossing his arms over his University of Denver T-shirt. "Doesn't seem like there's anything to talk about. It's the Peter, Paul, and Melinda show all the way. God, you guys sound like a lousy cover folk band."

Melinda briefly closed her eyes, remembering their couples therapy. *It's not about you; try to understand and reflect his feelings.* "I don't mean for you to feel steamrolled. I love this place. I want to keep it in our family and my brothers feel the same way. We don't want to sell to some hedge fund manager or bitcoin prince."

"You know I'm more of a mountain guy than an ocean guy." Luke ran one hand through his curly blond hair. "I thought we were going to decide together, that's all. You've made it clear I have no choice."

The back screen door flung open. "Choice?" boomed a voice. Peter strode into the kitchen wearing swim trunks and flip flops, a faded New Yorker beach towel wrapped around his neck like a silk scarf. A thin line of blood trickled down his leg from a gash on his knee. "If we're talking dinner, I choose lobster."

"Peter, you're bleeding." Melinda grabbed a paper napkin from the center of the table. "Here, take this."

Peter took the napkin and dabbed at his leg. "It's nothing, Florence Nightingale. I tripped on the path coming up from the beach. Too many roots and rocks. Should have put up a handrail years ago." He bestowed a wet kiss on his sister's head and corralled a seat beside her. "Anyway, I can pick up lobsters at the town dock. That is, of course, if Melinda does the cooking honors."

Melinda shivered despite the July heat. "Much as I love lobster, boiling those scaley critters alive has never been my forte. I couldn't even dissect a dead frog in high school bio."

Peter waved a hand. "No bother. I'll get Paul to do it. Speaking of science, guess who I ran into?"

"The creature from the black lagoon?" Luke offered in what Melinda assumed was an attempt to be funny.

Peter ignored his brother-in-law and leaned toward his sister. "Dr. Phil. He waylaid me on my way up from the beach. Before I tripped, by the way. Otherwise his presence might have come in handy."

"I'm surprised he speaks to you," Melinda said. "You tormented him when we were kids. Remember the time you rowed him out to Crab Rock in Dad's dinghy and left him stranded?"

"He could've swum back to shore if he had any nerve. And he got picked up eventually by that softhearted brother of ours. I'm still pissed that Paul took Dad's Zodiac out to get him." He shook his head. "Typical middle-child peacemaker."

"Who's Dr. Phil?" Luke asked. "You don't mean the TV Dr. Phil, do you?'

"He had some very pointed questions about what we intend to do with the house." Peter rose to take a chipped Pine Tree State mug from a cupboard. He picked up the French press before Luke could stop him. "Thanks, buddy. Don't mind if I do."

Luke reached out a hand like he wanted to grab Peter's mug but instead waited to pour his own cup. He shot Melinda a narrow-eyed look as he joined her at the table.

"Phil was another summer kid growing up," Melinda explained to her quietly seething husband. "I'm sure I've mentioned him. His family's house is the one right before the turnoff to the Point. We called him doctor because he had his whole life mapped out from the time he was about eight years old. Yale undergrad like his grandfather, then Harvard Medical School and then he was going to be a famous surgeon."

"I don't know about all that but he did end up in medicine, didn't he?"

"If you call anesthesiology medicine, yes." Peter shrugged. "He's not curing cancer. He's putting people to sleep so the big guys can come in. Anyway, he's definitely interested in this place."

Luke perked up. "Really? From what I understand anesthesiologists can make big bucks."

Melinda touched Luke's arm in a warning gesture. "Hon, we sorted this out last night."

He shook her off. "I just remembered a call I've got to make. See you guys later."

"Good luck finding decent reception," Peter murmured as the screen door slammed behind Luke. "What's up with hubby? He's not a happy camper this morning."

"You're not helping. You basically pretend Luke's not in the room, even if he's standing right next to you."

"Okay, so?"

"So Luke's not thrilled about our house plan. He thinks there might be better ways to use my inheritance. We're talking about having kids. If that happens I'd probably cut back my hours at work, and we'll definitely need more room. Brooklyn's so expensive."

Peter took a long swallow of coffee and wiped his mouth with his towel. "While I am childless by choice and by virtue of more than one divorce, I fully support any nieces and nephews you'd like to bestow upon my world. That said, I'd rather have your rug rats running around here in the summers like we did than in some needle-strewn city park."

"You do have a way with words," Melinda said dryly.

"Besides, it's our house and, frankly, our money. If Luke ever gets that novel of his published, then he can talk. He'll come around, you'll see. Now please excuse me. I'm going to find one of those Band-Aids Dad loved to hoard from the 1960s."

Although Melinda suspected her brother probably was right about Luke, she still worried. She went outside to search for him on the bluff overlooking the cove. The sea air tickled her nose and the sun shone on white sailboats skimming the sparkling water around the Point. In the horizon Melinda spied a pod of dolphins cresting the waves. Moments like this reassured her they were doing the right thing with the house. If only Luke felt the same way.

On the bluff she found her brother Paul instead of her husband. Paul sat shirtless and cross-legged on a large flat rock near the edge. His eyes were closed and she thought he could be meditating. His shoulder-length wavy dark hair and deep tan reminded her of an ancient prophet.

Before Melinda could creep away through the beach roses, he opened his eyes and gave her a lazy smile. "Hi, Mel."

"I didn't mean to disturb you. I thought you were still in bed. Have you seen Luke?"

"No bother and yes, I did see Luke wheeling that old bike of Dad's. He said he was going for a ride." Paul scanned her face. "Gotta say he looked a little sour. You guys okay?"

Melinda sank down beside his rock, the scrubby grass tickling her bare legs. "Yes, I mean, no. Luke's second-guessing keeping the house and all the work Peter's planning. Dad let a lot of stuff go over the years. Peter's repairs and renovations will eat up everything he left us."

"He always wants the best. He's not going to be content with new wiring, a few gallons of paint, and IKEA cabinets."

Melinda thought back to last night and the design sketches Peter laid out in the dining room's flickering candlelight. Although after a few glasses of wine she easily caught his enthusiasm, now his drawings seemed way over the top, even for a million-dollar location like Peregrine Point.

"What if we talk to him? Persuade him to cut back? Do we really each need en suite bathrooms? And what about that hot tub he wants for the back lawn?"

Paul climbed off his rock and held out a hand to help her to her feet. "One can only try."

"What do you want? Is this how you want to spend your share? Will you even come back here? Peter's in Boston so he can do weekends, and I can persuade Luke to come up every now and then. But you live so far away."

"Our older brother has always been a force of nature," he simply replied.

"A force of something," Melinda observed. "And you should know, after all those years down at the cove pretending to be in WrestleMania with him."

"Fortunately those days are long gone. He pretty much managed to whup me every time. Shall we head back to the house?"

While her brothers drove into town for lobsters and other provisions, Melinda spent a lazy day reading a musty paperback in a hammock underneath the side yard's red maple. Luke returned in the late afternoon, accompanied by a short, squat man wearing horn-rimmed glasses and an expression of mild trepidation.

"Is that who I think it is?" Melinda asked, peering through the screen door at two men approaching from the bluff. The siblings were in the kitchen prepping for dinner. At Peter's direction, Melinda shucked corn while Paul filled a huge pot with water.

Peter squinted out the window above the sink. "Indeed it is. Dr. Phil in the flesh. Again."

"Be nice," Melinda warned, sweeping a clump of corn silk into a paper bag.

Peter played the convivial host at first, insisting on cocktails for everyone. "Phil, you look like an Old Fashioned man." Without waiting for confirmation, he produced a bottle of Maker's Mark from an upper cupboard. He also mixed a pitcher of Mojitos.

"Shall we take these out to the veranda?" Melinda suggested.

"Excellent idea." Peter snapped his fingers. "Paul, be a good soul and grab us a tray of highball glasses."

As they headed to the wraparound porch at the front of the house Phil asked to use the bathroom, giving the siblings and Luke a few moments alone.

"Peter, do you always travel with a ready-made bar?" Luke lounged on a wicker couch and stretched out his legs. "Not that I'm complaining."

Peter poured Mojitos and passed them around. "The more important question is why did you bring Phil here?"

His sharp tone compelled Melinda to defend her husband. "Luke's not trying to make trouble. He's only being neighborly. Isn't that right, Luke?"

Luke took a sip of his drink and nodded. "Neighborly, yes. I met him on the main road while I was out for a bike ride. I also figured it wasn't a bad idea for us all to hear what he has to say about the house."

"Let's at least talk to him," Paul agreed.

Peter glared at his brother and then let out a heavy sigh. "Fine, fine. Let the doctor have his say. Don't forget, though, we already decided everything last night."

Phil reappeared, taking a seat at one of the random chairs scattered on the porch. It took him a while to warm up to his topic and Melinda feared Peter would boot him out before he even finished his drink.

"So," he finally said, removing his glasses and wiping them on his untucked polo shirt. "This isn't a purely social call."

Peter stood up to freshen his Mojito and put one hand to his chest in mock surprise. "Whatever do you mean?"

Phil replaced his glasses and cleared his throat. "I mean before he died your father and I struck a deal for me to buy this place. He knew my family always wanted to move out to Peregrine Point and frankly he doubted that any of you were truly equipped to take on the house and the upkeep it requires."

Melinda followed his gaze around the porch, noting the tattered wicker furniture, missing shingles, and gaps in the floorboards.

"And you are?" Peter challenged.

"Your dad and I had an oral agreement that I hope you'll consider honoring." He named a number that nearly made Melinda gasp. Luke sat up straight and Paul gave a low whistle.

Peter scoffed. "Although that's a nice fantasy and, I admit, a nice number, Dad never said anything to us. We're keeping the house."

"Uh," Luke said, "shouldn't we—"

Peter cut him off. "If that's all, Phil, thanks for stopping by."

"Don't you even want to consider it?" Phil asked.

"I'm afraid there's nothing to consider." Peter plucked the glass of bourbon from Phil's hand. "Nice chatting with you. We've got some lobsters to boil."

Dinner that evening was strained at best. Peter tried an imitation of Phil slinking away down the front steps but no one even cracked a smile. Melinda kept thinking about the price Phil quoted. She wondered if Luke and Paul were doing the same.

Luke wasn't beside her the next morning when she opened her eyes. Moving her head, she felt a telltale ache in her temples. The Mojitos had been stronger than she'd realized and those drinks, coupled with a generous pour of Chardonnay with her lobster, sent her to their room well before her husband.

Had Luke even come to bed at all? His side of the mattress looked untouched. Making it downstairs, Melinda found the kitchen surprisingly tidy. She vaguely remembered Paul and Luke volunteering to clean up. Peter, of course, failed to lift a finger. No one had started coffee yet so she must be the first one awake.

"Melinda, come quick. I need help!"

Through the back door screen Luke's face shone a bright red and his breath sounded ragged, like he'd just finished a long run. Jolted out of her hangover, Melinda dropped her father's jar of Maxwell House on the counter and joined him outside.

"What's happened? Where have you been?"

"Follow me." Luke took off toward the path leading from the bluff to the cove. Melinda scrambled to keep up with his long legs. Halfway down the path she stopped short. A few feet in front of her Peter lay face up on the dirt, blood pooling underneath his head and his eyes turned unblinking to the blue sky.

Luke knelt beside Peter. "I found him like this. I'm not sure he's breathing."

Heart pounding, Melinda shook her head, unable to comprehend the scene before her. "Jesus, Luke. We're not doctors. Did you call 911?"

"I don't have my phone on me and the service here sucks anyway." He slapped the back pocket of his khaki shorts. "Once I saw him all I thought about was finding you."

Luke stayed with Peter while Melinda raced back to the house to dial 911 from a landline in the foyer, which thankfully they hadn't disconnected yet. She paced the front hall while she waited for an ambulance. What happened to Peter? Had he tripped again on the path? And where was Luke all night? As sirens blared up the long winding driveway, Paul materialized at the top of the stairs in a ripped T-shirt and striped pajama bottoms.

"What's going on?"

Melinda looked up at her brother. In her turmoil she'd almost forgotten him. "It's Peter. Luke found him on the path to the cove. He's hurt. He might—he might be—" She couldn't get the words out.

To Melinda's relief, Paul took charge. He guided her to an overstuffed wing chair in the living room and went outside to meet the paramedics. Melinda slumped in the chair, suddenly exhausted. When Luke and Paul eventually reappeared, she knew from their faces that Peter was gone.

The following days passed in a whirl. The county sheriff called in the Maine State Police, who quickly concluded that Peter had stumbled on the path on his way up from his swim and hit his head on a large rock. According to the medical examiner, Peter died from massive craniocerebral trauma.

They buried Peter beside his father in a small cemetery not far from Peregrine Point. Although Peter's death drew some measure of media attention due to his business successes, the funeral service remained private. Melinda still thought she spied Phil lurking in a copse as Peter's coffin was lowered into the ground.

Paul left the next day to work on a movie being shot in southeast Asia. "It's on an island I can't even pronounce the name of. I'll be out of touch for at least a few months," he told Melinda while they waited outside the house for his Uber.

"What about this place?"

"You decide. Keep it, sell it to Phil, make it into a yoga retreat, whatever you want. With all that's happened here, I don't care anymore."

The vehemence in his voice surprised Melinda but he softened to give her a quick hug as the Uber pulled up. "If you need me to sign anything, send it through the studio. They'll be able to find me."

Melinda was grateful that Luke didn't bring up Peregrine Point on their long drive back to Brooklyn. After resuming the rhythm of their lives, however, the respite didn't last more than a week. She came home from work one day to find him waiting for her on the couch with a bottle of champagne and two of the long stem crystal glasses they'd gotten for a wedding present.

"What's this?" She set her workbag down on the small table inside their front door. "Do we have something to celebrate?"

"Maybe," Luke said with a sly smile. He patted the sofa cushion next to him. "Sit down."

Melinda complied while Luke poured her a generous glass. Veuve Clicquot, she noted with approval. A pleasing thought struck her. "Is it your book? Did you finish?"

Luke's face fell as he replaced the bottle on their coffee table. "Why does everything have to be about my book? Can't I be excited about something else?"

"Of course. I just thought—"

"Well, it's not about the book. It's Peregrine Point. I got a call today from Phil." He paused for emphasis. "He's willing to double the offer he made your father."

"Double?" Melinda's head spun. "That's insane. The property's not worth that much."

"Willing buyer and willing seller. That's the definition of fair market value."

"Now you sound like Peter. Why would Phil call you?" Then a much less pleasing thought dawned. "Unless you've been talking to him all along. Have you?"

Luke's cheeks flushed. "What if I have? Is that a crime? Peter was the one driving the plan to keep the house and now that he's gone, why not reconsider? We could do a lot with all that money."

"It's not all about money. Peter at least understood that."

"Did he understand that without a significant infusion of cash we're going to be stuck in this overpriced crappy apartment forever? And that if we ever have a kid it'll be sleeping in a closet?" Luke's voice rose to a shout. "No, not Peter. Not the Prince of Peregrine Point. He was looking forward to playing the benevolent lord of the manor and letting his poor little sister experience the good life on the few weekends she could find the time to schlep up to Maine."

Once he finished Melinda was silent for a few moments. "You really hated him, didn't you?"

"I'm not going to respond to that." Luke reached over to take her hand. "You must admit, though, his death presents us with a well-timed opportunity."

Well-timed opportunity. The words hung in the air and a cold feeling washed through her body. She snatched her hand back. "Speaking of timing, how did you happen to be on the path that morning? You never go down to the cove. You've always said you prefer the mountains."

"What are you trying to say? I got up early and I took a walk. That morning I decided to check out the water."

"And the night before? Where were you? You didn't come to bed."

"I told you. Don't you remember? Paul and I finished the dishes and I went up. You were snoring like a sick moose so I came back down to sleep on a daybed in the sunroom. You can ask Paul. He saw me."

Melinda furrowed her brow. Did Luke tell her that? She couldn't remember. Then again, she couldn't remember much from the immediate aftermath of Peter's death.

"I can't ask Paul anything. He's away for at least a few months."

"Do you really think I had something to do with your brother's death? Because that's what you seem to be hinting at. Let's look at the facts.

"Number one, the state police concluded it was an accident. He tripped and he fell. Unfortunately, his head hit something really hard. It's that simple. Number two, even somehow if it wasn't an accident, why me? What about Phil? He was no fan of your brother and he wants the house so badly he's willing to pay a huge premium. He was on that path with your brother the day before. And he's a doctor; he'd know plenty about head trauma."

Phil. Luke. Phil and Luke. Melinda dropped her head into her hands as the cold feeling intensified. They both hated Peter; they both wanted the house sold, albeit for different reasons. If it wasn't an accident, could they have planned it together? "Maybe it was both of you," she murmured, without even realizing she'd spoken the words aloud.

"Wow, you are incredible." Luke slammed his drink down on the coffee table. Shards of glass shot around the room. "You actually could see me ganging up with Phil to smash your brother's skull into a rock?"

Melinda flinched at his words. "I . . . I don't know."

Luke stood up and kicked over the coffee table. The champagne bottle spilled its liquid all over their rug. "Then I'm done. I'm really done."

Their divorce proved far easier than Melinda anticipated. They'd only been married a few years and had no children, not even a dog. Luke had signed a prenup in anticipation of her inheritance, ensuring it wouldn't be treated as marital property. After letting Luke take anything he wanted from the apartment, Melinda quit her job and broke their lease to move to Peregrine Point full time. Money from her father, plus the fact that some paint and modest electrical work was all she needed, would allow her to stay there indefinitely, assuming Paul really meant she could do as she pleased with the house. She managed to avoid running into Phil on her trips to town and was relieved to see his family home closed up for the season before the end of September.

She didn't hear from her surviving brother until the first snowfall. An SUV pulled up the driveway shortly after the snowplow left in the early afternoon. Paul emerged, more tanned than usual, wearing a plaid flannel shirt over a turtleneck and a gray wool beanie.

"Get inside," Melinda scolded as she opened the front door. "Where's your coat? You're going to freeze to death. How did you know I was here?"

"Since no paper work came through, I figured you ended up deciding to keep the place." Paul followed her into the living room where she'd lit a fire. "Plus, you've always said that as much as you loved summers here, you also loved it in winter."

Tinkering with the logs stacked on the andirons, Paul apologized for being away so long. The movie constantly teetered on disaster, he explained; unexpected monsoons and an outbreak of malaria plagued the set. "Picture Werner Herzog's Fitzcarraldo set in Indonesia instead of South America." He chuckled. "Now that I can laugh about it, Luke will appreciate this story. Didn't he once say Herzog was his favorite director?"

"I don't really remember," Miranda replied stiffly.

"Where is my brother-in-law, by the way?"

From the sofa, Melinda looked down at the faded Persian carpet. "We split up. We had a huge argument and he walked out. Probably for the best anyway."

"That's tough." Paul carefully replaced the fireplace poker in the tool stand. "What did you guys fight about?"

"This place, of course. Luke kept in touch with Phil after Peter died and Phil upped his offer to a crazy amount of money. Luke assumed I would take it. I didn't jump so he started screaming at me. Then I got this idea." She paused and took a deep breath. "I got an idea that he had something to do with Peter's death. Either alone or with Phil. I practically accused him of murder." She raised her eyes to Paul. "Could that be true?"

Paul's face wore a stricken expression. "No, you can't possibly believe that."

"I don't mean he deliberately set out to kill Peter. But what if Luke met him on the path that morning? Maybe he thought he could talk Peter into thinking more about Phil's offer. That wouldn't have gone over well with Peter. Maybe Luke got angry and pushed him down."

"It couldn't have happened like that."

185

"How would you know? You weren't there."

Paul didn't answer. He picked up the poker again to reposition the logs.

Her stomach clenched. "Oh my god, Paul. Were you there that morning?"

"You asked me to talk to him. About the renovations." Paul stared at the fire. "You were right that I'd be sinking a lot of money into something I'd barely use. He got angry, not me. At first he laughed and called me a weakling. Then he started towards me on the path with this look in his eyes, like he wanted to wrestle like we used to when we were kids. He thought he was still the big brother who could boss me around and take me down."

Melinda could barely breathe. "What happened?"

"He thought wrong," Paul said. "I'm not that little kid he could bully anymore. He fell over hard and his head hit a rock."

"Why didn't you go for help? He was our brother," she whispered. "He was our brother and you—you killed him."

Paul slowly turned toward her, still clutching the fireplace poker as he approached. "I'm sorry, Mel. Believe me, I never meant for it to end up like this. I only wanted to make everything right. Make us all a happy family."❖

Lessons from Nature

Mo Walsh

I spied my Sunday afternoon guest from the top of the steps leading up to the porch. I'd insisted on a proper front porch when I sold the farmhouse in New Madrid and moved to this neighborhood of brick homes just outside St. Louis. I'd left behind the breeze wafting over the bottomland from the Mississippi, but this porch was spacious enough for a guest or two and provided plenty of shade and protection from the heat.

"Hey, Betsy!" I called. "Come on up and join me in some iced tea." I held up a tall glass with a slice of lemon poised on the lip, the condensation easing just enough to create amber drip patterns on the frosted sides. "There's homemade shortbread, too."

"Well, don't that sound delicious!" Betsy smiled through the perspiration carving streaks in her Sunday church makeup. Since the morning service, she'd changed into an oversize cotton blouse and pedal pushers in muted shades of pink. She wore pink bobby socks with her beige tennis shoes and a worn straw sun hat over her bowl-cut gray hair. "We had plenty of heat in Oklahoma, but this is like a steam bath."

"Hot enough to roast a turtle basking on a log, as my granddad used to say. You'll get used to it, unless you plan to live most of the summer inside with the AC running. I know some people do." I fingered the top button of my sleeveless silk shift and curled my coral-painted toes in my new slim-strapped sandals. Along with the silt-rich farmland, I'd given up a lifetime of scrimping and saving in exchange for a comfortable independence. I gestured to the pair of rocking chairs with their plump new cushions. "Have a seat, please. I'll put your tea right here on the TV tray—though why I call it that when I've never eaten off one by the TV, I don't know."

We rocked and sipped tea in companionable silence, though we'd met only two months earlier when Betsy joined the Jubilee Gospel Church. I don't make new friends easily, but despite the gaps in our ages and circumstances, Betsy and I seemed to have much in common. Both of us were transplants from rural communities in transition, fields turned into housing tracts, town centers into quaint tourist attractions. We were both widowed without close family nearby, and our other relatives were too busy to visit often or talk for more than three minutes on the phone.

Betsy clinked the teaspoon against the sides of her glass and stared into her tea as if she expected to discover something disagreeable at the bottom. "I'm dreading next Saturday, you know," she said with a barely detectable quiver. "My Debbie would have been thirty-five years old. I'm sure she would have been married with the most beautiful children."

That was our strongest bond, of course. We were two mothers who'd lost daughters—how silly that sounds, as if we'd misplaced them like car keys or eyeglasses. Our daughters had *died*, they were *dead*, and we had to bury our dreams for them, too.

"I know you don't see your grandsons much, and that's a shame." Betsy darted a quick look in my direction. "And, of course, I have my nephew Christopher and he's sure to have a family someday, but, well, I just wish Debbie had experienced the love a mother feels for her own children." She gulped the rest of her tea.

I nodded and continued rocking. We'd had this conversation before in various forms, and I *did* take comfort in my Ruth's boys and knowing they'd had time to form memories of her they'd never lose. I was even happy my son-in-law had remarried a woman who loved them as her own and gave them a younger sister to torment and spoil by turns. But what could I say to what seemed to be a comparison of grief? "Some days are harder than others, but you get through them."

Betsy knuckled the corners of eyes grown misty. "That's why I'm flying to Polynesia on Tuesday. Usually, I go with a church mission team, but I need to be with my closest family this week, and I'll have such a wonderful surprise for Christopher!"

I pushed up from my chair and gathered the empty glasses. "I'll get us more tea."

When I returned with the refills, Betsy had recovered her composure. A scattering of crumbs remained in place of most of the shortbread, and Betsy hummed as she sorted through a handful of 4" x 6" photographs. "Here, Judith, I've got those pictures from Christopher I promised to show you. They've broken ground on the new Lazarus Mission School, and by the time I get there Wednesday, they should have the foundation poured!"

She passed me the first photo, showing a gangly young man with a sweet smile and with the freckled tan that so often goes with a naturally light complexion. With each arm he embraced a thin brown child dressed, as he was, in faded shorts and a T-shirt. Christopher wore a bucket hat and sandals, and a plain wood cross hung on a cord around his neck. The barefoot children flashed shy smiles at the camera.

"That's Moses Kiana and his sister, Susannah," Betsy said, pointing. "Christopher says they are the brightest little things, and so anxious to go to a proper school."

The next picture showed a rectangular hole dug in bare, sunbaked ground, and beside it piles of palm branches and a row of undressed tree trunks.

"The roof and walls will only be temporary for now, and they won't be safe when the typhoon season comes. That's what they call a hurricane."

I'd seen "permanent" buildings, immense structures of masonry, turned to rubble by tornadoes and engulfed by churning flood waters. "How soon will Christopher be able to get a real sturdy school built?" I asked.

Betsy's frown at the photo cleared. "With all the church members are doing to help, I know the Mission will soon have the bricks and lumber for a good, solid, *safe* school building." She waved a third photo in front of my face. "Look! This one's from last year when

I visited the Mission with some of my church family from Turley True Fellowship."

There was Betsy in another blouse and pedal-pushers outfit and what could be the same sun hat and tennis shoes. She was flanked by two older couples, closer to my age of seventy-seven than Betsy's relatively young sixty-two. Christopher knelt in front of them, his arms embracing three other smiling, thin brown children.

"Well, I don't want to overwhelm you," said Betsy, slipping the remaining photos into an envelope. "I just wanted you to see how much good you're doing with your donation to the Lazarus Mission. And I'll have more pictures next month when I get back—maybe even video!"

"I'm honored to be a part of it." I reached for the envelope. "Please, let me see the other pictures, while you finish your tea."

"Well, if you'd like to—only they're mostly shots of the island, the beaches and palm trees and things. It's tragic that poverty can exist in such beautiful surroundings." Betsy nibbled another piece of shortbread. "Their need is so great."

"It's hard to imagine such a place, except for the heat. We seem to have that in common." I sipped my tea. "Perhaps I could go with you and a Jubilee mission team next time?"

"Well, don't that sound wonderful! Then you could really see what you're doing with your generosity!" Betsy beamed. "As it says in Luke, 'Give, and it shall be given unto you.' And you know what?" She waved her hand over the envelope of photos. "I do believe the good Lord has given me grandchildren after all." She gulped her tea. "Now I'm just going inside to use the little girls' room."

"Of course." I continued sorting through the photos, reflecting that one white sand beach or palm tree soon began to look like any other. I returned to the photo of Betsy and her church family at the Lazarus Mission. They all had that "salt of the earth" look associated with charitable works and self-sacrifice. And those little children, smiling despite the difficulties in their young lives! How many times had I seen such faces and wished I could do something to help?

I carried the empty tea glasses back to the kitchen and refilled them from the cold pitcher in the refrigerator.

"Oh, thank you!" said Betsy, finding on her return another cool glass of tea and more shortbread. "In this heat, I seem to pour liquids into me just to sweat them out again."

"Ladies don't sweat, we glow," I said.

"I believe this muggy heat is getting to me. I think I'll mosey on home." She emptied her tea glass. "I hate to ask, Judith, but you did say you'd have the bank check today for the Lazarus Mission?"

"Oh, yes, I have it." I twisted my hands together in my lap. "Actually, Betsy, after seeing those photos and hearing how much still needs to be done, I was thinking about that $15,000 and—there's another $10,000 I can spare. I was going to take the family to Disney or maybe on a cruise, but the children are still young and I'm thinking what the Mission could do. Christopher could buy desks and books, a generator for electricity. I want Lazarus to have it all."

"Oh!" Betsy inhaled shortbread crumbs and fell into a coughing spasm. "You mean—the whole $25,000?"

"I can afford it now that the big home developer bought my land, as much as I hate to see more houses encroaching on the wetlands—but that's neither here nor there." I waved the thought away. "The problem, you see, is that I can't get the money from my savings back home into my checking account here before Tuesday. By then you'll already be on your way." My enthusiasm faded to frustration. "And from what you tell me, Christopher can't deposit a personal check in the Mission's bank."

"No, only bank checks. It all has to do with the currency exchange. I don't quite understand it myself." Betsy tapped her fingers against her check. "There has to be a way…"

"I could give you the $15,000 check now and get another to you later. We could even take it to Lazarus Mission on our trip there together!"

"Well, don't that sound lovely! But you know," said Betsy with a teary smile, "there's so much good the Mission could be doing with that money *now*. So much so, I believe I must put off my trip until you get that second check. I'm sure I can change my flight!"

I waited a full hour before calling the number given to me by the agent from Interpol. He contacted me two days after I gave Betsy my pledge for $15,000. "You were correct, Agent Renaud. She said she'll wait for the extra money. But that doesn't prove she's a phony. That money could do a lot of good for Lazarus Mission."

"Mrs. Gant, there is no Lazarus Mission." There was a gentle weariness in the agent's voice. "The photos are all faked—expertly, I admit—with good-hearted people who think they are making a brochure or a slide presentation for a legitimate charity. Your 'friend' Betsy has collected more than two million dollars in three countries for charities that exist only in her mind, the mind of a criminal. You must help us stop her."

As Granddad would say, it was time to dance on the griddle or jump over the fire. "What do you want me to do?" I asked.

"Thank you, Mrs. Gant!" The warmth in the agent's voice flowed through the phone line. "I will come to your home tonight to collect and certify the first bank check as evidence. I will meet you outside the bank on Tuesday to collect the second check and certify that one, too. You will inform me when this woman Betsy is meeting you again, and I will give you back the checks to witness the exchange. When she attempts to deposit or cash the checks, we will follow the trail of transactions until we can make the arrest."

I gnawed my lip. "You are sure you'll be able to do all that, Mr. Renaud? I won't lose my money?"

"Not one dollar," the agent assured me. "Quite the contrary: Interpol will pay you two percent daily interest, that is five dollars each day, for the loan of your money until it is safely back in your account."

"Very well," I said. "If you hadn't contacted me, I would have fallen for her scheme. I suppose it's my duty to keep some other pigeon from losing her nest egg. Please come over before nine o'clock. I believe I'll retire early."

Agent Renaud was an immaculate middle-aged Frenchman in a well-fitting but modest suit, as befitted a civil servant. His accent was slight, his long face shaved smooth, and his neatly trimmed brown hair was sprinkled with gray. This much I could see in the faint light from the street lamp when I greeted him on my porch. He made a slight bow as he briefly shook my hand in a way that reminded me of an old-fashioned gentleman greeting a lady.

"If you don't mind sitting in the dark, sir, we can talk here on the porch where it's cooler," I said. "I've lived most of my life without air conditioning, so now it gives me a chill."

"I will need light, Mrs. Gant, if I am to certify the bank check as evidence," the agent reminded me. "Inside, perhaps, so we do not invite the insects to join us?"

"We've time for that, and the bugs won't bother us with the lights out and the citronella burning." I gestured to the candles at either end of the railing. "There's a pitcher of iced tea here, and I've poured an extra glass if you'd like some. Help yourself."

"You do have the check, ma'am?"

"Of course, but please indulge me, Mr. Renaud. I'm that distressed over this business, and there's no one else I can talk to about it without sounding like a credible old fool." I waited till the agent tasted his tea and settled back in the other chair.

"Hush for a bit and listen. Hear the cicadas singing? I don't care if they're actually doing deep breathing exercises or belly dancing—to me it's pure music, free for everyone. We can learn a lot from nature."

Renaud stirred in his chair. "Indeed, ma'am. This is most pleasant, but the check—"

"Have you ever seen a snapping turtle?" I forged on without waiting for Renaud to respond. "Down in the Missouri Bootheel—that southeast corner that pokes down into Arkansas?—there's snappers everywhere from the mighty Mississippi to the slow-moving creeks and weed-choked ponds. Snapping turtles have a nasty temperament when they don't get their way, and they're opportunists. Your common kind lurks in the underwater vegetation, feeding on plants and bugs and just waiting for a big, tasty fish to come along. Then he shoots his neck out and snap!"

"How interesting, but the time, Mrs. Gant." A blue disc flashed on Renaud's wrist. I had noticed his watch was in a higher price range than his suit. "I must be going—"

"That's another problem with people who live in cities. You're always in a hurry. Well, you can't rush me tonight, Mr. Renaud. Have some more tea." I rocked in silence till I heard the trickle of liquid and the plunk of ice cubes into a glass.

"I've never had much extra money, so I don't know a great deal about investments and dividends and what they call wealth management. I understand tithing and charity and those who have much giving to those who have little, and that's always worked for my family and me."

"Your sentiments do you credit, ma'am."

"They also set me up for nasty opportunists who try to snap up some of my money or pull an outright swindle. This affair is not just about cheating me and the good-hearted people from our church! It's stealing from children who have almost nothing, and that I don't tolerate." I stopped rocking and took a deep, clean breath.

"You got to be careful with a snapping turtle, Mr. Renaud. Catch him, and he'll claw and snap till one of you can't fight anymore. But he makes a soup considered a delicacy in many parts of the world. Did you know there's a black-market trade in our snapping turtles going to China?"

"I did not know that," said Renaud, apparently resigned to hearing out my monologue. He loosened his tie and shirt collar. "That is handled by a different branch of Interpol."

"Then you must have more branches than the transcontinental railroad," I said. "I couldn't find the Bureau of Fraudulent Transactions listed anywhere. Not that I was surprised. Your little pitch sounded an awful lot like some of the scams I read about online when I was figuring out Betsy's angle."

"No . . . Mizzuz G-G-Gant . . . you mistake . . ." Leather scrabbled against wood as Renaud tried to rise from his chair but collapsed backward in the seat. I ignored his boneless sprawl and his mumbled noises of distress. Maybe the tea was too strong.

"I would have liked to make a friend here, but there were just too many coincidences between my life and Betsy's. How many young women die from rare brain tumors? Way too many, but not enough for two mothers from different states to connect at the same church line-dancing class. That was a real cruel thing to do to a mother's heart." I sighed for what could have been. "I might have believed it—coincidences do happen—if Betsy hadn't tried to hook me into sending money to some unknown charity. They've got a name for that, you know—Affinity Fraud, going after the folks in your church or your work place or your rich country club. Or joining up just to defraud folks of their money."

"N-N-Noo . . . helpppp . . ." Well, he got that right. I sipped more tea.

"Now, this extra little scam of yours? What is that, some variation on the Badge Con? Just in case I don't feel the affinity with Betsy, you hope I'll turn over $25,000 in 'certified evidence' bank checks to a man with a badge—which I couldn't tell from the real thing anyway?

"See, Mr. Renaud, I don't know much about money management the way Wall Street does it, but I know to be cautious and look closely and watch out for danger camouflaged as something harmless or appealing. Living with nature teaches you that."

I leaned close and raised his tea glass to Renaud's lips. "You're sweating buckets now, Mr. Renaud. Drink up." I trickled the rest of the liquid into his slack mouth. "Relax now. We're almost done. Let's just listen for a minute."

The thirteen-year and seventeen-year cicadas must have overlapped cycles this summer to produce such a loud and varied chorus, I thought, or perhaps I'd allowed the sounds of city life to block them out. Now they took me back to the farm ponds and stream beds, hunting snappers with Granddad to make into tangy soup with tomatoes and fresh vegetables, butter and sherry, and the secret ingredients that never blended the same way twice.

I could picture his favorite spot to drop a line or a jug—the old fallen-tree bridge, where the influx from the stream carried the bait scent to all the inlets and stands of trees. In the dry season, Granddad would poke into the mud with a rake to find the alligator snappers, just for show. I'd seen him pry a sixty-pounder from the muck and toss her to higher ground. I'd try to get a "snap" shot with his old Kodak Brownie before she crawled back in.

"You listening, Renaud?" I said, my voice dreamy with memory. "A couple more things you should know about snappers. Granddad would never let me help with the butchering, saying the turtle would keep on crawling around after his head was chopped off. And the snapper was so mean, the head would still bite. Best not to take any chances, he said.

"Granddad must have cooked up a couple hundred common snappers, but the alligator snapping turtle appealed to his soft spot." I spread my hands beyond the width of my shoulders. "She's much bigger and heavier for one thing. Clever and efficient, too. She makes herself comfortable down in the mud where she blends right in. Then she opens her mouth and waits for the fish to swim right in.

"You might be thinking even a fish is smarter than that. See, inside on the bottom of that alligator snapper's mouth is a piece of red tissue that wriggles in the water like the world's most delicious worm. The greedy fish goes after the worm and snap! Hardly any effort at all.

"You and Betsy went after the worm, Mr. Renaud. And this old lady caught you, SNAP! Betsy's inside sleeping off her iced tea, and I'll stick a cushion under your head out here. You'll both feel better when you wake up in the county jail."

I stood and gathered the pitcher and tea glasses. I blew out the citronella candles. "In the old days, Mr. Renaud, I would have rounded up some men, given them rope and a sack of rocks, and told them to dump you two in the nearest pond.

"Those snappers love carrion." ❖

Obscura Eclipse

Connie Johnson Hambley

The call came in at midnight.

"We have your son. Do not contact the authorities. Do not make any public statements. You will receive instructions to pay his ransom within the hour. His life is in your hands." The call disconnected.

Annie Granger fumbled the phone away from her ear and groped the bed stand for her glasses. "Silva. Silva! Wake up! Someone has Desi." Her lamp crashed to the floor. "Wake up, dammit! Desi's in trouble!"

Silva didn't move. "Desi's always in trouble."

And her Silva was always there to get them out of any jam. Expecting to be an undesirable widow saddled with a toddler, she was amazed when Silva showed interest in more than the string of coding that once spewed from her fingers. Then, as now, he was the head of Red Dart Industries, owner of the massive data farms responsible for the ginormous processing required for Bitcoin transactions and for the zillion terabytes of storage every company from Google to Facebook to Microsoft needed to mine the massive trove of meta data that provides the "customized" and "free" services to their billion-plus users. Silva was famous for being the first to observe that if a service or product was free, then the user was the product. He became a gazillionaire by selling troves of meta data to the highest bidder knowing bulk data sales provided an exception to the pesky privacy rights of individuals.

She scrambled out of bed, tearing the covers to the floor. "Voxnay! Bedroom lights on!"

Silva's eyes squinted against the sudden light. "Annie? What's going on?"

"That call! Desi's been kidnapped!"

She watched Silva's face as he sifted through the possibilities. He had more than enough haters and few would be surprised that hatred spilled over onto his wife and her son. Environmentalists hated him because the data farms sucked up more energy than the adjacent wind and solar farms created. Privacy advocates hated him because the information stored told the inner workings of private thoughts that, once mined, could be used for coercive targeting. Law enforcement felt shafted because Silva's legal team's demand for excruciatingly precise and narrow warrants thwarted their efforts to access any information that focused on an individual and not the nameless meta. Red Dart stored years of likes, clicks, and searches. Governments from Albania to Zimbabwe shifted uncomfortably in their seats at what secrets Silva's data farms held.

Silva had plenty of enemies.

"Okay. Let's take this one bit at a time. Who was on the phone? Man? Woman?" Silva scrubbed his palms against his face, stubble making a scratching sound.

"I don't know. The call woke me up."

"Accent?"

"I said I don't know! I can't think!"

Silva propped himself up on his elbow. "Take a deep breath. Tell me what you remember about the voice, and then we'll get to what they said."

"It was weird." Annie thrust her arms into her robe and cinched the belt tight.

"AI generated? Human? Altered?"

"I don't know! I couldn't tell. They said they're going to contact us again with details about how to pay." She gripped her hair at her temples. This was pure Silva. Methodical. Focused. Practical to the point of maddening.

"Calm yourself, Annie. Picture him in that walled campus with its ivy-covered buildings and stone chapel you love so much."

She chose the picture-perfect campus as a safe place to mature, and Lord knew Desi needed plenty of space to do just that. "My Desi! I should be there! How long will our jet take to get ready?"

"Flying from California to New England takes hours we don't have, and we've got to work together."

She wrapped herself in his words. As much as she loved having her son around, she also loved having all Silva's attention. She wondered if Silva's toss-'em-in-the-deep-end style of parenting would soften if he had had his own children. Probably not. His company was his baby and he ruled it with the same sink-or-swim maxim.

Silva swung his legs over the edge of the bed and sat hunched, shaking his head free of sleep. "We'll figure this thing out." He looked at her phone. "The call log shows it came from Desi. It's three in the morning there." He tapped the phone icon and put the call on speaker.

Desi's nasally voice filled the room. "Hey! Yo! Desi here. Leave a message and I might call you back."

"Desi's not answering his phone!" Her robe rose and fell with her panicked breath. She crumpled into her reading chair. The damask fabric and extra thick cushions gave her none of their usual comfort. "Is this really happening?" she said, words barely a whisper.

Silva glowered. "All we know for sure is that you got what could be a crank call from Desi's phone or his number could have been spoofed."

"Trace it! Find whoever or whatever made that call!"

"You know as well as I do that spoofs happen all the time and are hard to trace." He tried Desi's number again. Unsuccessful, he grabbed the covers off the floor. "Hey. It's finals week. If history proves right again, he's about to flunk out, realizing that going to class matters more than walking in the woods." He stared at her with tired eyes. "What's his major now, anyway? Theater? Forestry? The Lyrics of Taylor Swift?"

Annie stifled a sob. "I . . . It's just that call. Spoof or not. I'm afraid. They said not to call the authorities!"

"They didn't say anything about our security people." He grabbed his cell.

"Brace here." Bracebridge Snow, head of Red Dart's security, sounded alert and ready despite the hour. In less time than it took for Silva to update him, he responded, "I sent you Desi's last known. See it?"

"Yeah," Silva said. "He's on campus?"

"Hold on." Brace's voice muffled. Annie had seen Brace in action many times. She envisioned him now with computers and tablets set up around him juggling multiple phones, getting up-to-the-second information. "At least his phone is. I'll send some of our men to check on him."

"Thanks, Brace. Call when you know more."

"Will do." The call disconnected.

"So, that's it? Should we do more? At least you should postpone the shareholder meeting!" Her maternal urge pushed her into action.

He patted the bed beside him. "You know our world doesn't work like that, Bananny. Smelling weakness only makes them stronger."

She nibbled on her cuticle. "Does Stone Cold have enough sway with the board to force a takeover?"

"It's still my company even if the shareholders want to feed on me like a school of piranhas. The employees aren't exactly on my side either. It's anyone's guess." He sat up and opened his arms to her. "You must be terrified."

Her heart softened despite her fear. Being enveloped in his big bear hug was exactly what she desperately needed. She crawled beside him and nestled her face into his chest, inhaling the ambrosia of his skin. With one kiss, the sweet lovable bear she married was back. She pulled the covers over them, relaxing in his warmth. "Oh, Silva. You're right. It's just one call and Brace is working on it. Still, I can't stand the thought of something happening to my little boy!"

Silva chuckled. "At six foot six, he's hardly a 'little boy.' C'mon. Let's get some sleep." He snuggled her closer to his chest. "Voxnay! Bedroom lights off!"

As soon as the room plunged into darkness, both of their cell phones chimed. "What now?" he grumbled, reaching for his phone. Annie found hers and gasped.

The emails were identical but sent from different addresses. The video of Desi bound, gagged, and shoved into a car's trunk was fuzzy in the low light, but clear enough to show the terror in Desi's eyes and carry his muffled protests. A voice floated over the images. "Silva and Annie. Your phones and computers are being monitored. If you call the authorities, Desi will die. We require five million US dollars transferred according to the attached instructions. You have until the markets close." The call disconnected.

"Sweet Lord." Silva threw off the covers. "Voxnay! House lights on! Wake Avi." The house blazed to life. He pulled on sweats and looked at Annie. "Don't panic. We still don't know what we're dealing with."

A soft buzz sounded. Annie pressed the button on the night stand. "Mr. and Mrs. Granger? Is everything all right?" Avi, their house manager, sounded alarmed despite the sleep that filled his voice.

"No, Avi. Things are not all right. Make some coffee. We'll update you." Annie's voice shook.

The yellow bowl of lemons set in the center of the Calacatta marble island provided the only pop of color in the cavernous white kitchen. It had been meant to look sleek and modern when Silva helped her update their Tuscan-themed kitchen, but now it looked sterile, almost surgical, in the glare of the lights. Even the black coffee that dripped from the Breville Barista Express seemed swallowed by the paleness of it all.

Avi swept around the kitchen pulling out mugs and the silver cream and sugar set. His eggplant-colored silk robe highlighted his graceful former-dancer movements. The elegance he had since he and Annie were in the same dance troupe hadn't diminished. Avi had been trying to make it big and Annie was dancing off the stress of her job at the start-up eventually purchased by Red Dart. Silva pulled up a stool, opened his laptop, and played the video for Avi, pausing each frame to examine every detail.

"Oh! Annie! Our boy! Our sweet Desi!" He embraced her and turned to Silva. "Track him! Use that Family Finder app you're so proud of and tell the police!" He grabbed Silva's phone and held up the screen showing a map of the campus and local police phone numbers.

"No police." Silva took back his phone and placed it on the counter. "Brace, any update?"

"Hold on," Brace said. "Got it," he said to another call. To Silva he responded, "I sent our guy to Desi's dorm. Room was messy but not torn apart. Phone was on the closet floor. Seemed like he dropped it. Roommate hasn't seen Desi. He figured Desi went spring skiing."

Silva tapped a few keys. "Nope. His ski pass wasn't activated, and he hasn't used his debit card since Saturday morning to buy his usual latte and croissant."

"What about his Matrix? Anything there?" Brace asked, referring to the program Red Dart had created for governments looking to identify contacts and networks of terrorists.

Matrix had been in development when Annie first met Silva. She was fascinated how Red Dart's tech nerds scoured public information to look at one individual, then outward at their public messages, websites, and social media posts. Internally, they referred to it as Matrix Lite.

It had piqued Annie's interest. The marketing folks loved Matrix Lite because it whets the appetite of Red Dart's customers for more details. She learned the nerds had gone deeper and developed Matrix Dark, the beta version no one admits to. Dark mines Red Dart's hoarded meta data by first focusing on an individual's public footprint, then gathering info via AI that instantly hacks passwords, app encryptions, and stored histories. Silva learned secret fetishes, obsessions, and neurotic tendencies that, once discovered, became very, very valuable.

Annie watched Silva twist in his seat as he spoke. "I don't want to use Dark."

"Are you kidding me? Now is the exact moment to use it." Brace's irritation crackled through the phone.

"For exactly the wrong reasons."

"Wrong? What's wrong with trying to find kidnappers? And your kid!"

"It's just, I don't . . ." He sighed. "Fine. I'll activate Dark and send you the reports."

"Good. I'm sourcing a match on the car's trunk configuration to see if we can get a make and model. Then I'll run that against the school's security footage. I'll expand outward from there." He paused. "I'm real sorry this is happening, Mr. Gardner. We'll pull out all the stops to find Desi. I'll check in when we know more." The line disconnected.

Annie took the offered cup of coffee from Avi, sloshing some over his hands. "Oh! So sorry!"

He wrapped his hands around hers to steady them. "Easy, Bananny. He'll be okay." He turned to Silva. "How much are they asking for?"

"Five mil." He didn't look up.

"Only five million? Oh, honey. Just pay the fuckers and be done with it. Desi will be home by daybreak." Avi swept through the kitchen, opening and closing cabinets as he arranged cheese, French bread, and red grapes on plates and set them in front of the distraught parents. "Seriously. Can't you just click a few icons and do that? Forbes said you make more than that in a day."

"If it's that easy, whoever it is will come after me again."

Avi huffed. "Not if they know who they're dealing with! They might get your money, but they'll never get peace again in their life. You'll lock onto who they are, and they'll wonder why they just got audited by the IRS or why their face just went viral on a racist meme or why their electric car has a mind of its own or why their medical records no longer list fatal allergies. Let me guess, they said pay in untraceable Bitcoin." He chuckled to himself. "Amateurs."

"Avi has a point." Annie looked over Silva's shoulders at the glowing screens. "Five mil seems like a sucker's sum to ask from us."

"What I'm not seeing bothers me." Silva rolled his shoulders. "Whoever did this is clever. No tells. No fingerprints."

The next hours passed on a torrent of nerves and caffeine. Annie clutched her phone, knuckles blanching white from the effort. No notices chimed or vibrated. Even her news feeds seemed less active than usual, as if giving her the space to process all that was happening around her.

She watched as Silva jabbed at screens and screamed to whichever poor sap was on the other end of the phone.

"Don't ask me again! I'm not telling you how I know you met with Stone Cold's CEO or that you're screwing around on your wife. No. This isn't about the meeting today. Your son was in touch with Desi last week and I want to know what they talked about. . . . I could give a fat fart about your vote. . . . Wake your kid up or I will."

Silva raging at allies hours before a critical vote was not good for him. He was burning bridges he desperately needed if he was going to keep his company and stay on as CEO.

Another call came in from Brace. Silva put it on speaker. "Well?"

"School cameras show him leaving his room with a backpack, then joining a group of students. He went to the library. Then nothing. We ID'd the students and followed their phones. Two went skiing and we found them at their lodge. The others are still on campus. All of them deny knowing anything about Desi's whereabouts."

Silva read off the names of the students he had gleaned from Dark.

"Yeah. That's them. Seems like a tight group. They're all pretty shocked that Desi's missing, so no leads there."

"How about new or unusual traffic on campus?"

"We're following three cars that left the campus around the time we think Desi went missing. One stopped at a hotel. Nothing unusual. Hotel registration and cameras verify parents visiting their kid for the weekend. Another stopped at a residence. All internet traffic is normal and doesn't point to contacting you or Mrs. Granger. We accessed their Ring and security cameras and nothing suspicious shows up. We're still working on the third car. That one's the most interesting as it traveled deep into New Hampshire where there's limited cell and GPS service. We haven't ruled out AI generated calls made remotely."

"Deep Fake videos are easy enough, too."

"True, but the video of Desi meant they had to have decent connection to upload. We're still digging. The information from Matrix Dark is gold. We'd never be this far into the investigation without it."

"Yeah, well, keep it to yourself. I don't feel like quadrupling my problems by getting busted for the kind of hacks we're doing."

"Gotcha. I'm deleting history as I go."

"Good. Thanks, Brace." He clicked off the phone and slumped in his seat.

Annie rubbed his back. "Deleting history? Is that enough to keep Matrix Dark from discovering the origin of calls and actions?"

"Yeah. Matrix Dark is real time. It must be activated before it starts gathering info. I'm exhausted. Today is going to be a disaster if it wasn't already."

"We'll work it out. We always do." She brushed his forehead with her lips.

He kissed her palm. "Red Dart's been my oasis and you've always been my rock."

If she was being honest with herself, she'd admit to being jealous of the company. An oasis was in the middle of nowhere, so where did that place her?

Avi swept away dishes of barely touched food and placed down ever more tempting dishes of crepes, eggs, and pastries he'd made in an anxious drive to keep moving.

Silva glanced at his phone. "Brace just updated me on the car model. Configuration and carpet type most align with a Ford Fiesta." He grumbled. "That doesn't make any sense."

"Why not?" Avi asked, pausing midstroke in wiping the counters.

"Because the picture of Desi doesn't show him crammed into it. He'd be folded over like a piece of origami to fit into a Fiesta."

"Do you think the image was AI generated?"

"It's possible, but this one doesn't seem to be."

"How can you tell?"

"AI uses Generative Adversarial Networks to create an image. Some generators use distinctive coding to create an image. Our filters look down into the pixels, almost like a fingerprint, for clues as well as looking for the typical tells like extra fingers, surfaces that are unnaturally smooth, backgrounds or items that blend together like eyeglasses that appear absorbed into skin. Desi's face and his expression are real, but the background is too generic to get any kind of ironclad answer."

A tear rolled down Annie's cheek. "So Desi was truly terrified."

"Yeah. I'm sorry to have to say that."

Speakers in the house sprang to life. "Silva. This is a reminder. Your board meeting will start in sixty minutes at nine a.m. sharp. Your car arrives in five minutes."

"Shit." He looked at the clock. "I don't have time for a shower."

"You're still going?" Judgment mixed with anger creased her words.

"I have to."

"But what about the ransom? It's going to take time to get that cash together."

"The instructions were clear. I'll schedule the transfer now to happen before close. Brace will continue to work on finding Desi. I'll cancel it if we learn something."

Annie sank into his arms. She uttered a soft "Thank you." Moments later, she watched Red Dart's car service's sleek Mercedes-Maybach EQS680 SUV hum down the driveway.

Her phone chimed as Brace called in. "Any news?" she asked.

"No. We've tracked out the emails, phone calls, and images looking for origination points, language similarities, communication intersections, or anything that would point us in the direction of who would or could do this."

"Aren't there any other leads?"

"We've looked at patterns of chatter that may have involved Silva, Desi, or Avi."

"The family? Are you kidding?"

"We'd be negligent if we didn't look at every close connection. Even you."

"So that's it then?" Annie took a deep breath. "We just pay the ransom and cross our fingers they'll release Desi?"

"Pretty much."

"How can you sound so fatalistic?"

"I'm realistic, not fatalistic. We have more digital investigation horsepower than the FBI, Homeland Security, and CIA combined. We looked at any connection to Desi, and the list of Silva's enemies who could benefit from today's meeting is very long. The timing can't be a coincidence."

"What do you mean?"

"There was more activity than average because of the eclipse."

"Eclipse? What are you talking about?"

"Northern New England is in the path of totality and that's generated a lot of digital traffic. It's complicated our search by giving us more to look at, but the basics are the same. Plus, the ransom ask is tiny compared to what Silva has access to, so that made us think it was someone closer to Desi. Inexperienced. Naïve. But the communications have a level of sophistication we rarely come across."

"So?"

"So that makes us think that whoever did this is intentionally trying to throw Silva off his game for the vote today. If it goes south, Stone Cold gets control and Silva's not only lost control of his company, but he'd be replaced immediately."

"Meaning he'd be out of a job, too."

"Right."

"I asked him to postpone the meeting. Surely the board would understand that a kidnapped child would merit a delay."

She could hear Brace typing. "No," he said, staccato clicks filling the silence. "The strike price for the stock is tricky. If word got out or if there was any delay, the price would drop. Silva was stuck. The meeting had to be today."

Annie bit the inside of her cheek. "Stone Cold is poised to pick up the pieces to gain a majority interest. It's what they want regardless of how they get it."

"If they did that, all suspicion lands on them, so they'd be stupid to be involved." Papers shuffled. "It's no surprise that Silva has more than his share of enemies. But would any of them stoop to kidnapping? I don't think that's their style. Hostile takeovers? Yes. Kidnapping? Nope. I just don't see it."

"Silva called his friends, though. Right? Just to make sure they were on board?"

Brace laughed. "Yeah, right. He chewed them up, threatened their kids, and spit them out again. I think he lost a few."

"Oh, no." Annie moaned. "Red Dart is everything to him."

"Almost everything. You and Desi mean more to him than you know."

"Really? You think so?"

"I know so. I've known Silva since we were kids. He's never loved anyone the way he loves you."

"And Desi?"

The slight pause said more than his words. "He loves Desi because he's your son. Hey. Hold on a sec." Annie heard him answer another call. "Look. We're still following leads. Sit tight, okay? I'll keep you posted through the day if we learn anything."

"I should be out there. I can take the jet and be there by dinner time."

"And do what? Pace around a hotel suite? No. We've got the bases covered there. It's going to be a long day. Stay for Silva. Win or lose, he's going to want to be with you."

"I hope you're right. Thanks, Brace." She disconnected the call while waving off the fresh cup of coffee Avi placed in front of her. "I'm too jittery as it is, Avi." Her outstretched hand fluttered like a leaf in a breeze.

"Ah, Miss Annie. You need to take your mind off this. Take a walk. Go to the stable and ride. Do something aside from obsessing."

"Oh, my Avi. You've never steered me wrong." She gave him a hug and walked out the door, checking her battery life and connectivity. Normally she'd leave her cell phone in the house when she walked. She hated feeling like she was being tracked, monitored, and spied on. She valued her privacy, but today wasn't a day to be unplugged.

She bent over, bracing herself against her thighs with arms that shook with the effort to hold her upright. "Just pay the ransom already. Do what they want!"

She decided to ride her horse to her favorite peak to see what she could of the eclipse, but sunny California was well out of the path of totality. She and Desi both loved the wonders of nature, and she gave a wistful smile at the thought of him reveling in the rare event.

Gratitude for the life she led pushed aside her fears. Silva had given her everything she could ever have imagined, but it was almost too much. The homes, cars, and travel weren't what she yearned for. She loved the simplicity of nature and the connectedness she felt to something larger than herself. Desi shared her love for the outdoors and Silva was happy to buy whatever high-end camping gear Desi wanted. The only thing Silva didn't buy was more time to spend with her.

Thoughts of Silva facing a hostile board tightened her chest. She had suggested April 8 for the meeting because her horoscope said the date was auspicious. They would be okay together no matter what happened.

They had to be.

After checking her phone for the umpteenth time, she shook off the tension and rode back down the mountain.

She was washing the horse grit from her hands in the kitchen sink when Silva's car wound up the driveway.

Avi swept in beside her. He had a bourbon on the rocks poured before Silva sat down at the counter.

Silva opened his arms to Annie. "Brace called. The ransom's been paid. So, we wait."

She burrowed into his embrace. "Thank you, Silva." She pulled back to look into his eyes. "And today?"

Tears welled then spilled down his cheeks. "It's gone. Red Dart is gone. They took over the island and voted me off." He gave an exhausted huff. "I have nothing." He held Annie tighter to his chest. "That's not true. I have you and Desi." He muffled his cry against her shoulder.

She met Avi's eyes as he silently set a charcuterie board on the counter. He blew her a kiss and slipped away.

She would have stayed in Silva's quiet embrace forever, but his phone chimed. She listened in. "Brace here. Desi's safe. We have him. We got word that Desi was spotted walking along a road about an hour north of here. I sent a team to get him."

Silva grasped Annie's face and kissed her in a way he hadn't in so long. Warmth spread through her.

"That's wonderful, Brace. Thank you."

"But, er, I don't know what to make of it." Brace slowed his words in a way he always did when bad news was going to follow.

"What's wrong, Brace?" Annie reached over and angled the phone to her.

"Desi says he wasn't kidnapped."

Silva stood up so quickly Annie almost fell to the floor. "What? What are you telling me?"

"The images? The recordings? All fake."

"Brace," Silva growled, "I'll have your head for this."

"Don't shoot the messenger. You and I both ran the images, calls, emails, recordings through every filter and program we had. That was Desi's face and voice. No question. Cyber kidnapping is a thing. The purported victim is manipulated or tricked into being off the grid and not discoverable for a period of time giving the alleged kidnappers a window to extort a ransom. You and Desi were the perfect targets. They look to college-aged kids going to school in another country or just far enough away to make travel there difficult."

Annie leaned into Silva. "Desi is safe. You're home with me. That's all that matters."

Annie pressed the door to the bathroom closed, secured the lock, and turned on the faucets to the tub full blast. She treated herself to an extra scoop of bubbles.

She tried Desi's number three times before he answered. "Hey Mom! What's all this about me being kidnapped?"

"I know! Crazy, right? How was the eclipse?"

"Mom! It was the best! You were totally right about being unplugged. I just walked out of my dorm and kept walking on that cool trail Avi found behind the library when he was here doing that acting workshop with me. Then I hitchhiked some, too."

"To the granite domes?"

"Yeah. That's the place. It was just me, a compass, and a map. Full dark in the middle of the day. I wanted to video it, but you were right about being present in the moment without tech. It was tough at first, but that old-school mindfulness stuff rocks! I was in this place of Zen. On my way back to campus I felt swept into a tornado. Brace's men demanded to know who took me when I was just being off grid. Crazy." He paused. "What's up with Dad?"

"Oh, honey. The meeting didn't go well. They took Red Dart and booted him to the curb."

"Wow! I'm sorry to hear that, but I don't think you are."

After they said goodbye, Annie reached under the vanity, loosened a board, pulled out a tablet, and replaced its battery. With a few strokes, she admired the string of code that created the images and scheduled the calls that had made her life perfect.

Then she pressed delete.

A moment later Annie was startled by a hard banging on the bathroom door.

"Brace just had another conversation with Desi," Silva said in a voice Annie had never heard him use with her before. "You'd better come out now. There's no point in waiting to face the inevitable."❖

Public Affairs Homicide

A Vermont Radio Mystery

Nikki Knight

We'd call my first big interview in Vermont a #MeToo situation now.

It's too bad I realized twenty years later, in the middle of another public affairs interview, that it was also a motive for murder.

But I didn't see any of it coming on a warm spring day at the lake house.

"Jacqueline, I'd like you to meet Martha Edwards," Will said, beaming at bringing his old mentor and new partner together.

I forced a smile and held out my hand, slouching a little as I always did when meeting someone much shorter than my six feet. "Jaye, please."

My full name, pronounced the French way in a silky whisper, Zhak-leen, was Will's endearment for me. I couldn't stand the thought of it coming from her.

"You're Jaye Jordan."

"Yes." I watched her green eyes widen as the recognition hit.

Remembered looking over her creepy husband's shoulder as he moved closer and closer during the taping twenty years ago, gazing into those same clear green eyes as the man's hands moved under the table, willing her to do something, say something, just remind him of her presence and make him stop. Realizing she wasn't going to act and I was on my own.

That I didn't matter.

Even after my ex-husband's cancer and the betrayal that followed, I'd still never felt so alone and powerless in my life.

"Oh. Will always refers to you as Jacqueline." She pronounced it the English way, all sharp consonants and angles as she pulled herself back into professional demeanor. "Really nice to meet you."

"Same here." I kept my voice steady and forced myself into the usual preinterview patter.

I've done hundreds of public affairs interviews. They're a staple of local radio, an easy way to fill a half-hour on a Sunday morning, and generate some good will by promoting the food bank, the craft fair, or whatever community-service thing is going on at the moment. As a DJ who started off as a journalist, I was usually the go-to person for them, and now that I own my own station, I'm all there is. But I do a great job with happy talk about good works. Fully expected I would do the same for State Senator Martha Edwards and her women's charity, WEVermont. Chat up preschool programs, scholarships, whatever.

Then forget this—and her—for another twenty years.

I set up the mics in Martha Edwards's bright comfortable living room.

Started the recording.

And opened my mouth to do the intro.

Nothing came out.

I've been on the air since I was a teenager, and that's never happened.

But I'd never been on the air with Martha Edwards.

Never had a flashback before, either.

The spring weekend at Lake Champlain had started out pretty well. That morning, I'd driven the three hours up from Simpson, where I own and run the local radio station, WSV, for my monthly stay-over with my guy. Most other weekends, Will Ten Broeck, yes, the governor, let's get that out of the way right now, comes down to visit me, because his schedule is a bit more flexible.

Hard to believe but it's true. The governor has a certain degree of control over his days. If he wants, say, to make sure his late Saturday and early Sunday events are usually in the southern part of the state, within a short drive of a certain small radio station, his staff can manage it.

I, however, can't tape my nightly all-request love songs show very often without cutting into the good will that keeps local radio alive. So I manage to sneak away once a month to join Will at his wonderful old clapboard house on the lake.

Saturdays are usually our private time, but Martha Edwards was important to Will.

I knew, because he'd mentioned her occasionally, with a special note of admiration in his voice. When he asked me to book an interview for my weekly public affairs show, giving her a chance to talk up her women's empowerment charity, WEVermont, ahead of its big annual fund-raiser, I agreed. Said I didn't mind tossing the recording kit in my Jeep along with my go-bag, or even giving up a couple hours. The Edwards house is also on Lake Champlain, a quick drive from Will's place, so it wasn't a major interruption.

None of it was a big deal.

That's what I told myself.

Until I walked into the room and saw Martha Edwards.

I'd honestly thought I could fake it for Will's sake.

Martha's late husband, State House Minority Leader Chase Edwards, had recruited Will into politics when he was a geology grad student at UVM, a transplanted New Yorker still finding his way.

That first state house race, now more than thirty years ago, had changed everything for Will, showing him what he really wanted to do—and who he could be. Speaker Edwards, as he was always known, despite serving just one term before the Republicans became a near-permanent minority, was a mentor and more. In the photo of Will's first inauguration he displays in his office, Edwards is standing beside him, looking prouder than his actual dad.

A year or so later, Edwards died suddenly, and Will appointed Martha to fill out her husband's term. It was the formal beginning of her own political career and led to her current long tenure as a state senator. She'd always been a women's advocate, founding WEVermont years before. (The irony was not lost on me then, or ever.)

Martha backed up Will through his shooting-star career: hot young governor to Interior Secretary to national party chair . . . to crash-and-burn when the party took a hard turn to the right. She might even have been the one who convinced him to run for governor again when he came back to the state, sadder, wiser, and divorced.

Meaning I owed her, at least a little. If Will hadn't been back in Vermont when I returned, after my own professional and personal meltdown, it would have been a lot colder. The less said about my perfect storm, the better: my husband survived cancer and decided he needed to recover with blondes and my New York City station's corporate overlords decided all-sports was better than light rock.

I took my buy-out and broken heart and bought WSV, moved up here with my ten-year-old daughter, and started over. Not easy, but it worked.

Recent history wasn't my problem right now.

Nope, the long-ago past was coming after me.

My first week on the job at WSV back then, I was desperate to do well, a girl from the Western Pennsylvania back country firmly convinced it was succeed or die trying. I arrived in Vermont with the ink still wet on my degree from Pitt, a big fat kid with a big fat voice and not much idea how to use it. (Eventually, a good voice coach and some bad food issues fixed those.)

WSV's owner at the time, the old local guy who would later sell it off for satellite talk, had booked Speaker Edwards for a public affairs interview. Light and friendly way to get to know the players, he'd said.

Friendly for sure. Light, not so much.

Of course I didn't tell him what really happened. Pretended it was fine.

Less than a month later, Chase Edwards was dead anyway.

It was my first huge state story.

And the first time I had to keep my mouth shut about what the faithful departed was really like.

"Jaye?" Martha Edwards asked.

I held her gaze. She looked concerned.

Did I matter now? Because I mattered to Will?

I stopped the recorder.

Walked out onto the deck without a word.

Spring sunshine, warm but with that cold edge Vermont still has in early May, trees still slightly yellowish green with new growth, water faintly ruffled like silver-blue taffeta. Gorgeous day on Lake Champlain.

Clean breeze off the water.

Deep breath. Calm the fight or flight reflex.

"Jacqueline?"

Will.

"What's wrong?" he asked.

I kept my eyes on the water. No way I could look at him as I destroyed his mentors.

"We'd—" My voice wobbled a little, but it was there. Good enough. "We'd call it a #MeToo thing now. It was my first interview here, a public affairs show taping like this one. He loomed over me, put his hands on me, the whole deal. It wasn't anything that would legally qualify as sexual assault, but it was pretty damn horrible. And she just sat there the whole time."

"Chase Edwards?" Shock and at least a little disbelief in his voice.

I turned. "Yes, Chase Edwards."

"I heard a few whispers, but it was a long time ago," Will said. His face was tight. Processing. "Different time."

"Not that different. And she was there."

Will shook his head. "I'm sure she didn't understand what was going on."

"What's to understand? Her husband had his hand on my knee and his face practically in my cleavage."

"She may have misconstrued it . . ."

216

"Seriously? That's the oldest male dodge in the book." I stared at him. "I never expected to hear it from you."

"It's not a dodge. You were so young at the time. Maybe you didn't—"

"Didn't what? Didn't understand that he was putting his hands all over me while his wife sat there and did nothing? I was twenty years old, not twenty minutes."

"I'm sorry, I just have a hard time seeing Chase—"

I turned away from him, looking off the deck.

"It's not that I don't believe you, Jacqueline," Will said carefully. "I'm sure you experienced it that way. But—"

I wasn't sure if I wanted to cry or slug him. Or throw him off the deck.

Off the deck.

Looking down at the clear water of Lake Champlain, brownish in the shallows near the rocks, I remembered Chase Edwards had been found floating face down.

Unlike a lot of the houses on the lake, including Will's, the Edwards's home didn't have stairs or a walkway to the water. The deck was a good ten feet above the surface, with a simple rail separating the floor from the sheer drop.

No easy way to go for a swim. It wouldn't be safe to jump off into such shallow water. The house didn't even have a little deck for a rowboat.

So . . .

"How did he get into the water?" I asked Will. "Was he walking on the lakeside path?"

"He who?"

"Chase Edwards. He was found in the water. That was all anyone said. The medical examiner and police reports weren't made public after it was ruled accidental."

"I don't remember." Will looked off the deck.

"It happened maybe a week after the—incident—in Simpson." I took a breath. "I didn't pay a lot of attention to the details."

Will stared down at the water. "I'm sure they investigated."

I didn't say anything. I knew how things could be handled when important people were involved. So did he.

"Are you all right?" the assistant, a scruffy kid like I'd once been, poked her head out the sliding door. "Senator Edwards has a dinner meeting and—"

"I'm sorry," I said quickly, moving toward her. "Just needed a breath of air. Getting over a stomach bug."

Will rested a hand on my back. For the first time in our relationship, I pulled away.

"You all right?" he asked.

"I'll be fine."

Deal with him later.

As I walked over to my chair, I almost tripped over my purse strap. I didn't think I'd left it hanging out like that . . . further evidence of how distracted I was, I guess.

I heard Will's footsteps after me. Saw his plainclothes state trooper driver, Len Fortescue, usually his only security, nod to him as he walked back inside.

All right. Get this going.

"Good morning and welcome to Simpson Focus. I'm Jaye Jordan. Today, I have the honor of interviewing Chittenden County Senator Martha Edwards, founder of WEVermont, the state's premier women's empowerment charity."

My decades of on-air training kicked in, and I was able to dissociate enough to deliver the canned intro smoothly, and get into the first question, a softball about what WEVermont meant to her.

Martha smiled, thanked me for the opportunity, and started talking in the warm, friendly tone she used for interviews. But her eyes gave her away.

Not absent like they'd been on that day twenty years ago.

Intensely focused on me.

Trying to see what I was thinking. What I planned to do with my memory of that day.

I glanced around the room. Will was just out of direct sight, tapping away on his phone, Fortescue watching him with one eye and a bird on the deck rail with the other. Be anywhere but here.

Wish I could.

The memory of Chase Edwards's hand scrabbling up my leg as his wife sat idly by was bad enough. And now, I had all these new questions about what had happened to him just a few weeks later.

Was I wrong? Maybe it really was an accident. Or maybe she'd had enough. Maybe seeing him climb all over some poor scruffy new kid was finally more than she could take.

Maybe that horrible day meant something after all.

Not exactly a win.

My throat was dry.

I picked up my coffee. Almost took a sip before I caught the faint creamy scent over the smoky roast. I always drink it black, except for an occasional fancy latte as a treat with my daughter.

How—

Martha Edwards's gaze had sharpened from intense to scorching, a complete disconnect with her cheerful tone as she talked about some preschool program.

Waiting.

"What's in the coffee?" I asked.

"What?"

"I know you did something to my coffee." Now it made sense that my bag had been moved. I motioned to Len Fortescue. "Look in my purse."

"Jaye?" Fortescue asked, puzzled.

Martha froze.

"I'd bet the farm there's something in there that shouldn't be," I said. I put the coffee mug back on the side table, kept my gaze on Martha, returning her defiant stare.

It didn't even take ten seconds.

The sight of the pills in the trooper's hand should have been enough.

"What does that have to do with me?" Martha snapped. "Your drug problem—"

"She doesn't have a drug problem." Will, his tone soft, shocked, finally believing instead of offering excuses.

"Are you sure?" Martha's tone was cold and deadly. Not just challenging me but challenging Will's judgment. And everything between us.

He nodded to the coffee. "She does have an eating disorder, and she'd never drink the calories from cream."

"Well!" A huffy snort as she puffed herself up, preparing for some serious indignation.

"You killed him," I said.

Stopper.

Her jaw dropped.

"There's no easy way for him to get into the water on his own. The cops believed you because it was you."

Silence. A breath where everything could have gone differently. Where the last twenty years didn't matter—and neither did I.

And then:

"He had head trauma. And no water in his lungs." Will's voice was calm. Sad. "The truth has been sitting in the state ME's files all this time."

He'd checked the records online while I was starting the interview.

"I'll call Major Crimes," Fortescue said.

"I will not dignify this." Martha stood, looked to Will. "I will not let your new chippie ruin thirty years of work for WEVermont."

"She's not a chippie. She's an accomplished professional, the mother of a ten-year-old, for God's sake—and not incidentally the woman I love. What the hell ARE you?"

"What I am is a leader. A person who does far more for the women of Vermont than that—girl—can imagine." Martha spat out the words, with at least a little actual spittle.

I couldn't remember the last time anyone referred to me as a girl. "I was a woman of Vermont twenty years ago, too, Martha."

That shut her up.

"Senator, should I call somebody?" the assistant asked.

"Call her a good lawyer," Will said. "She's going to need it."

"Oh, will I? Why don't you just pardon me?" Martha let out a bitter little laugh. "You wouldn't be where you are without us."

"I didn't know—"

"You didn't want to know," she said. "It was always out there. He didn't even try to hide it."

"Well, that's the truth," I said. "And you just sat there."

"No, honey. YOU just sat there."

"I was twenty and trying to keep my job. What's your excuse?"

"You should thank me. I took care of it."

"Stop." Will snapped. "Do you understand that we're all witnesses and Fortescue is a sworn officer?"

"He should appreciate this." Another bitter laugh as she looked to Len. "It's a public affairs homicide."

"Ma'am, the term is public service homicide." Fortescue's voice was calm, controlled. "And we don't say that anymore. At least not here."

"Just be quiet, Martha," Will said, his voice turning gentle and imploring on her name.

"You didn't care what Chase was doing back then—and you wouldn't care now if it didn't involve your precious Zhak-leen."

Her bitter use of Will's endearment was a gut punch in the way the rest of the confrontation hadn't been.

Suddenly, I couldn't be in that room any longer.

I grabbed the recorder and mics, stuffed them in the kit.

"What—" Will started.

"No." I forced the zipper far enough to keep the equipment inside. The last thing I needed was to have to find the money for a new recording kit.

Well, next to last.

Staying here, with her—and him—was the real last thing I needed.

I grabbed my purse and the kit and started walking.

"Jacqueline?" Will asked.

I looked at him. Just then, it didn't matter that he believed me. It mattered that I'd had to convince him.

"I'm sorry. I shouldn't have questioned you." Will held my gaze. "Are we okay?"

"Not right now." I shook my head, took a long breath as he bit his lip, wincing as the realization hit.

"Jacqueline . . ."

"We might be later."

Tuesday night, three very long days later, I'd ignored a dozen phone calls and texts, and emailed a very cool thank-you for the vase of big red-tipped white roses that had been waiting for me when I returned to the station.

I'd also led our news updates with the arrest of Martha Edwards and her confession to the murder of her husband. A Chittenden County prosecutor had called and told me they might also bring an attempted murder charge for the coffee, but she was likely to take a plea.

Of course, there was also the possibility of a pardon.

The card on the roses, and most of the messages, said the same thing: "I screwed up. I'm sorry. Forgive me?"

Thanks to my divorce, I knew from real deal-breakers, so when my phone buzzed after Tuesday night's first break with a simple "Can we talk?" I replied "Yes."

Only a little surprised to see the doorbell light up a minute later.

Will was on the porch, alone. Just a guy who'd really messed up. And knew it.

The message was a little diluted by the big SUV at the base of the steps, running, with Fortescue at the wheel, but still good enough.

Will started to reach for me, then thought better of it. "Give me a chance to do better?"

"Okay. But this was a big one."

"I know. My daughter says I'm a schmuck. And that I'd better not pardon Martha."

"She's right on both counts."

"I never even considered a pardon. I don't believe in public service homicide." He shrugged. "Still a schmuck?"

I opened the door. "You're my schmuck, and you're doing the work, and that makes all the difference."

"I love you, Jacqueline."

"I love you. That's why I'm letting you in." ❖

A Capital Offense

Hans Copek

Dresden, Germany, November 1943

At three minutes to ten, Frieda moved the dial on her radio to the forbidden wavelength. Under a weak 25-watt lamp, she had laid out her steno pad and an array of short but freshly sharpened pencils. She waited.

Promptly at 22:00 hours, she heard the four drumbeats of the BBC, followed by *Hier ist London mit dem deutschen Programm.* For the next fifteen minutes, a man read a list of German soldiers held in prisoner of war camps in Britain.

Hunched, her gray hair touching the coarse fabric in front of the speaker funnel, she had turned the volume way down. She feared the tattletale in the apartment next to hers might have her ear pressed against the wall. An ardent admirer of Hitler, this woman might report her neighbor to the authorities. Listening to foreign stations had been made a capital offense at the beginning of the war.

With a mixture of shorthand and long hand, Frieda took down the names of the captured soldiers and the addresses of their relatives back home. For the past three months now, Frieda had made it her mission to bring relief and happiness to families unaware of their loved one's fate.

Tomorrow morning, at her kitchen table, she would write their addresses on plain envelopes. Each contained a simple note: Your husband (or son), the name of his unit, is alive and is a prisoner of war in England.

She was already on the third page of her note pad. Her anxiety grew as the list reached the letter O.

"*Oberdieck, Horst, Unteroffizier, Luftwaffe, Ehefrau: Ursula Oberdieck, Mittel Strasse 34, Hildesheim.*

"*Oske, Herbert, Bootsmann, U-boot 340, Eltern: Dr. Walter Oske, Welfenallee 2. Hannover.*"

Not tonight, she sighed. Read alphabetically, the name she hoped to hear was not among them. Her son's name, Oelkers, Gerhard. Missing in Action. Somewhere in the cold North Atlantic Ocean.

She kept scribbling down more names.

"*Rodenwald, Wolfgang, Gefreiter, Luftwaffe, aus Berlin-Pankow, Waldweg 13.*

Sellmann, Winfried, Soldat, 6th Grenadie—"

The broadcast stopped in midsentence. Her lamp flickered and went out. The dial screen on her radio dimmed, then faded from view.

At the same moment, she heard someone hammering at her apartment door. "*Aufmachen!*"

A man's voice: "Open up! Open up!" He never stopped pounding.

Fear shot through Frieda's veins. She heaved herself off her chair. Then, in total darkness, with her hands stretched out in front, she stumbled through the entry hall of her apartment.

"Coming, coming." Frieda quaked.

Whether the man heard her or not, he kept up his pounding.

"Open up! NOW!"

What an idiot. Why didn't he ring the electric bell? He'll wake up all the other tenants in the house.

She turned the key and opened the door. With his flashlight pointed to the floor, she couldn't see the face of the man who held it. Whoever he was, he barged forward, flattening her against the wall. A second man emerged from the darkness. While still on the landing, he turned and yelled to someone downstairs, "Lights on!"

Ahead of her, she saw the lamp in the living room glowing again. The second intruder grasped Frieda's arm and led her back to the radio. She had her first look at the two. They weren't policemen. The leader wore a leather coat, shiny with rainwater. The one who had guided her down the hall had the empty sleeve of his trench coat pinned to his left side. Their broad-rimmed hats shadowed most of their faces. Drops of water were still gathering at the hats' rims.

The man in the leather coat sat down in front of her radio. The low hum told her that the device was warming up. Then, barely audible, the announcer in London came on again:

"...*orst, Winfried, 82nd Infantry Regiment, Mutter: Lottie Windhorst, Stein Strasse 3 Magdeburg.*"

The leather-coat man turned up the volume. Now the radio blared.

"*Sieger, Walter—* "

"I've heard enough." The leader clicked the receiver off. He had a rasping, high-pitched voice.

"Are you Gestapo?" Frieda managed to croak. No answer.

"You have to come with us. Are you aware what the penalty is for listening to enemy broadcasts?" asked the man, who was clearly the leader of the two.

Frieda nodded. She knew only too well. The papers had made a big case about an old man in Leipzig. Three weeks after his arrest, his life ended under the *Fallbeil*, the German name for the guillotine. She had ignored the warning.

Now she sat sobbing, her plump body filling an armchair. The man rapped his knuckles on the table next to her. "Get your coat. We'll take you to headquarters. We don't have all night."

She looked up and saw his face for the first time. Chinless, with a long nose and eyes close together, he made her think of a bird, a large bird, a turkey? No, a vulture!

"I need to use the toilet first." She heaved herself to her feet.

"Martin. Stay with her," the leader ordered the one-armed man, who looked embarrassed. "But Herr Siebert . . . "

His superior relented. "All right. Let her go."

Turning to Frieda, Siebert barked, "Be quick!"

She locked the bathroom door behind her and reached for a bottle of sleeping pills. She poured several handfuls into her palm and gulped them down with cold water. Her hands were trembling as she replaced the glass. I'll die on my own terms and not on the scaffold. She flushed.

When she joined the men, a feeling of calm suffused her. Martin helped her into her brown wool overcoat. He also reminded her of the rain outside, and she went back and pulled galoshes over her best leather shoes. Finally, she tucked a gray cloche over her straggly hair.

"I'm ready," she told them.

Vulture-faced Siebert gathered her notes, a stack of envelopes, and a sheet of twelve-pfennig stamps. They pictured Adolf Hitler's profile. He shoved everything into an outsized envelope. Martin switched off the lamp by the radio and turned on the light in the entry hall. The young man made Frieda think of her two sons. Then she noticed that one of his eyes didn't follow her. It was made of glass. Poor man, she thought. While of no more use to the army, he now apprenticed to become a henchman for the Gestapo. Well, at least his mother must be glad he wasn't killed.

Two uniformed policemen sat in a car waiting by the curb. The driver stayed behind the wheel while the other got out to supervise the loading of the prisoner. First, Siebert crawled into the back seat. Then Frieda was shoved in next to him, and finally, the task for the other gendarme became clear. With Martin barely squeezing in, the policeman, with all his might, rammed his butt against the door until its lock clicked shut. Three people in heavy coats in the backseat made breathing difficult. To make it worse, the car reeked of stale tobacco.

"I forgot my keys. I didn't lock the apartment door." She gasped as the car started to move.

"We'll take care of it," whispered Martin. It earned him a harrumph from the other side of their prisoner.

"Where are we going?" she asked once more. Both men ignored her question.

A jumble of thoughts raced through her head. Someone had betrayed her. But who? What if Gerhard returned from the war and she was dead? What would happen to her belongings? How did they surprise her? It had to be that the house's front door was still unlocked at ten. This allowed the two agents to creep up to her second-floor flat.

When the men barged in, the policeman downstairs turned off the electricity for the entire house. And when the light went on again, the radio dial was still set for the BBC. Bastards.

The car moved hardly faster than a horse-drawn carriage. Its headlights were masked save for a narrow slit. The city was in total darkness, with no streetlights or traffic signals. Peering ahead past the heads of the two policemen, she saw snowflakes flit among the raindrops. At long last, Frieda made out the bulky city hall. The car came to a halt by a side door. Frieda felt drowsiness coming on. She stumbled on the slick pavement as she stepped over the curb. Martin used his only arm to steady her. "One step at a time, Oma."

"Oma!" he had said. Grandmother. There won't be any grandchildren ever to call her that name. Tears blurred her vision as her two captors led her down a short flight of stairs into the basement. Siebert opened a door at the end of a dark corridor. The only light in the small room came from a lamp at the ceiling. Frieda faced a plain wooden desk with a massive chair behind it. Against the back wall stood two large lamps with reflectors the size of kettledrums. They were not turned on.

Siebert ordered Frieda to take one of the two chairs facing the desk. When she sat down, she let out a long yawn. Then, after a few minutes, she unbuttoned her heavy winter coat. The two plainclothes men remained standing in the corner, waiting, and once in a while, exchanging a few mumbled words.

When the door flew open, the men snapped to attention. A tall officer in the black prewar uniform of the SS entered the room. He turned to Siebert. "I've taken over this case from *Sturmführer* Schmidt. You two take up your position outside." His voice had a harsh, north German sound, not the melodic Saxon accent.

"Yessir, *Sturmbannführer*. Stay outside." Siebert and Martin hurried out of the room.

Siebert was awed and confused. SS-*Sturmbannführer* Engelhardt was the head of the Gestapo for the province of Saxony. This had to be a major case.

With her eyes closed, Frieda heard the man shuffling papers. *What will he do to me? Ha, he can't do anything anymore.* She was at peace and smiled briefly.

Finally, Engelhardt cleared his throat and spoke with a soft voice, "As the arresting officer explained, I had you picked up because we were informed that you are listening to enemy broadcasts."

Frieda was too tired to answer and merely nodded her head.

"Why did you do that?" he kept probing.

After a long yawn, she mumbled, "I'm trying to find out whether my son is alive."

"The enemy will tell you that?"

"Yes, the English radio reads a lisht of prisoners of war."

She opened her eyes briefly.

"Yes, and . . ." The man prompted her to go on.

"My shon served on a U-boat. I wash notified that he . . . is mishing in action."

"When was that?"

"Oh, fffour months . . . ago."

"Do you recognize this letter?" He slid a small envelope across the table. It had been stamped at the Meissen post office.

After adjusting her glasses, Frieda recognized her handwriting. She nodded her head but couldn't stifle another yawn. A few times, she had taken a train to nearby towns so the packets of letters didn't all show a Dresden postmark. She thought herself very clever for doing this.

"Did they turn me in?" Her voice was down to a whisper.

Her interrogator merely shrugged his shoulders.

"You weren't very careful."

What did he say? He sounded like he was far away.

Engelhardt waited a while until he spoke again. "Do you have any next of kin?"

"I'm a widow. I live alone." She no longer bothered to cover her mouth when she yawned.

After a pause, she labored to add, "My oldest shon . . . fell in Shtalingrad."

"Anyone else?"

Her eyes were closed. A smile appeared on her face.

"I hear birds singing."

Her interrogator waited.

Frieda sat up, squinted, and asked her interrogator, "Whooo are you?"

No answer from him.

"Where am I? The cuckoo?" Her head lolled to the side.

"You aren't well. Can I get you a glass of . . ."

He jumped up when Frieda slid off the chair. The back of her head cracked against the floor.

"Siebert!" Engelhardt yelled. His minion burst through the door, bent over Frieda, put his ear over her mouth. "She's not breathing." He looked up.

"What did you idiots do to her?" Engelhardt fumed. "Didn't Schmidt tell you she is harmless?"

Siebert felt for her pulse.

After a minute, there was no doubt. "She's gone, *Sturmbannführer*."

"Call an ambulance." His boss's boss snapped.

"Cause of death, the usual?" Siebert needed instructions.

"Yes, the usual. Heart attack." On the threshold, he turned around. "Burn the files. This case is closed." With that, Engelhardt stalked out of the room, leaving Siebert to deal with the dead woman.

Upstairs, in his office, the *Sturmbannführer* pulled a piece of paper from his tunic. The same handwriting as on the envelope.

"Ihr Sohn, Werner Engelhardt, Waffen-SS Division 'Hermann Göring,' in Messina, Italien" . . . Engelhardt picked up the framed photo on his desk. "Captured in Italy. Thank God you are alive," he whispered, looking at the image of his son.

He struck a match and held it to the edge of the letter. When the flame got close to his fingers, he let the paper go. Black flakes fluttered into his ashtray.

Looking at the picture again, he said, "She never gave me a chance to thank her."❖

The Ave

Sean C. Harding

Sloane spotted Roshi Rossi panhandling with a grimy fedora by the bus stop at Boston Medical Center. Roshi looked nothing like the pudgy, pink-faced model of tranquility Sloane knew from their mindfulness classes in prison. Now he looked like one of those alien life forms you see in memes—gray, big-eyed, and emaciated. Shoulder length hair greasy-wet. Unruly beard. Clothes hanging off him like a child playing dress-up. No doubt, Roshi had picked up the needle again.

Call him a cold-ass bastard, but Sloane just spent thirty minutes with an infectious disease doc discussing an antiviral combination for Hep C and wasn't in the mood to hear a tale of woe. So, he pulled his Scally cap low, hung his head lower and tried to pass without—

"Sloane! Is that you, Sloane?"

Goddammit.

"Oh, hey Roshi." Sloane squeezed out a smile. "How are yah?"

Roshi didn't answer. He didn't need to. He teetered up to Sloane and offered his hand. He smelled like vinegar and dirty sidewalk. Strong enough to notice even through a blustery autumn wind and bus fumes.

Eventually, Roshi said, "Long time no see, brother. When you get out?"

"Couple weeks ago."

"Hope you handle it better than I do. I'm not doing too well."

"I hate hearing that, bro. What's it been for you, three months?"

"Almost four."

"It's easier if you're clean, but I'm sure you know that."

"Yeah." Roshi looked down at his now charcoal-colored sneakers, nodding. Sloane felt a question coming.

Sure enough. "Listen, Sloane, since you're here, I can really use your help."

Saying "since you're here" like Sloane's paying him a visit. Sloane patted his pockets and shook his head. "Sorry, Roshi, but like I said, I just got out. I can't even say I'm tapped 'cause I haven't had anything to tap."

Roshi put his hands up and waved them. "No. No. I wouldn't take no money off you, brother."

That didn't put Sloane at ease. "What then?"

"I need you to help me find my girl."

"Huh?" Sloane squinted. "Your girl?"

"Yeah. Pam, she's my girl. I haven't seen her for two days."

"Listen, I hope it works out for you, but I'm not getting involved in any lovers' beef, if that's what you're saying."

"It's not like that. She isn't pissed at me or anything. She's missing. Went out last night to get us a fix, and hasn't come back."

"Since last night? I wouldn't call that missing."

Roshi raised his voice. "I'm telling you she's missing. She knows I'd be getting the agonies by now. She wouldn't leave me hanging like that. If she couldn't find none she'd at least tell me she whiffed." His face contorted and his eyes became slick with tears. "Please, Sloane. She's my life. I can't let anything happen to her."

Sloane's gut stirred. A missing heroin addict didn't bode well. A bad bit of dragon in your dope and that's all she wrote. He knew of seven acquaintances on the street who bit it in the forty-four months he spent in the can. That didn't include the two prison buddies who OD'd inside. The life span of an addict those days was that of a fuckin' fly.

He sighed. "What do you want me to do, Roshi?"

Roshi took him by the elbow and started down the loud, traffic-laden Mass Ave toward South Bay. "Just help me find her."

"Just help you . . . How?" Sloane took his elbow back and released a sigh. "Okay, tell you what, give me some clothing with her scent on it and I'll lead your ass right to her." Sloane looked around and frowned. "Where the hell are we going anyway?"

Roshi pointed. "Down a couple blocks there."

Sloane stopped walking. "Not the Ave? Aww, hell no. Are you shitting me, Roshi? I'm on friggin' parole, bro. I can't be seen around there. Shit, I shouldn't even be seen with you."

"Believe me, Sloane, I wouldn't ask you if it wasn't, like, life or death."

Sloane stayed stiff in place and Roshi said, "You know what Monday is?"

"Halloween?"

"No. That's Tuesday. Monday's the day they send in the storm troopers to tear down the tents and clear everyone off the Ave."

Sloane read that in the paper just the day before. After years of a spiraling free-fall of crime and overdose, a city ordinance planned on cleaning up the several-block area of homeless encampments in the South End. A secular Hell with its nucleus at the intersection of Mass Ave and Melnea Cass Boulevard. The infamous Mass and Cass. Even when using, Sloane avoided the place like Chernobyl.

'I can't, Roshi. I'd like to help but—"

"Look, Sloane, you don't have to do nothing with nobody there, okay? I just want you near me when I ask around. You're a big guy and look like you still got your prison fitness. No one's likely to fuck with me if you're around."

The kiss of death right there.

Sloane lifted his cap off his head and rubbed his thinning buzz cut. Half of him sympathized with Roshi, the other half wanted to beat the bejesus out of him for the emotional manipulation. The kind voice of Tracy Duboise, his and Roshi's mindfulness teacher in the can, sounded in his head like an angel encouraging him toward compassion and aid for his friend. The primitive voice of species survival commanded him to turn his ass around and run. The last time he ignored the primitive voice he tried to rob a Bank of America in Cambridge and wound up getting a nickel and a day.

But how could he say no to Tracy Duboise?

Sloane checked the time on his new phone—almost noon. "Was there a regular guy Pam would cop from?"

"Yeah, Tommy Boy. That's who I want to see. We call him Tommy Boy cuz he looks like Chris Farley."

"Good. I'll go with you to talk with this guy, but then I'm gone. Even if he's not there, I'm bailing. You hear me?"

"Fine. Thanks, Sloane. I owe ya."

"You don't owe me shit. This is for a friend out of the goodness of my heart."

"Well, just the same, the Universe will give you serious karma points for this."

"What, you're in charge of doling out karma now?"

They reached the corner of Mass Ave and Albany Street when a statuesque Black woman with a huge scrub of hair came sprinting around the corner hollering like a manic Paul Revere. "Them mothahfuckahs are coming! They're coming!"

She stuck her face in Sloane's without stopping and screamed. Sloane stood six-two. She was almost the same height—maybe taller with the big hair. She continued her banshee dash down the street. People cleared the sidewalk like she was a runaway horse.

Sloane turned to Roshi with brows high. "What. The fuck. Was that?"

"Oh, that's just Foxxy Cleopatra."

"Foxxy Cleopatra? Like in the Austin Powers movie? Beyoncé?"

Roshi shrugged. "I don't know what her real name is. We just call her Foxxy Cleopatra cuz she looks kinda like her with that Afro. Well, you know, if Beyoncé got shipwrecked maybe. The girl's bat-shit crazy."

"You think? Seems like all your friends are named for people they look like. What do they call you?"

"Gandalf."

Sloane laughed. Perfect. They continued down Southampton Street, past Melnea Cass. They could barely hear one another over the rumbling and horns of trucks going up and down the street, but the sights of the homeless commune bombarded Sloane immediately. The sidewalks were lined with tents, tarps, and beach umbrellas of all shapes, sizes, and colors. Unsteady, disheveled men and women, also of all shapes, sizes, and colors staggered, slumped or lay prone all about. Drug transactions took place in the open, with buyers and sellers hollering and haggling like a Middle Eastern Bazaar. Cop SUVs were spaced up and down streets, watching it all as if guarding the city from a zombie outbreak.

Sloane's head spun. It was like he was no longer in Boston. Like he'd been knocked out and dropped in some third-world country. These poor souls were in a harsher prison than he'd ever been in. He'd never felt such gratitude for being clean.

"You live here, Roshi?" Sloane couldn't keep the disturbance from his voice.

"Nah, not no more. I spent last night near South Station. Pam's staying at her cousin's place in Brighton. Spofford Road. Know where that is?"

"No."

"Corner of Comm Ave. Right across from the Hopewell Bar.

"Yeah, I know the Hopewell."

Averting Sloane's eyes, Roshi said, "Pam thinks, you know, after a shower and clean clothes, I might be able to stay with her at the cousins for a few days. Oh, hold on, Sloane. Luis! Hey Luis!"

Roshi shuffled over to a plump, balding guy wearing a blue backpack, and a clear, healthy olive complexion that made him stick out around there like a diamond among pebbles.

While Roshi made introductions, he told Sloane that Luis served as an outreach worker.

"He and his team save lots of lives on the Ave," Roshi said and tapped Luis's backpack. "This is filled with Narcan kits. You seen Pam around, Luis?"

Luis hesitated before shaking his head. "No, sorry, man. Not for a couple of days, at least."

Roshi grimaced and thanked Luis, then continued down the street looking to and fro. Sloane walked by his side.

Roshi pointed up Atkinson Street. "See the piss yellow tent there? That's Tommy Boy's."

A stringy, shaggy kid lay on the curb outside Tommy Boy's tent. An unsteady Roshi needed to step over him. Sloane watched, certain Roshi would fall on the guy. He didn't.

"Tommy! Yo, Tommy Boy!" No response. Roshi pulled open the tent entrance. Sloane took cautious steps up to the tent behind him and looked inside.

A guy, Sloane assumed to be Tommy Boy, mainlined a sleepy-eyed woman in her extended neck. Sloane turned away as soon as he saw the needle.

"What the fuck? You mind?" Tommy Boy said.

The pulse in Sloane's own neck throbbed. His body grew warm and tingly. He felt that old tickle in the bowels.

"Gotta go, Roshi," Sloane said and strode back in the direction he came.

Sloane's half-way house mandated its residents to attend a twelve-step meeting every night for their first ninety days. That night, Sloane went with a couple of guys to a Narcotics Anonymous meeting at the Faulkner Hospital. He normally thought meetings were a pain in the ass, hated most of them, but he welcomed the one that night. Seeing the girl getting high with Tommy Boy really poked the beast—even after the misery he witnessed on the Ave that morning. How friggin' sick was that? At the break, he poured his fourteenth cup of coffee that day from the large metal urn in the hall outside the meeting room, nearly crushing the Styrofoam cup with a shaky hand. Someone tapped his shoulder and he jumped.

Luis, the outreach worker from Mass and Cass, stood frowning at Sloane, shaking his head, face stretched tight with strain. It didn't surprise Sloane to see him at an NA meeting. There needed to be a reason a guy would do what he did. A recovering addict giving back would be the first guess.

"It's Sloane, right?"

"That's right."

"You hear about Roshi, Sloane?"

"No. Did he find her?"

Luis looked down and shook his head. "He found something, but it wasn't Pam."

"What are you talking about?"

"He's dead. Murdered. Stabbed up real bad, man."

Sloane stopped breathing for a second. That, on top of the caffeine, made him dizzy. He braced himself with his hand on the table and thought it might tip over.

"Let's go outside," Sloane said.

They stood outside in a thin fog. Boston skyline lights peeped through to the north, and headlights shimmered past them below on Centre Street. Sloane asked, "What happened?"

"I feel really bad," said Luis and blew on his hands. "When he asked me about Pam earlier—you was with him then—I said I hadn't seen her but that was bullshit, man. I saw her real early that morning with Ruffin."

Ruffin? Sounded familiar.

"I lied for Roshi's sake, man," Luis said, "cuz Pam and Ruffin were looking real friendly. Know what I'm saying? Anyway, Roshi came around asking me again. You weren't with him then. He looked so desperate. I thought he'd be looking for her all night, so I told him what I saw that morning. The dumb bastard probably went looking for Ruffin." Luis smacked his own head. "I'm even dumber than he is. Friggin' loco."

"Who's this Ruffin guy?"

"Who's Ruffin? Ruffin is a bad, bad dude. That's who Ruffin is. I don't know his first name. He deals around the Ave. People around there say the guy robbed and murdered at least two other dealers over the summer. He's probably killed five times that many with the fentanyl-cut heroin he pushes."

"Wait a minute. Tall, curly red-haired dude?"

"Might be right." Luis put his hand way above his head. "Big—even bigger than you. He may have been ginger once, but his head is shaved now and has eighty-eight with a lightning bolt under each eight tattooed at the base of his skull."

One of many symbols for the Aryan Brotherhood. Eighty-eight meant "Heil Hitler" and two lightning bolts, like sharp angled S's, were the symbol of the Nazi SS.

"He's AB?"

Luis nodded slow. "He's plain evil, man."

"Why would he kill Roshi?"

"Why? Cuz if you know Roshi, you know the kind of mouth he's got on him. If he went yapping with it to Ruffin and Ruffin felt disrespected? It don't take much for Ruffin to kill somebody."

Sloane couldn't concentrate on his book in bed that night. He kept thinking about him and Roshi reading, trading, and discussing all the philosophy books they got from the Prison Book Program. So, he lay in bed, bedside table light on, staring at the water-stained ceiling and listening to his roommate snore like a warthog. The way Sloane figured it, if he'd been with Roshi to speak to Ruffin, his buddy could still be alive.

Sloane remembered Ruffin from about six or seven years back when they were both being held at Nashua Street jail after Sloane got pinched for a bullshit possession of stolen property charge. Ruffin thought himself the shit among the detainees back then, acting like he was some high and mighty gang lord. Sloane wanted to bust up the scumbag's larynx, but everyone wanted to do that to everyone else in that shit-pit, so the name hadn't stuck with him.

He wouldn't forget it now, though.

Nuh-uh.

Luis had called Ruffin a nocturnal predator who roamed the Mass and Cass area anytime from sundown to sunrise. So, Saturday night, Sloane flipped the script and made the predator the prey.

First, he blew off a twelve-step meeting and took the T to Andrew Square. To burn off the hype, he killed an hour on the speed and heavy bags in Pat Walsh's boxing gym on Dot Ave. Then amidst the stink of sweat and smacks of leather striking leather he chilled his racing thoughts by sitting on a mat facing a bare, yellowing wall, minding his breaths. From there he trekked up Southampton, with detours on streets off of it, scanning every person and tent, nook and cranny, for someone who could be Ruffin.

His phone read nine-thirty. Curfew at the house was eleven-thirty on Saturdays. Can't be late.

One thing he wasn't going to do was go back behind the wall. He spent nine of his thirty-two years locked up already. More than a quarter of his life. More than enough.

He also couldn't kill Ruffin. Once you crossed the murder line you were capable of anything.

No killing and no prison.

Still plenty of options to work with in between.

Out on the Ave, it didn't look like the campers were showing much urgency to pack up their stuff. At least, Sloane couldn't see much difference from the previous day. People still roamed up and down the street looking to cop or fence or borrow.

When Sloane reached Albany Street, a corpse-lookin' kid approached him. He recognized the kid from the Southie projects back in the day—only he looked about fifty years older. Bobby something. Sloane heard he died. He pretty much heard right.

Bobby Something asked, "Hey, hey, got a nail?"

"Nah. Quit 'em in the can."

"Hey, that's cool, yo. Ize got johnnies and roxies. You lookin'?" Bobby Something clearly didn't recognize Sloane, or if he did, would rather not show it.

"Yeah, I'm looking, but not for johnnie or roxy. I'm looking for Ruffin."

"Roofies?" He smiled with piano teeth. "Shiiit, Ize can probably hook you up with someone for a broker's fee, yo."

"Not roofies. Ruff-in. A big, bald white dude. Tattoo on the back of the head."

"Shiiit. You a narc? Pffft. Fuck you, dude. Folks don't ask no questions 'bout Ruffin, and they sure as fuck don't answer them." Bobby pivoted like a soldier and hustled away.

Good seein' ya again, Bobby Something.

Sloane walked back down Mass Ave. A girl anywhere between fifteen and fifty and weighing as much as a Barbie doll stood out front of the Hampton Inn on the corner of Melnea Cass. With a dark brown hoodie and dark brown hair beneath the paltry lighting, her ashen face looked disembodied. "Hey dude. You lookin' for a date. A big, handsome guy like you shouldn't be alone on a Saturday night."

"No dates for me."

She clicked her tongue. "Why not?"

"Maybe I'm a priest."

"So, I don't mind." She hugged herself, looking cold in the hoodie, and nodded down the street. "Fine. Then you got a few bucks for me to go to McDonald's, Father?"

"If that's what you'll do with it. You wouldn't lie to a priest, would you?"

She crossed her heart. Sloane handed her a Hamilton, keeping a few singles for the train home. "You seen a guy named Ruffin?"

"Careful buying from him, dude. His dirt is deadly. One of my girls OD'd on his shit."

"No worries." Sloane shrugged and smiled. "I just want to hear his confession."

"I think I just saw him going down Newmarket."

He fast-walked a block to New Market Square. Three streets—all named New Market Square—intersected to form a triangle. The namer apparently lacked imagination besides a basic knowledge of geometry.

Numerous businesses with red brick and stone buildings, large lots, and chain link fences comprised the area. Prison looking but without the razor wire. With the businesses closed, the area held a gloomy silence. Sloane made his way down the New Market Square off Southampton chiding himself as a fool. Poor lighting made his task like seeking a shadow in the dark. This time of year it's autumn in the day and winter at night. He wore only a T-shirt under his old pea coat. The ancient, knit Bruins beanie on his head provided the insulation of a paper napkin, and the black cotton gloves on his hands weren't for providing warmth.

Then he spotted movement in the distance beneath a street light. Two moving figures, both appeared tall. They crept into the gravel-covered lot of a building where large rigs and box trucks were parked for the night. Sloane hustled to get close enough to check them out.

The two moved toward the back of the lot outside the view of the building's security camera. The privacy they sought suggested they weren't making a drug deal. Those transactions didn't require discretion on The Ave. No, they probably had something far more intimate in mind.

Sloane followed.

They disappeared behind one of the last row of vehicles at the edge of the property. Sloane moved from truck to truck for cover, before finally stopping twenty feet from the pair, leaning his back against a box truck, gloved hands in coat pocket, waiting, listening.

He really didn't want to see what they were doing.

After five chilly minutes a voice said, "Gimme mine now."

A rough female voice. Sloane peeked. One of them stood with his back to Sloane looking down, hands on hips. The other kneeled before the guy. The big fella standing had to be Ruffin: six-four, wide back, a head and ass like full moons, pants lowered to his knees.

Foxxy Cleopatra kneeled before Ruffin with her palm out. Sloane just assumed a male being with Ruffin because of Foxxy's height.

"Sure, baby," Ruffin said as he reached down for his pants. Only before pulling them up he yanked his belt from the loops. Said, "Here's you go, bitch," and lashed Foxxy across the head with the buckle.

She screamed and recoiled.

Foxxy, head covered by her arms, yelled, "You promised a g, lyin' moth—"

Ruffin whipped her another time. "This is what you've earned, bitch. I ain't giving you my good dope for no bull shit hummer. Think I'm a fool?"

A bomb went off in Sloane's chest. Bile burned his throat. God, he hated bullies. Prison was a septic tank filled with them. Low lifes feeding on the vulnerable. Ruffin, so damn smug, stood absorbed in his sadism. Sloane's legs shook with rage while he crouched and crept up behind his prey.

Then made a stealth rush.

Sloane reached the unexpecting thug and made a little hop before driving his heel into the inside of the psychopath's knee. Ruffin didn't make a sound. Did he not get the bastard as good as he thought? Oh, yeah he did. When Ruffin tried to turn on his knee he began to collapse. Before the big tree went down, Sloane grabbed hold of Ruffin's hoodie collar, bent low and drove a hook to the body, putting everything behind it and getting that sweet feel of knuckle on rib. Bone on bone. A groan followed the blow. Sloane let go of the hoodie and backed away in a fighter's stance. The punk teetered back and forth and fell to the ground. There he remained, sideways on the cold dirt and gravel, holding his knee with one hand and his ribs with the other, staring up with a slack expression, like Sloane wasn't from this world.

Foxxy, whimpering and watching, ran off before Sloane said a word.

In gasps, Ruffin said, "If you aim to rob me, you're shit out of luck, muthafuckah. I ain't got shit."

"Just want info, freak." Sloane saw a black leather biker jacket lying on the hood of a truck cab beside them. He picked it up. Shiny new leather, no emblems or patches. An iPhone in the front pocket, a burner and a hunting knife in the inner pockets. He removed both phones and placed them on the ground. "Although, I gotta say this is a nice looking jacket. New?"

Sloane tossed it aside. "Okay, straight-up, punk. Did you kill Roshi?"

"Who?" Ruffin sounded asthmatic. Sloane may have busted a rib or two.

"You might know him as Gandalf."

"Don't know who the fuck you're talking about."

"No?" Sloane kicked the hand that covered the ribs. Hard. Ruffin squealed, tried to get up but couldn't. "He went to you looking for Pam, his girl," Sloane said.

"Pam," Ruffin wheezed as he spit the name. "That whore is the reason I'm empty. Bitch robbed me. Acting all sweet and shit. She played me."

"That right? When?"

"Yesterday morning. Early."

"Ohh, I get it. That's why you stuck Roshi. Payment for what Pam did." He looked in the direction Foxxy just ran. "I mean, obviously you don't have a problem with violence against women, so you must not have been able to get your filthy hands on her. Roshi was the next best thing."

For a while neither spoke. Ruffin panted and Sloane waited. Eventually Sloane grew impatient. "I asked you a question." Sloane faked another kick in the ribs, still getting a moan.

Shaking his head, Sloane said, "Looks like I'm gonna have to move all the kicking up to your head, or we'll be here all night." He took two steps.

"Fu . . . Alright. Alright," Ruffin said between coughs. "It was self-defense, man. Straight-up. The chatted-out bastard came after me. Wait. Hear me out. That boy was buggin', talking all kinds of crazy shit." More shallow breathing. "Come on. You know he was crazy. What was I supposed to do?"

"You're full of shit. I did time with Roshi. He had his issues, but he wasn't crazy and he wasn't violent."

At least the drug-free road-dog Sloane knew back then wasn't. Whatever. He was going to give his friend the benefit of the doubt. Sloane picked up the phones he took from the jacket and hefted them in his hands, displaying them like a magician before making cards disappear. He smashed them on the ground, then shook the knife from the coat and kicked it under a truck. Maybe an anonymous call could get it to the cops? Think that out later when less tired. With Ruffin's jacket over his shoulder, he started to walk away.

"Hey, where you going with that jacket, muthafucka? I can't walk or call nobody.

"You're gonna have to slither then, snake."

Ruffin yelled to Sloane's back. "I'll freeze to fuckin' death, man."

"It'll be warmer in Hell."

Reaching the end of the lot, Sloane exhaled a loud sigh. No doubt he would be on the AB hitlist after tonight. Like life isn't hard enough as it is.

Loud footsteps and growls came toward him. Jeezus, what now? He felt like an avatar in a friggin' video game. He braced himself.

Foxxy. Left cheek swollen, she marched like a Roman legionary past Sloane into the lot. Over her head she carried what looked like the leg to a coffee table. Went past like she didn't notice him there.

Sloane watched Foxxy striding with vengeance in each step, then disappearing behind a rig. Should he stop her? No. Let nature take its course.

Shit, look at the time. Sloane needed to get back to the house—fast. He looked at Ruffin's jacket in his hand, thought of a good home for it and headed back toward Mass Ave while a harsh wind carried Ruffin's screams across Mass and Cass.

The girl from the corner looked out the window from a counter in McDonald's. It warmed Sloane's heart that she bought herself some food. Sloane walked up to her and laid the jacket on the stool beside her.

"That's for telling me the truth. It should keep you warm. Warmer, anyway. It's hot, so if someone asks where you got it, tell them it was a payment for services rendered. Understand?"

She nodded. Sloane left her sitting there, speechless while she put the jacket on. He started to hustle for the train along the busy Saturday night street. He passed New Market Square.

Ruffin had grown silent.

News of Ruffin's fate didn't make it into the following morning's Sunday *Globe*. Sloane wasn't sure he wanted to know the fate of the piece of scum anyway, but he did want to know what became of Pam. He owed that to Roshi.

After the Sunday morning in-house meeting, Sloane jumped on the Green Line into Brighton. Roshi had told him Pam stayed in her cousin's crib adjacent to the Hopewell Bar. He got off the train and crossed Comm Ave—always death defying—to get a coffee at Dunkin'. He guessed he might be waiting a while for Pam.

With a large black coffee in hand, he hiked up Comm Ave to the apartment building. As expected the front door was locked. Needing to wait for someone to come in or out, he took a seat on the steps

The first who did, an elderly guy, looked at him so suspiciously he thought better of saying hello let alone asking to be let in. Ten minutes later a frosted-hair, middle-aged lady in yoga pants and thigh length sweater came out the door.

"Excuse me, miss," he said. "I'm looking for my friend Pam. She said she's staying here with her cousin. You wouldn't know her, would you?"

The lady's jaw dropped. "Pam, you said?"

"That's right. Sorry, I didn't get her cousin's name."

"Oh shit, hon, I don't know, but a girl named Pam died here Friday."

Sloane's gut sank. "What?"

"Yeah, I think it could have been your friend. A girl on the second floor came home Friday evening and found her cousin dead. An overdose, I believe. I'm pretty sure they said the name Pam."

"Who said?"

"My neighbors. They were here when the first responders got here and one of my neighbors spoke to Laura. That's the cousin."

He thought of Luis and the girl on the corner calling Ruffin's dope poison, and Ruffin saying Pam robbed him. "Do they know when she died?"

"Friday—late morning or early afternoon, I think. Around then."

"While Roshi was getting killed over her," Sloane said under his breath. "She was right here."

"What's that, hon?"

"Nothing. Thank you for telling me."

"I'm so sorry to have to. Such a tragedy."

"Yeah. That about sums up The Ave, I guess."

The lady tipped her head to the side at that. Sloane checked the time on his phone and hurried off. He could still make the Loonie Noonie meeting in Southie.

And damn did he ever need it. ❖

The Business of Others

Gabriela Stiteler

It was Gary who told me Jessica Miller had gone missing.

It was around five-fifteen on a weekday and I was driving back from rec half-listening to my boys try to convince me Mr. John had grossly exaggerated the bad report he'd given, which had something to do with the propagation of poorly timed your-mom jokes. Said to each other. Which, I wanted to tell Mr. John, was funny. But I could read a room and the man wasn't amused and so I nodded sympathetically and said I'd deal with it at home. They were mostly good kids. It was just they liked to figure out where, exactly, the line was and tiptoe up to it, and sometimes over it, to see what would happen.

And then there was the dog to walk. And dinner to make. And three job-related emails that required some attention. And my husband, who had been working late. And the house we couldn't actually afford, thanks to student loans and interest rates and car payments and afterschool care and medical bills and all of the things that whittle away paychecks.

We were doing everything right. Playing by all the rules as we understood them.

But we were still broke as shit.

And we needed a new roof.

This is what I was thinking when I turned onto our street, a dead end a few blocks from the bay. I did not have time for trouble that belonged to somebody else. I did not, if I was being entirely honest, have time for trouble that was my own. And so I was determined to keep my head down.

However, Gary, our mailman, had other ideas.

He was taking his sweet time on my stoop so I knew something was up. His interest in neighborly gossip was probably illegal or at the very least unprofessional but there was no way I was going to be the person to say something about it. If Gary wanted to put his nose in the business of others, that was on his conscience. Besides, the last thing I needed was my mailman's wrath.

I pulled into the driveway and willed Gary to move on. But he did not.

The kids exploded from the car, said hi, and ran to the back yard to kick around a soccer ball. I pretended to look for something under my seat. Gary was not dissuaded, so I resigned myself to my fate and got out of the car.

"You've got good kids," Gary said by way of greeting. And like that, I softened.

"Thanks," I said.

Gary went on conversationally, "We're having an early spring."

He always slow-walked to the point, hitting sports and weather before the juicy bits.

I nodded.

"Little league starting up?"

"Two weeks." I was juggling my bag and two backpacks and a pair of muddy boots. I shifted on my feet and made it a point to look at the door.

"Dan working late again?" he asked, studying my load.

I nodded and shifted again.

He picked up on the hint and got to the point.

"You know Jessica Miller?" He jerked his head toward the house two doors down.

"Sure," I said.

"You notice her car hasn't been around in a few days?"

I hadn't.

"The police were just here. Talking to Mike. Apparently he reported her missing."

Mike and Jessica and their daughter, Maggie. The Millers. We went to dinner at their house from time to time. They both worked and were swimming in all the same things we were. Youth sports and school and jobs. I wouldn't have said we were friends, exactly. It was more like we were trains running on parallel tracks.

"Sharon thinks she left," Gary went on.

Sharon was the neighbor between us and the Millers who was half-retired, loved gardening and cats, and couldn't help herself when it came to gossip.

"Does she?" I asked.

Gary nodded. "She said about two weeks ago, she could hear them fighting. Loud. And then Jessica left. With a suitcase. And Sharon hasn't seen her since." As Gary went on about Ron's DUI and Mary's unpaid hospital bills, a feeling of concern unfurled in the pit of my stomach and clawed its way up to my brain. Where it wouldn't let go. Jessica wasn't a friend. Not really. But she was devoted to her kid. And that was something.

I was still thinking about her when Dan got home from work, when we were eating a frozen pizza from Hannaford's with one of the bagged salads that didn't taste great but it counted as something green. Which was good enough. After the chaos of showers and reading and bedtime, which took longer than it should have because our younger son remembered he was afraid of the dark.

Dan was on the porch with a bottle of beer staring at the horizon. Maggie, Mike and Jess's daughter, was practicing her violin with the windows open and the sky was the pinkish orange of a sunset and there were seagulls and the smell of salt and wet earth.

"You got something on your mind?" he said after a minute.

I told him about Jessica. "You think she left him?" I asked.

He shrugged.

"It's just I wouldn't take her as the sort of person to leave her kid."

Maggie stopped playing and the gray fox that our neighbor and his wife fed strolled toward the trail system that our street abutted, as though he hadn't a care in the world.

"Maybe you can check on Mike?" I suggested, not taking my eyes off the fox. "Just to see if everything is okay?"

Dan finished his beer and put the empty bottle down. I got the feeling he didn't like my suggestion from the way he sighed. Sometimes, when we were alone, it felt like we were walking on ice, the two of us. A wrong step in any direction, and it'd crack.

"Just to see if he needs anything," I said. "Can you imagine if I vanished and you had the kids? If you had to do this alone?" I threaded my fingers with his and it took a minute for him to soften and squeeze, like he had when we were first dating. We went to our room and closed the door and were as quiet as we could be.

Later that night Dan told me he'd talk to Mike next time he saw him.

Six months ago, I'd been walking the dog through the trails. It was dark and the ground was frozen. A man and a woman were on the gravel path, standing close and talking. She took a step back when I approached. The man was tall and lean and handsome, with black boots and a canvas coat. He was smoking.

The woman was Jessica. Looking guilty as hell and not meeting my eye.

I nodded and kept moving and didn't say a damned thing. Not my business, after all.

Besides, when I got home, Dan was still at work so there wasn't a soul for me to tell.

When we first moved to town, Jessica invited me out for drinks at a restaurant down the block. It felt good to get dressed up and go out.

We were two glasses of wine into the evening when she said she'd almost left Mike the year before. "We tried everything," she said. "Couples therapy. A vacation. Date nights."

I took a long sip of my wine and thought hard on how to play things. I could have said it was a phase or it would get better or that sometimes marriage was just that. One of the obligations we held sacred because we said we would. But having two younger siblings who fell in and out of love with some degree of regularity, I'd learned the hard way it was better to keep my opinions to myself when it came to matters of the heart.

"Oh," I said carefully.

Apparently, it was the right thing.

"It's just he's more like a friend. More like a brother." She went on. This comment, coupled with the fact that she'd been looking at her phone all night, led me to believe she had somebody on the side.

"Uh huh," I said again, thinking of a way to extricate myself from the conversation. I did not want to be in the middle of somebody else's marital strife. I did not want to be the secret-keeper for somebody else's infidelity.

Again, I had enough trouble of my own.

"It's just I'm in my forties," she went on. "And I'm going to get to a point when men will stop noticing me. When I am not attractive. What about you and Dan? Are you happy?"

I considered the question. For me, Dan was it. I said as much.

"Is this *it*?" she went on. "We don't sleep in the same room. I don't want him to touch me. But then we've got a kid and this house and I don't know what other options there are." Her phone buzzed again. She looked at it. Then she looked at me and forced a smile that just about broke my heart.

I thought about my own parents and their divorce and the string of men that entered and exited my life from the time I was six until I left home. It was easier not to learn their names, to expect nothing.

"Look," I said, "maybe things will get better. It's the winter. It's cold and dark and a little hopeless right now. But maybe come spring . . . "

I could see her pull back.

"Sure," she said. "Maybe it's just the weather. Winters in Maine are always hard."

That night, I went home and sat on the couch next to Dan and put my head on his chest and listened to the steady sound of his heart and wanted very badly to cry.

The day after Gary told me about how Jess had gone missing I was at Kristine's house. She was drinking that room temperature Chardonnay from a box. I was eating stale Goldfish. The kids were outside tossing around a football and getting muddy as hell.

She was the one who brought up Jess.

"They separated last summer. Did you know that?"

I said no.

"They got an apartment and were switching weeks off and on with Maggie."

I couldn't imagine a world in which Dan and I could afford a second home. I said as much.

Kristine nodded. "I think that's what they decided. Not that they wanted to be together necessarily so much as they couldn't afford not to be."

Then, somebody got a bloody nose and all hell broke loose. Kristine finished her wine and I said my thanks and took the kids home.

Mike was sitting on his porch alone. Drinking. He was looking gaunter by the day. I waved and he nodded and went back to staring at the empty spot in his driveway.

Dan was quiet when he got home from work and I was staring out the kitchen window.

He asked about my day. I told him about my conversation with Kristine. And then I went for a walk alone.

Two days after Gary told me Jessica was missing, the police found her car on a residential side street a few blocks away. Sharon had taken to sending Mike food.

She caught me one night when I was pulling the trash can back up the driveway.

"I cannot imagine what it would take for me to just leave like that," she said in a low voice. "I wonder if she had some sort of a breakdown."

I didn't say anything.

Jessica was a little scattered and flighty and maybe even a little self-absorbed. She was not a good wife but she tried hard to be a good mother. Leaving her husband was one thing. Leaving her daughter was something else entirely.

Dan took Mike out for a drink and I watched the kids. My boys had reconfigured the pieces of the marble maze to look like weaponry. And I'd closed the door to their bedroom and left them to it.

Maggie stayed downstairs with me. She was a quiet kid with big brown eyes and a serious expression. She was drinking milk and I'd made myself a cup of tea with lemon and honey. We were sitting on the couch watching the Great British Bake Off.

"How's school?" I asked.

"Fine," she said.

"Are you in any sports?"

She shook her head.

Upstairs the boys poured the bucket of Legos onto the floor. I took a sip of my tea.

"You know my mom left, don't you?" she asked.

The comment startled me. I considered telling her how sorry I was. How her mother loved her. How everything would be okay. But something about the way she was looking at me gave me pause. And I decided she was not the sort of kid who needed to be spoon-fed little white lies.

And so I nodded and said nothing.

"She was dating somebody else. Tom. Did you know that?"

"No," I said. "Did you meet Tom?"

She nodded. "He came over a few times. Stayed the night. I didn't really like him." She turned thoughtful. "I don't think he really liked me much either. I wonder if that's why she left."

"It's not your fault," I said. "Sometimes people need a break. That's all."

She turned her attention to me fully. "Do you? Need a break?"

I put my tea down. "Look. Maggie. Here's the thing. Dan. The guy I'm married to. He's pretty much it for me. It's how I'm wired. I don't know how else to explain it."

"And is it the same way for him?" she pressed.

I felt bad for the kid but wasn't about to jump into an analysis of my marriage.

"Hey," I said. "I'm sorry about your mom. Really. I know she cares about you a lot. And if you want to talk about it, I'm here. But my marriage is between me and my husband. Okay?"

The kid shrugged and snapped her mouth shut. Tight. I don't think she said another word to me the rest of the night.

Later, when Dan and Mike were back and Maggie had left and our kids were in bed, Dan dragged me to the bedroom like he was drowning and I was a piece of driftwood. There was a desperation to the act that I wasn't used to and afterward, when we were lying there, I said as much.

Usually Dan was a measured man. But his words came out in a torrent, as though he'd been holding them in for some time.

"She was sleeping with him. In their house. In their bed. Bringing him over to be with their daughter. Without him knowing. Like none of it mattered. She told him she didn't love him. That she didn't want him. That she didn't want any of it. Not anymore. Mike's wrecked."

He was holding me while he said this, like he was afraid I would leave.

"It's not us," I said.

He let out a breath. Like he wanted to say something.

I squeezed his hand. "It's not us," I repeated.

Everything around us was quiet and still, like we were the only two people in the world.

"No," he said finally. "It's not us."

That night I dreamt that Jessica was dead.

The next day, Mike showed up at our doorstep at seven. Early morning joggers found her body in the Bay and he wondered if we could help with Maggie.

Mike went to identify the body and talk to the police. He looked awful, with circles under his eyes and the stuttering steps of an ill man. Dan and I kept as much to a routine as we could and folded Maggie into our lives, picking her up from school. Helping with homework and laundry and lunches.

Dan stopped working late. Little League started.

One night at bedtime, my younger son asked why Maggie cried so much.

"Because her mom is dead," my older son said, very matter-of-factly.

Dan and I ended up sleeping on the floor in their room that night.

Dan checked in on Mike every morning. Every night he'd reveal another detail in the dark of our room as we lay together, breathing the same air.

"The police think it was the boyfriend."

"Did you know she left him alone with Maggie?"

"She'd been texting him for two years."

"Mike knew about it the whole time."

"He didn't want her to leave."

"He had forgiven her for everything."

"She said she wouldn't do it again."

"How could he forgive her?" Dan asked one night. And it was impossible to miss the guilt in his voice. I considered telling him then, that I knew about the late nights and other woman. That there were all sorts of reasons to forgive somebody. That I never doubted we'd sort things out.

Instead, I curled into him and held his hand. I said, "These things happen. It will be okay."

He was quiet after that, like he wanted to say more.

I pretended to be asleep.

It was early on a Sunday and the kids were watching television. Dan had gone out to get donuts, something he used to do when we were first together and living in DC. He'd run to the corner store for pastries and

255

coffee and bring them back and we'd eat them in bed and read the paper.

I heard the car door and the birds and the footsteps and him talking to the boys in a low voice and the boys laughing. I turned to watch him come in, with his baseball hat and sweatshirt and jeans slung low enough on his hips to remind me he took care of himself.

"Sharon was out this morning," he said. "Early."

He was upset. I could tell from the stiffness in his voice and the way he held his body.

I pulled back the covers and he sat next to me.

"The boyfriend's dead, too. They found him. Farther down in the Bay."

The quiet that filled the room was heavy.

"Did they take Mike in?" I asked as softly as I could.

"Picked him up first thing this morning. How long have you known?" He asked in a low voice.

"Since the beginning," I said. "Since Gary told me she disappeared. I knew Jessica wouldn't leave her kid. And I knew Mike wouldn't leave Jessica."

Our boys were laughing and I knew we only had so much time.

"It's over," he said.

"I know."

"I'm sorry." He said it so softly I almost didn't hear.

So softly we could pretend he didn't need to say it. ❖

Coda for a Love Affair

Susan Oleksiw

The thumping beat of Elvis Presley's "Heartbreak Hotel" on her transistor radio accompanied Emmy as she rode her bicycle along the old road. She spotted the Brewster mansion through the bare trees and the Delaney home just beyond.

Emmy missed the Delaneys. Vicky had been her best friend, and the only playmate her age in the area. During their last Girl Scout weekend, in the spring, before Vicky moved away, the troop focused on camping skills, creating flints and building a fire. They were doing pretty well until it came time to get the fire started. The pairs of young girls, each squatting around their own pit, struggled to get the damp wood lit after a week of on-again, off-again rain.

"We'll starve if we don't get this going," Vicky said.

"We can't let that happen," Chief Mosley said. Keeping watch lest a cooking fire got out of hand, he squirted liquid on the kindling. "It's all right to use a shortcut once in a while if you've shown you can do what you have to do," he said. He handed each girl two matches. Vicky lit one of hers, threw it down, and the kerosene-doused wood flamed. The girls cooked beans and made pan bread. But now the Delaneys were gone, and Emmy was without a best friend. She shut off the transistor when she spotted Mrs. Brewster deadheading roses by the front door.

"And now, how is your brother? I read he scored a winning touchdown. Is that correct?" With her hands clasped together at her waist, her black-shoe-clad feet aligned, Mrs. Brewster stood poised like Emmy's fifth-grade teacher.

Her older brother, Ed, was a sports star in their little town, and Emmy often received compliments meant for him. He was on track for early admission to a small midwestern college with a full athletic scholarship. He was becoming insufferable.

Emmy cycled up to the Delaney house. No one had purchased the place, which was half the size of Mrs. Brewster's, painted white with arched windows and a slate roof. Emmy was about to visit the little pool in back when a car drove down the hill coming off the old fire road. The driver slowed, and Emmy looked in at the police chief.

"You know they moved away, Emmy."

"I was just looking."

"Well, it's not good to hang around an empty house. Go on, now."

She started back down the hill. He passed her and was soon out of sight.

Emmy reported seeing Mrs. Brewster that evening. "Chief Mosley came by up by the Delaney house," she added. "Can Vicky come visit?" Her parents glanced at each other, silent, so she had to repeat herself.

"Maybe, sometime," her mother said.

"That might not be a good idea," her father said.

"Why not?"

Her brother laughed but a look from their dad put a stop to it.

"What?" Emmy asked, confused.

"I'm going out with the guys." Ed stood up. He'd been warned college would be different, harder, and he should study more now, but he was confident. Emmy was jealous.

"Bunch of knuckleheads," she said.

"Twerp," Ed said, and then he was gone, out the door at the sound of a horn honking.

Emmy was not without friends, so weekends now meant longer rides to other neighborhoods. She worked on her Girl Scout badge for public speaking, and on more camping skills. Caroline Parrelli had a tent in the back yard where the girls slept on weekends.

"You need to get moving if you're going to make Sunday school," Mrs. Parrelli told her one Sunday morning before she and Mrs. Mosley, the chief's wife, left for their early morning walk. Emmy liked Mrs. Mosley. She had thick, curly brown hair that framed a warm expression, and her eyes were always smiling, not just her lips. She asked after Emmy's mother, complimented the girl on her badge work, and promised to buy cookies again next year.

It was only seven-thirty, but Emmy gathered up her things, stuffed them into her basket, and raced for the fire road, the shortcut home running through the woods.

She loved the quiet, the tree branches dipping low overhead, the occasional deer stopping to look before darting away, the twittering of birds, and sometimes the sound of hunters. She sped along. At a sharp corner she came wheel to grill with a police car. She skidded around it.

"We were just about to come and get you," her mother said when she bounced into the house.

"I saw Mrs. Mosley at Caroline's. She said to say hello. And then I passed the chief on the fire road."

Her mother shook her head and sighed. "I don't know how that woman puts up with him." She told Emmy to hurry up.

The end of Halloween meant the beginning of Thanksgiving and the holiday season. It also meant tracking down firs and berries for decorating. The Delaney property had an especially nice row of holly bushes, which Emmy and Vicky had harvested together for almost six years. By the Friday after Thanksgiving Emmy had persuaded herself that it was perfectly all right for her to continue the tradition, and she packed up her pruning shears and baskets and string and headed off to the Delaney house.

The day was cool, but the ride up hill had her standing on her pedals and pumping hard. Just below the Brewster mansion the road leveled off and she heaved great breaths as she neared her destination.

She pulled her bike off the driveway and leaned it against the side of the house. A once well-tended arrowwood had grown scraggly in the months since the Delaneys left, and it now concealed the path to the back yard. Heated by her ride up, Emmy left her bright yellow sweater draped over the handlebars.

The terrace seemed forlorn without the cast-iron chairs and tables where Mr. and Mrs. Delaney had entertained friends. The small rock pool was still filled, and she hoped the tadpoles would arrive on schedule in the spring. She knelt on the edge to peer into the shallows, hoping for a sign. Nothing. Then a frog jumped, and Emmy did too. Cheered, she grabbed her tools and headed to the holly bushes.

The berries seemed brighter and bigger this year, as though the bush had burst forth red tears of sorrow at the Delaneys' departure. Emmy began snipping. At first she wanted to take limbs that wouldn't leave the bush looking hacked up, but then her clippers seemed to work on their own. Nothing to worry about, she told herself. No one would ever know. There wasn't even a For Sale sign to tempt passersby to stop and look, not that this road had anyone just passing by. It was too out of the way. She soon had everything she'd come for.

She went back to the terrace, and then she saw it. She had missed this on her way in, but it was hard to miss now. Mrs. Delaney— or someone—had forgotten to close a window when they left. With a gap just tall enough to let a bird hop in, as well as snow and rain and pipe-bursting cold, the window, she knew, gave a view of the dining room. Emmy carried her things to her bike and then returned to the window. The house stood high on the foundation, the window almost too high for her to reach, but standing on her toes she might be able to reach it. She was about to jump up to the sill when she heard voices— murmurings.

"He's at work." A woman's voice.

"Where I should be."

She knew those voices.

"It's not that far. It's just the awkwardness of it, timing and all that."

"Yes . . . timing . . ."

Emmy strained to hear.

"Well, he already knew. It was time to be honest. We agreed, darling."

The man's voice grew faint.

"But we agreed. You told me you loved me."

The man's voice now sounded impatient, his words more a growl than speech.

"I don't understand what you expect me to do?" she said.

Lower and lower his voice fell.

Emmy thought they must have left the room. But then she heard him again, his voice low and sounding kinder but still a growl.

"Is that what you think of me? Don't you understand what I've done? I've told him everything so we could have our life together. And you expect me to—"

"It's not like I'm asking you to—"

The sound was unmistakable. A slap, hard. Silence.

"You shouldn't have done that, Sally."

And then they did leave the room, their voices rising and falling in incoherent bursts of anger, dismay, resentment, panic. Emmy slid down the granite foundation and sat with her arms around her drawn-up knees, her forehead resting on them. She knew those voices.

A car started up. Emmy peeked around the corner of the house just in time to see a blue station wagon pull out of the driveway. The chief followed it a few steps, standing on the other side of the overgrown arrowwood. Emmy froze, praying "Don't see it, don't see my bike, please don't see it." Moments later another car started but it didn't pass the house. The driver went the other way, up the hill.

When she stood, the terrace seemed smaller, dirtier, less welcoming. Someone had forgotten a steel pail and she carried it to the spot below the window and stepped onto it. She was a good girl, so she reached up and closed the window. The glass rattled but didn't break as it should have, to her mind.

The holidays proceeded as they usually did, with Saturday evening parties, large bags coming into the house and being whisked away upstairs to a closet, and afternoons and evenings spent writing and addressing holiday cards.

"I need more stamps," her mother said one afternoon. "We can still make the post office and stop at Bell's Market." They found a parking space and hurried in. "You can pick out the stamps, Emmy, when we get to the counter."

"Afternoon, Mrs. Wallenski." Chief Mosley nodded and smiled. Emmy's mother greeted him in return. "And hello there, Emmy."

"Well, say hello, Emmy."

Emmy looked at her feet, her hands held tightly in front of her. She mumbled hello.

"She hasn't been feeling well."

"Oh, and just before Christmas. That's too bad." The chief tapped Emmy on the shoulder but she pulled away, keeping her eyes on the floor. He wished the family a Merry Christmas and left.

Once in the car, her mother turned to her. "What was that about, young lady? You were very rude to Chief Mosley." Emmy took a quick peek at her mother. She looked angry but something else too.

"I don't like him."

"Did something happen that I don't know about?" Her voice softer, she leaned toward her daughter.

"He upset Mrs. Delaney."

Her mother gasped. "How do you know this?"

"I heard them talking." She narrated her afternoon collecting holly branches. Her mother was silent for the rest of the trip. Both parents were quiet that evening, and Emmy was glad not to be interrogated.

The following week Emmy's father went off to the hardware store looking for whatever he needed to fix the tree stand. He got home around five o'clock looking grim.

"I thought we were going to have to send out a search party," her mother said, but her smile faded when he failed to respond to her light teasing. "What's wrong?"

"Nothing." His eyes slewed to the right, toward where Emmy sat at the kitchen table wrapping a handmade potholder to give Mrs. Parrelli. A car door slammed, and he turned toward the front of the house. "That'll be Ed. Go upstairs, Emmy."

"What? Why?"

"Just go." Her father pulled the chair she was sitting on away from the table, rustling her out of the kitchen. From her place on the stairs she could hear her mother asking him the same question just as Ed slammed into the house.

"I've been benched," her brother announced from the living room. He threw himself into an armchair and scowled.

"Benched?" Emmy's mother trailed into the living room after her dad. "Did you know about this, honey?"

"I heard, this afternoon in the hardware store." He sat down on the sofa and leaned toward his son. "Ed, you haven't done anything wrong."

"That's not what the coach says." He slammed the heel of his shoe into the carpet, once, twice.

"Oh, Ed." His mother reached out to take his hand. Ed struggled not to cry.

"You've done nothing wrong, son. I've watched every game. I've seen every move you've made. You're a good player, a fair player."

"I'm benched."

"Get ready for supper. We'll talk about this and you'll see I'm right."

Not yet ready to believe him, her brother thrust himself out of the chair and marched up the stairs, ignoring Emmy.

In the quiet Emmy's mother repeated her questions, and finally her dad responded.

"Chief Mosley told the coach a few parents had complained that Ed was too rough, taking advantage of his size and skill. He suggested the boy not play for a while." She glimpsed her father sitting in his chair, all long limbs like a Daddy Longlegs, his elbows resting on his knees as he clasped and unclasped his hands.

Neither parent said anything for a while, and Emmy was about to continue her way upstairs when she heard her mother's voice.

"It's about the post office, isn't it?"

"Yeah. I think so."

"What're we going to do?"

"Ride it out."

"But his scholarship? He could lose it if . . ."

"We'll deal with that when it happens."

"You don't seem very concerned."

"I am very concerned, Mona. Steve Delaney called to let me know he was coming out this weekend to make sure everything was all right and to rent the place to a family he met."

"Well, that's good." She sounded almost cheerful.

"He had a call from the chief earlier in the week warning him about how dangerous it was for an old house like that to be left empty, especially in a remote place like it is." He shook his head, his brow furrowed, his lips like a crack in a sidewalk.

"Foolish woman," he whispered.

"You can't blame Sally for this," her mother said.

"You're right, but it sure is a mess."

"What're we going to do?"

"First, we're going to have a family meeting."

The meeting came after supper with all four of them sitting around the dining table, and Emmy taking center stage with her recitation of her encounters with Chief Mosley on the fire road, the conversation overheard, and their meeting in the post office.

"I'm screwed because she wouldn't say hello to him?" Ed's mouth dropped open.

"No, son, you're being punished because Chief Mosley is a spiteful man. It's a lesson in how not to behave."

"Well, what am I going to do about college and my scholarship?"

"Son, you have a right to be upset. The coach is treating you unfairly because of a rumor. But this isn't about you. It may feel like it is, but it isn't." He swung around to Emmy. "And it's not about you either, young lady."

"I wish she'd just leave him," her mother said.

"And it's not about Mrs. Mosley, either, Mona."

"Honestly, Richard, I don't know why she puts up with him."

"That's not our concern. Our concern is this family."

By Saturday morning, Emmy was bursting with curiosity about the new family moving into the Delaney house. Even though her dad had insisted that nothing was settled, Emmy had pushed aside the encounter with the chief and now thought only of having a family with children her age nearby. At seven o'clock in the morning she was on her bike racing up the hill, ready to greet the new arrivals. She came to the Delaney driveway—the empty driveway.

Deflated by finding no one, she dropped her bike against the front step. The house was quiet, the woods asleep for the winter, Christmas only a week away. She leaned back against the storm door, resolved to wait until Mr. Delaney and the new tenants arrived. She was getting restless when she smelled something. She sniffed, stood up, and sniffed again. She went out to the road and looked down toward Mrs. Brewster's house but the chimney was just a chimney, and no extra cars were parked there.

Curious, she went around the back of the Delaney house. Beneath the window where she had heard Mrs. Delaney and Chief Mosley argue was a pile of dried branches and other kindling, with flames taking hold, scarring the white clapboards. She pulled apart the kindling but the fire was already established. She ran for her bike and pedaled to Mrs. Brewster's house and banged on the door till the maid opened it.

Mr. Delaney arrived soon after the fire engines and stood by looking grim on the edge of the crowd of curious neighbors. Emmy watched from inside the protective arm of her father, who refused to leave until he was reassured that the area was safe and the fire under control.

"You the little girl that raised the alarm?" the fire chief asked when the men were recoiling hoses and taking final safety walks through the property. "Mr. Delaney's lucky you spotted it."

"I could smell it," she said. The fire chief thanked her again, congratulating her dad on raising such a fine, responsible girl.

"I could smell it, Dad," Emmy said when he was gone. She motioned for him to lean down, and whispered, "kerosene."

"Lucky you came by, Emmy," Chief Mosley said. He came over to them just as they were turning to leave. "Not many people around this area and at this hour." His smile was barely halfhearted. "You see anyone?"

Emmy shook her head.

The chief stepped back and addressed her dad in a formal tone. "The fire chief thinks there was an accelerant used. I tend to agree that some person had a hand in it. My deputies check the house regularly, make sure no one has broken in, and no one recalls seeing a pile of debris up against the house. We would have moved it if we had." He glanced down at Emmy and she leaned closer to her dad.

"I'm sure the fire chief'll make a full report," her dad said.

"Tell me again when you came up here, Emmy? Why were you riding your bike up here?"

She glanced up at her dad, who nodded. "I wanted to see the new family. I miss the Delaneys. Vicky was my friend."

"No one was moving in today," the chief said.

"She knows that. She just wanted to get a look at them. She was excited at having another family in the area and wanted to know if they had a girl her age."

"I see." The chief looked over at the house, the trampled shrubbery, the firefighter closing the front door. "You learned how to build a fire in Scouts, didn't you?"

Her dad's arm tightened around her.

"If there's nothing else, Chief, we'll be on our way. It's been a long morning." Before the chief could answer, her dad took hold of her shoulder and turned them both to walk back down the hill.

Her dad didn't send her to her room but he and her mom whispered at length in the kitchen. When they broke apart and saw her staring at them, her dad said, "You did the right thing, Emmy. I'm proud of you."

"I tried to put it out."

"That was stupid," Ed said.

"Did you burn yourself?" Her mother hurried to examine her hands.

"I put some of the stuff in a pail, the matches and little sticks and it went out, but the rest was still going."

"Matches?" Her father took a step toward her. "You found matches?"

The Delaney house once again stood alone in the woods when Emmy and her dad and brother revisited it later that afternoon. She led them to the pail lodged among the holly bushes. Her father pulled it out and peered into it. Ed did the same.

"Those sticks are hexagonal. The coach's are round," Ed said. "He uses them to light the wood stove in the clubhouse during the winter."

"That's right," her dad said, as though his mind was somewhere else. "There are lots of different kinds of these, with different chemicals on the tip."

"Chief Mosley's are like that," Emmy said.

"How do you know?" Ed asked.

"He gave two to each of us when we were doing our camping tests. We had to build a fire."

"Do you still have them?" her dad asked. She nodded.

That evening she was once again excluded from adult conversations, but then so was Ed, so she didn't feel quite as bad. The two sat at the top of the stairs trying to understand the muted voices of the guests, who arrived in uniform, never sat down, refused all refreshments, and asked a lot of questions. They took the metal pail and Emmy's leftover matches, and the two children were told to never speak of the visit.

After the holidays life returned to normal. The Delaney house was sold to a family with three boys, one close to Emmy's age, the chief announced his early retirement, and Mrs. Mosley developed cancer. She died in the summer. Ed went to an in-state college, gave up football, and stopped calling Emmy a twerp. She earned all her camping badges, and in the fall she joined the girls' soccer team. ❖

Contributors' Notes

Christine Bagley publishes short stories in both crime anthologies and literary journals. She holds a Master's Degree in Creative Writing from Lesley University, and was a fiction contributor to the Bread Loaf Writers' Conference. She also taught writing and presentation skills to Harvard Medical School foreign national scientists and physicians. Bagley's stories have appeared in *Briar Cliff Review, Bryant Literary Review, Untoward Magazine, Fiction on the Web* in the UK, and in numerous editions of Best New England Crime Stories. She was also a finalist for the Al Blanchard Award for Short Crime Fiction. A member of Mystery Writers of America, Sisters in Crime New England, and the Short Mystery Fiction Society, Bagley enjoys reading, swimming in any beach she can find, and attending national and international tennis tournaments.

Nancy Brewka-Clark is a member of the Short Mystery Fiction Society and New England Horror Writers. Her work has been featured in numerous publications across the USA, UK, Canada, and Australia, including Level Best Books 2009 anthology Quarry. Her poetry collection, *Beautiful Corpus*, was published in 2020.

Bruce Robert Coffin is the award-winning author of the Detective Byron mystery series. A former detective sergeant with more than twenty-seven years in law enforcement, he supervised all homicide and violent crime investigations for Maine's largest city. Following the terror attacks of September 11, 2001, Bruce spent four years investigating counterterrorism cases for the FBI, earning the Director's Award, the highest award a nonagent can receive. Winner of Killer Nashville's Silver Falchion Awards for Best Procedural, and Best Investigator, and the Maine Literary Award for Best Crime Fiction Novel, Bruce was also a finalist for the Agatha Award for Best Contemporary Novel. His short fiction appears in nearly a dozen anthologies, including *Best American Mystery Stories 2016.*

Hans Copek has published a number of short stories in various anthologies. His family insisted that he write down what he remembered about his years in WW II and becoming a soldier in Hitler's army at age thirteen. When the memoir was done, he discovered that writing was fun, and turned some of his adventures into fiction—greatly embellished, of course. "Capital Offense," in this anthology, is based on a true story. The story illustrates the saying, no good deed goes unpunished—when the Gestapo knocks on the door.

Michael Ditchfield is a writer of novels, plays, haiku, essays, and short stories. A quarter-century of practicing social work taught him that life is fragile, life is dangerous, everyone is wounded, yet people do heroic, selfless, and beautiful things. He tries to capture that spirit in his writing. He won the Stonecoast Writers' Conference Humor Award, published in *Borders to Bridges: Arts-Based Curriculum on Social Justice* and *Wolfsbane: Best New England Crime Stories 2023.* He won the William Faulkner—William Wisdom Writing Contest for his essay "Zen and the Art of Dementia," and this year he won for "No such Agency," a novella featuring private investigator Abraham "Jolly" Lucky. Lucky appears in other short stories and a novel in progress, as well as a story in this anthology.

Christine Eskilson's stories have appeared in numerous magazines and anthologies, including Best New England Crime Stories and Malice Domestic. Her work has garnered awards in the Al Blanchard Short Crime Fiction Contest, the Women's National Book Association Annual Writing Contest, and the Bethlehem Writers Roundtable Short Story Contest.

Kate Flora's fascination with people's criminal tendencies began in the Maine attorney general's office. Deadbeat dads, people who hurt their kids, and employers' discrimination aroused her curiosity about human behavior. The author of twenty-six books spanning many genres including crime fiction, true crime, memoir, and nonfiction, and many short stories, Flora's been a finalist for the Edgar, Agatha, Anthony, and Derringer awards. She won the Public Safety Writers Association award for nonfiction and twice won the Maine Literary Award for crime fiction. She received a lifetime achievement award from the New England Crime Bake and the Lea Wait Award for contributions to the crime writing community at the Maine Crime Wave. She is current president of the SinCNE, and a founder of the New England Crime Bake and Maine Crime Wave. She blogs with the Maine Crime Writers. Flora's books include the domestic suspense novel *Teach Her a Lesson*, and *Such a Good Man*, the eighth Joe Burgess police procedural. She divides her time between Massachusetts and Maine, where she gardens and cooks and watches the clouds when she's not imagining her character's dark deeds. www.kateclarkflora.com
https://www.facebook.com/kate.flora.92
http://www.mainecrimewriters.com

Connie Johnson Hambley's short stories appear in *Mystery Magazine*, several Best New England Crime Stories, and the Anthony Award-winning Mystery Writers of America's anthology *Crime Hits Home*. Her writing also appears in *Bloomberg BusinessWeek, Financial Advisor*, and *Nature*. Connie is a long-time New England Crime Bake committee member, a past president of Sisters in Crime New England, and a passionate fan of (fictional) crime. Learn more about Connie's award-winning novels, where family secrets link a world-class equestrian to a Boston-based terrorist cell, at www.conniejohnsonhambley.com and follow her on Threads @conniej.hambley and X/Twitter @ConnieHambley.

Sean Harding spent over two decades as a clinical social worker working with people in the Massachusetts criminal justice system. Lately, he has devoted time to writing crime fiction. Sean has lived his entire life in the Boston area, and currently lives in a Metrowest suburb. He is the proud father of an adult daughter. His first mystery story was published in *Wolfsbane*.

Nikki Knight is an author/anchor/mom, not in that order. An award-winning weekend anchor at New York's 1010 WINS Radio, she writes short stories and novels including the Vermont Radio Mystery *Live, Local, and Long Dead* from Wild Rose Press. As Kathleen Marple Kalb, she writes the Ella Shane and Old Stuff series, both from Level Best Books. Her stories have been in *Alfred Hitchcock's Mystery Magazine, Mystery Magazine, Black Cat Weekly*, and anthologies including *Deadly Nightshade: Best New England Crime Stories 2022*. Active in writer's groups, she's Co-VP of the New York/Tri-State Sisters in Crime Chapter and past VP of the Short Mystery Fiction Society. She, her husband, and son live in a Connecticut house owned by their cat.

Chris Knopf has published eighteen mystery/thriller novels and numerous short stories in publications such as *Ellery Queen Mystery Magazine* and *Alfred Hitchcock Mystery Magazine*, as well as in anthologies from Crime Spell Books and Akashic. He has won several awards, including the Nero, and has been shortlisted for the Derringer. Additionally, Chris writes a biweekly blog post for SleuthSayers and contributes essays to various publications.

Alison McMahan is the author of *Guy Blaché, Lost Visionary of the Cinema* (Bloomsbury 2002), translated into Spanish and Japanese and made into the documentary *Be Natural* (2018). Her short mysteries have been anthologized by Level Best Books, Wildside Press, Down-and-Out Books, *ThrillRide Magazine*, and in the *Scream and Scream Again* middle-grade horror anthology edited by R.L. Stine for HarperCollins. She's a two-time Derringer finalist and her short fiction was listed in "Other Distinguished Mystery Stories," *Best American Mystery Stories 2018.*

Paula Messina does not come from a long line of fishmongers, just an extremely short one. Her father and uncle owned a fish store in Ball Square, Somerville, for less than a year. She doesn't come from a long line of writers either. Her humorous caper "Which Way New England?" appeared in *Wolfsbane: Best New England Crime Stories 2023.* She is the fiction and non-fiction editor for *Indelible Literary and Arts Journal* and is the Derringer Awards Coordinator 2024. You can listen to her dulcet tones on LibriVox.org where she records audiobooks of works in the public domain.

Susan Oleksiw writes three series. The Pioneer Valley Mystery series features Felicity O'Brien, farmer and healer. Anita Ray, an Indian American photographer, uncovers murder in South India. Susan is also the author of the Mellingham series set in a small coastal New England town. Susan's short stories have appeared in *Alfred Hitchcock Mystery Magazine* and anthologies and other magazines. She is currently VP of SinCNE. She co-founded Level Best Books and more recently Crime Spell Books, and serves as co-publisher and co-editor. She received a Lifetime Achievement Award from Crime Bake, where she serves on the programming committee. She is a member of Sisters in Crime, Mystery Writers of America, and The Authors Guild. You can find her at https://susanoleksiw.com

Eugenia Parrish has published three books in her crime series The Del Sueño Files and is working on the fourth. Her mystery short story "A Death at the Crossroads" received an Honorable Mention for the 2022 Al Blanchard Award and was published in the anthology *Bloodroot* by Crime Spell Books. You can find her essay "The Desert or the Deep Dark Woods?" in the spring 2022 issue of *Mystery Readers Journal.* Originally from Ohio, she has traveled extensively and now lives in Vermont.

Ang Pompano is an Agatha Award-nominated and Helen McCloy Award-winning author of the Blue Palmetto Detective Agency series and the Reluctant Food Columnist series. He is the co-publisher of Crime Spell Books and co-editor of the annual anthology Best New England Crime Stories. His short stories have been featured in numerous award-winning anthologies, including one that won the Anthony Award. A member of Mystery Writers of America and Sisters in Crime, he is on the planning committee for the New England Crime Bake Writing Conference and serves on the board of SinC-Connecticut.

Stephen D. Rogers is the author of the story collection *Shot to Death*, and the author of more than eight hundred additional short works. His website, www.StephenDRogers.com, includes a list of new and upcoming titles as well as other timely information.

Emily Ross is the author of *Half in Love with Death* (Simon & Schuster), which was an International Thriller Writers Thriller Awards finalist. She received a Massachusetts Cultural Council finalist award in fiction for the novel. Her work has appeared in *Boston Magazine, Five South*, and other publications.

Clea Simon, a Boston Globe-bestselling author of fiction, was a journalist and penned three nonfiction books before turning to a life of crime (fiction). Prior to launching her new amateur sleuth in *Bad Boy Beat*, her thirty-first mystery, her crime fiction has been divided between cozy mysteries (most recently her Witch Cats of Cambridge series) and psychological suspense, including *Hold Me Down* and *World Enough* (both Massachusetts Center for the Book "must reads"). A graduate of Harvard University, she has contributed to publications ranging from Salon.com and *Harvard Magazine* to *Rolling Stone, Yankee*, and *The New York Times*. Born and raised in New York, she now lives in Somerville, Massachusetts, with her husband, the writer Jon S. Garelick. Find her at www.cleasimon.com, @Clea_Simon (Twitter), and @cleasimon_author (IG).

Sarah Smith's books, international bestsellers, are published in fifteen languages. She's won the Agatha for best teenage mystery, the Massachusetts Book Award for best teenage novel, and numerous other honors, including New York Times Notables and various Best Book of the Year lists. She lives near Boston, Massachusetts, and is working on a big fat fantasy set in nineteenth-century Brazil. Look for her on FB and BlueSky and practically everything except TwitX, IG @sarahwriter. www.sarahsmith.com

Shelagh Smith's previous publishing credits include "Fall River," a retelling of the Lizzie Borden story from Quill & Crow Publishing House (forthcoming early 2026), and *Dark Reads* by Thin Veil Press (2024). Her work has also been featured in Best New England Crime Stories (2017 and 2018), *Tales of Sley House 2022, Embracing Writing, Don't Forget About the Adjuncts,* and *Tempest.* She is the winner of the PEN New England Susan P. Bloom Discovery Award. Shelagh holds a Master's degree in Professional Writing and currently teaches writing at Massachusetts Maritime Academy and Bridgewater State University.

Gabriela Stiteler's first mystery story was nominated for the Robert L. Fish award in *Ellery Queen Mystery Magazine.* Her fiction has appeared in two anthologies from Crime Spell Books: *Wolfsbane* and *Devil's Snare.* She is active in the New England writing community as the newsletter editor of SinCNE, co-chair of Crime Bake, and a member of MWANE and the Maine Writers and Publishers Alliance.

Mo Walsh's first crime story won the Mary Higgins Clark Mystery/Suspense Contest and was published in *Mary Higgins Clark Mystery Magazine.* Other stories have appeared in print and online in *Woman's World,* and in Best New England Crime Stories,

Malice Domestic, and Sisters in Crime anthologies, and the middle-school collection of *Super Puzzletastic Mysteries* from Mystery Writers of America. She is a coauthor of the "killer trivia" book, *A Miscellany of Murder*. Mo belongs to Sisters in Crime and Mystery Writers of America and is a past-president of the New England MWA Chapter.

Leslie Wheeler is the award-winning author of two mystery series: the Berkshire Hilltown Mysteries and the Miranda Lewis Living History Mysteries. Her short crime fiction has appeared in numerous anthologies including the Best New England Crime Stories anthologies, published by Level Best Books, where she was a co-editor/publisher for six years, and now by Crime Spell Books, where she holds the same position. A member of Mystery Writers of America and Sisters in Crime, she serves as Speakers Bureau Coordinator for the New England Chapter, and as a co-founder of the New England Crime Bake Committee, she coordinates the Crime Bake sponsored Al Blanchard Award Contest. She divides her time between Cambridge, Massachusetts, and the Berkshires, where she writes in a house overlooking a ponds

www.ingramcontent.com/pod-product-compliance
Lightning Source LLC
Chambersburg PA
CBHW022102280326
41933CB00007B/228